Critical Muslim 16

Turkey

Editor: Ziauddin Sardar

Deputy Editors: Hassan Mahamdallie, Ehsan Masood, Shanon Shah

Senior Editors: Aamer Hussein, Ebrahim Moosa, Samia Rahman

Publisher: Michael Dwyer

Managing Editor (Hurst Publishers): Daisy Leitch

Cover Design: Fatima Jamadar

Associate Editors: Tahir Abbas, Alev Adil, Nazry Bahrawi, Merryl Wyn Davies, Abdelwahab El-Affendi, Marilyn Hacker, Nader Hashemi, Jeremy Henzell-Thomas, Vinay Lal, Iftikhar Malik, Boyd Tonkin

International Advisory Board: Karen Armstrong, William Dalrymple, Farid Esack, Anwar Ibrahim, Robert Irwin, Bruce Lawrence, Ashis Nandy, Ruth Padel, Bhikhu Parekh, Barnaby Rogerson, Malise Ruthven

Critical Muslim is published quarterly by C. Hurst & Co. (Publishers) Ltd. on behalf of and in conjunction with Critical Muslim Ltd. and the Muslim Institute, London.

All correspondence to Muslim Institute, CAN Mezzanine, 49-51 East Road, London N1 6AH, United Kingdom

e-mail for editorial: editorial@criticalmuslim.com

The editors do not necessarily agree with the opinions expressed by the contributors. We reserve the right to make such editorial changes as may be necessary to make submissions to Critical Muslim suitable for publication.

C. Hurst & Co. (Publishers) Ltd., 41 Great Russell Street, London WC1B 3PL

ISBN: 978-1-84904-543-8 ISSN: 2048-8475

To subscribe or place an order by credit/debit card or cheque (pound sterling only) please contact Kathleen May at the Hurst address above or e-mail kathleen@hurstpub.co.uk

Tel: 020 7255 2201

A one year subscription, inclusive of postage (four issues), costs £50 (UK), £65 (Europe) and £75 (rest of the world).

The right of Ziauddin Sardar and the Contributors to be identified as the authors of this publication is asserted by them in accordance with the Copyright, Designs and Patents Act, 1988.

A Cataloguing-in-Publication data record for this book is available from the British Library.

IIIT PUBLICATIONS

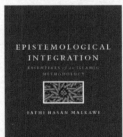

The Barbary Figs

by

Rashid Boudjedra

Translated by
André Naffis-Sahely

Buy a copy of Rashid Boudjedra's *The Barbary Figs* at
www.hauspublishing.com or by calling +44(0)20 7838 9055
and a recieve a copy of Khaled al-Berry's memoir
Life is More Beautiful than Paradise free.

RASHID AND OMAR are cousins who find themselves side by side on a flight from Algiers to Constantine. During the hour-long journey, the pair will exhume their past, their boyhood in French Algeria during the 1940s and their teenage years fighting in the bush during the revolution. Rashid, the narrator, has always resented Omar, who despite all his worldly successes, has been on the run from the ghosts of his past, ghosts that Rashid has set himself the task of exorcising. Rashid peppers his account with chilling episodes from Algerian history, from the savageries of the French invasion in the 1830s, to the repressive regime that is in place today.

RASHID BOUDJEDRA has routinely been called one of North Africa's leading writers since his debut, *La Répudiation*, was published in 1969, earning the author the first of many fatwas. While he wrote his first six novels in French, Boudjedra switched to Arabic in 1982 and wrote another six novels in the language before returning to French in 1994. *The Barbary Figs* was awarded the Prix du Roman Arabe 2010.

CM16

October–December 2015

CONTENTS

TURKEY

ARTS AND LETTERS

REVIEWS

ET CETERA

Subscribe to Critical Muslim

Now in its third year, *Critical Muslim* is the only publication of its kind, giving voice to the diversity and plurality of Muslim reporting, creative writing, poetry and scholarship.

Subscribe now to receive each issue of Critical Muslim direct to your door and save money on the cover price of each issue.

Subscriptions are available at the following prices, inclusive of postage. Subscribe for two years and save 10%!

	ONE YEAR (4 Issues)	TWO YEARS (8 Issues)
UK	£50	£90
Europe	£65	£117
Rest of World	£75	£135

TO SUBSCRIBE:

CRITICALMUSLIM.HURSTPUBLISHERS.COM

41 GREAT RUSSELL ST, LONDON WC1B 3
WWW.HURSTPUBLISHERS.COM
WWW.FBOOK.COM/HURSTPUBLISHERS
020 7255 2201

TURKEY

INTRODUCTION
SUN AND THE SHADOW

Tahir Abbas

'So, you are Pakistani?' Almost every day, when I meet Turks for the first time, I am asked 'where are you from?' Almost without fail, the conclusion is reached before I can say anything. Even though I was born in Britain, and have spent less than ten months of my entire life in Pakistan, I agree for simplicity's sake. But there is another more significant reason: Turkey is one of the few places in the world where being a Pakistani is celebrated. Turks are taught in schools that it was money and gold sent as donations from what was Muslim India, and is now Pakistan, which significantly helped the War of Independence. With all that cash and bullion Mustafa Kemal Atatürk (1881-1938), the founder of the Republic, established Türkiye İş, Turkey's first national bank, in 1924. After the initial introductions, the conversation turns quickly to focus on my religion. Some go on to ask my name. Then they probe, 'this is a Turkish name. Are you Turkish? Why do you have a Turkish name but you are not Turkish?' I smile and reply 'my name is from Arabic'. Then they ask, 'are you a Muslim?' I reply, 'of course.' They smile warmly and declare, 'Salaam-alaikum'. After this initial exchange many Turks declare, 'We love Pakistan. You are my brother'.

In Turkey, talk can quickly move to religion; and people are judged in terms of whether they are for or against religion. For most Turks faith identity is critical. After all, Turkey is a Muslim country where the majority of the people are content to call themselves Muslim. Those with strong faith identities also tend to have strong emotional attachment to the Ottoman past. However, a large segment of the Turkish population also subscribes to a brand of secularism which regards certain Muslim symbols with absolute dread – the very sight of a headscarf sends them into an enraged spin. These secular Turks look at the secular republic and its formative phase with a high degree of romanticism.

Known as Constantinople at the time Istanbul was captured in 1453 by the nineteen-year old Ottoman Fatih Sultan Mehmet (1432–1481). This is when the history of Turkey begins for vast swathes of the Turkish population, for whom their only education is high school or early secondary schooling. Constantinople was the seat of the Eastern Roman Empire for a thousand years before the arrival of the Ottomans. The majestic Aya Sophia still stands on the grounds upon which it was built, in spite of numerous earthquakes and reconstruction mishaps. The Blue Mosque, also known as Sultanahmet, built to pay homage to the Aya Sophia, is arguably one of the most symbolic images of the country today, in the same way that many associate the Taj Mahal with India or the Statue of Liberty with New York.

When Ottoman Turkey conquered Egypt, taking charge of the Caliphate, it became an immense economic, cultural and political power in the region, spreading Sufi philosophy east and west. The Ottomans positively incorporated other religions into wider society, namely Jews expelled from the Iberian Peninsula and Christians who joined the ranks of the civil service. The Ottomans were open and inclusive in recognising different religions as part of a millet system of governance, where each community abided by its own laws – Shariah, Christian Canon law, or Jewish Halakha.

In the early part of the twentieth century, Turkey was re-founded as a secular republic by Atatürk - a war hero who inspired the Turkish War of Independence (1915-1919), defeated the Allies in the 1915 Battle of Çanakkale, abolished the Caliphate and modernised society according to European ideals by introducing secularism based on French laicism. In contrast to the Ottoman Empire, Atatürk forged a monocultural and monolingual society, ultimately defined, formulated and operated in opposition to centuries of Ottoman rule based on Islamic and Sufi spiritual norms and values. Kemalism disregarded ethnic differences among the Muslims, suppressed public expression of religious sentiments and symbols and effectively expelled religious differences from society. But the fabric of society could not be changed without significant implications. Atatürk used an authoritarian system that projected and implemented a top-down idea of Turkey. By changing the language, both its content and script, he arguably removed from everyday use approximately thirty per cent of the vocabulary that had much of its roots in Arabic and Farsi. Overnight, in adopting the Latin alphabet instead of the Turkish form of the Arabic script, a significant body of the population became illiterate. Over the decades, the state apparatus, which served the interests of an elite cadre, brutally enforced Atatürk's form of republicanism. The state reproduced itself through the formalisation of institutions in its own image, namely the military, academy, judiciary and media. Bourgeoisie secular groups, located and operating out of the centres of Istanbul, held both industrial and commercial power, and garnered political and cultural influence as a result. In the meantime, the secular republic subjugated religious and cultural minorities, which were crucial to the expansion of the Ottoman Empire. They were oppressed or forcibly assimilated until the opening up of the economy and society that began in the early 1980s and accelerated after the end of the Cold War.

Strict authoritarianism led to reliance on the military as a means of seemingly protecting the nation from hostile others. But during the twentieth century Turkey witnessed three military coups. The late 1970s and early 1980s also saw the emergence of the PKK (Kurdistan Workers' Party). Its efforts moved beyond a Marxist-Leninist political and ideological cause to one of guerrilla warfare against the Turkish state. It was civil war in all but name in the south east region of Turkey until 2011, when a ceasefire was declared and a new peace process initiated, which subsequently deteriorated in September 2015.

This history of political turmoil is well described by Edip Asaf Bekaroğlu in his examination of Turkish secularism. Historically, as Bekaroğlu notes, the secularists have had the upper hand, buttressed by the military. But since the turn of the millennium, the majority in Turkish society has moved towards the centre ground. The emerging 'Islamists' embraced democracy and citizenship, and politically squeezed out the hard-line secularists and nationalists. From 2002, the Justice and Development Party (AKP) ruled Turkey with stability, vigour and enthusiasm unprecedented in recent Turkish history. The economy boomed, Turkey flourished, the AKP won three consecutive elections and there was a growing sense that a persuasive political, social and cultural project was bearing fruit for the many. The 'Turkish model' was touted as a potential future of all Muslim societies.

'What today is a cautious Turkish bid to become part of history', wrote Swedish critic Parvez Manzoor in the first issue of *Critical Muslim*, 'may one day become a model for all Muslim states to emulate'. Alas, poor Abdullah! It was not to be. Power corrupted the Islamists – as it does ideologues of all other shades. The 2013 events of Gezi Park, when citizens across the country demonstrated against turning a much loved small park into a leisure complex, brought the true controlling nature of the AKP to the fore. Soon after a host of corruption scandals that implicated people at the very top of the party surfaced. The then-Prime Minister Recep Tayyip Erdoğan curtailed press freedoms, oversaw a particular brand of neoliberalism and disillusioned many in society with his intense authoritarianism. In addition, his rather public feud with the Hizmet (a Turkish transnational civil society movement headed by Sufi scholar, Fethullah Gülen) was seen as unnecessary in-fighting between two progressive Sunni Muslim fraternities, one political and the other community-oriented. As Ahmet Kuru points out, Erdoğan tried to 'take various spheres of life under his control from soccer to judiciary, from religion to construction, and from media to education'; and 'replace the parliamentarian regime with a presidential one and to make himself the ultra-powerful president for ten years (2014-2024)'. Kuru outlines an array of Erdoğan's misdemeanours and concludes that the promise of the 'Turkish model' has turned out to be false; 'after a decade in power', what Tayyip Erdoğan 'has actually built is a 1500 room palace for himself at a cost of around $1 billion!'

The struggle for power between Hizmet and AKP played into the hands of the undecided and the critically minded in the 2015 elections, while also encouraging a Kurdish vote for a Kurdish party. Hizmet is led by Fethullah Gülen, described by Sophia Pandya as 'a Sufi theologian known reverentially as Hocaefendi (respected teacher) to his millions of followers', who has 'inspired a civil society humanitarian movement, called Hizmet, or service, which has founded thousands of educational centres and owns dozens of media institutions, in Turkey and abroad'. The AKP is led by Erdoğan, former Prime Minister and now President. The two leaders were allies for years; 'their alliance was based on their common traditional and religious inclinations, not to mention their shared political enemies'. Indeed, the AKP's electoral success was due, at least to some extent, to the support it received from Hizmet. But they had a 'furious fallout' in 2013; and 'their ultimate breakup was informed in part, by their contesting forms of masculinity'. This struggle for power represents, notes Pandya, 'their contesting visions of Turkey, but also their differing performances of masculinity, leadership, religion, and values regarding alterity'.

The Kurds have sought equality, status and recognition since 1923, when the modern republic of Turkey was founded. Arguably, the 2015 election is the first time their voice has been truly heard. The Kurds are resilient, determined people as I discovered when I visited Yüksekova, a town deep inside 'Turkey's Kurdistan', 200km further east from Van, far into the Hakkari province. At the bottom of Turkey, the town is approximately 60km from the borders of both Iran and Iraq. After flying to Van, reaching Yüksekova proved a treacherous journey. It meant traversing mountainous terrain, approximately 2,000 feet above sea level. Rivers flowed beside us as we drove on the rocky roads, finally arriving in Yüksekova, which is on a flat plain surrounded by snow-topped mountains on all sides. According to recent estimates, it contains approximately 60,000 people, all of Kurdish origin. I stayed with the family of Ismail Hakki, a former colleague from Fatih University in Istanbul. A well-built man in his late twentiess, he is a proud Kurd, as are all the Kurds I have met in Istanbul over the years. I was afforded the warmth, peace and nobleness of his most generous family, including his five brothers who were variously aged from their mid-twenties to forties. Their mother and father gave me the freedom of their home as if I were one of their sons. Steeped in traditional Kurdish and Sunni family culture, we ate together, young and old, on the floor while seated on elegant kilims and cushions.

I spent some time talking to the local community about the 'Kurdish issue'. Various responses came back, including the idea that current discussions are better than ever before, it is possible to be optimistic at some level, and a solution could be found. This was soon after the current peace talks began in 2012. Others blamed the PKK, stating that they were the problem per se. Some were of the view that no solution could ever be achieved. For them the status quo would remain as it has done since the emergence of the secular Turkish state. Although there was no overwhelming consensus, it was evident that the residents wanted to decide their own issues and run their own affairs. In truth, a local Kurdish leadership was in place in Yüksekova, but there remained a great deal of tension under the surface. Sadly, a day after I left the town to return to Istanbul, PKK guerrillas and Turkish soldiers exchanged gunfire in the Dağlıca village of the Hakkari province, some 50km south-west of Yüksekova, close to the Iraqi border. It left 26 dead, with casualties on both sides. The incident was one of the fiercest exchanges between these opposing groups in recent years. It is apparent that the spirit of the people deep in Kurdish territory will not be diminished. Kurdish land is in their blood and it pumps through their collective veins with vigour despite numerous attempts to make them think or believe otherwise.

Since the advent of the modern secular republic, ethnic and national conflicts have periodically re-surfaced, thwarting the development of a confident citizenship at ease with religious and ethnic pluralism. At the turn of the twentieth century, out of a population of approximately 15m people, there were as many as one million Jews, Christians, Armenians, Circassians and other minority groups loyal to and in service to the Ottoman Empire. Today, there are no more than 100,000 ethnic and religious minorities throughout the whole of Turkey. In 2007, the renowned journalist Hrant Dink was assassinated in broad daylight in the centre of Istanbul. His young assassin declared 'I have killed an Armenian'.

However, you do not have to belong to a minority community to be discriminated as pious Muslim women who wear the headscarf will tell you. Atatürk tried to reform the position of women, taking them out of the 'Islamic dark ages' as he saw it, encouraging them to enter the world of education and work. But he also banned the veil, or the headscarf, for teachers and civil servants working in public institutions. The ban was finally removed by the AKP in 2014. As Yusuf Sarfati notes, the headscarf has been a site of ferocious battle for the last three decades. While Sarfati provides a detailed historical account of the 'contentious issue', his analysis can also be seen as a powerful critique of 'difference-blind liberalism'. He suggests that a more positive approach to the headscarf issue is to push for 'institutionalise[d] counterpublics' – 'parallel discursive arenas where members of subordinated so-called social groups invent and circulate counter-discourses to formulate oppositional interpretations of their identities, interests, and needs'. Counterepublics, suggests Sarfati, would directly link marginalised veiled women to decision-making bodies, help in opinion formation and shape new strategies to combat the headscarf ban. Instead of seeing the headscarf ban solely as discrimination on the basis of 'freedom of religion' or 'gender discrimination', Sarfati argues, we should see it as discrimination against 'religious women'.

If Kurds are the internal 'Other' of the Turkish Republic, Europe, as Melek Saral argues, serves as the external Other. Many Turks see themselves as European and wish to be Europeanised, and rapidly so with individualism, urbanism and internationalism supplanting existing notions of collectivism, traditionalism and localism. Turkey's ambivalent relationship with the EU integration process is as much about Turkey's search for an identity at the end of the Cold War as it is about the European expansion project. Given that Turkey has experienced years of unprecedented economic growth, low inflation, stable interest rates, rising wages, increasing consumerism, improving living standards, a remarkable health service, a growing higher education sector and strong geopolitical confidence in recent years, one would think that it is the ideal candidate for membership of the Union. Western Europe could also look towards Turkey as a positive partner in the integration of its own Muslim minorities, which are now close to 25 million. The EU could take advantage of a young and skilled Turkish workforce in beleaguered Western European economies undergoing the effects of ageing populations and low birth rates. But the EU remains reluctant for a simple reason: Turkey has always been seen and represented as the Darker Side of Europe. As Merryl Davies shows in her analysis of the advertisements for Fry's 'Turkish Delight', European racism towards Turkey has deep roots. English statesman and philosopher, Francis Bacon (1561–1626) described the Ottoman Empire as a pressing 'terror of the world'. The Ottomans were seen as stultified in superstition hidebound by tradition, slaves to their past, and Europe recoiled in horror at their alleged savagery, despotism and violence. Contemporary Western Europe has similar views about Turkey – it is where European civilisation ends and barbarism begins. In contrast, writes Soral, 'European civilisation has always been a very important factor in the formulation of Turkish identity - going back to the Ottoman Empire. Modernisation, and to this end Westernisation, has not only been the major goal of the political elite in the modern Turkish

Republic, it was also an objective of the Ottoman Empire. To be Western and European was regarded as a panacea for all the problems of the country; a path from underdevelopment to the civilised, modern world'.

However, all of Turkey's overtures to the EU have been met with tea and sympathy at best and disdain and horror at worse. Not surprisingly, Turkey is looking elsewhere. Indeed, one could legitimately ask, given the crisis in the Eurozone and the all too evident fractures in the Union, what benefits could Turkey possibly gain by joining it? Particularly when Western Europe is arguably becoming more racist, xenophobic and intolerant towards its own minorities, especially towards Muslims since 9/11.

Thus, apart from its traditional allies, Pakistan, Iran, Malaysia, Turkey has begun to forge ties with Africa, where it has invested heavily; with Egypt after the 'Arab Spring' where it supported the short lived government of the Muslim Brotherhood; and with Latin America and the Caribbean (LAC), particularly Cuba. The ostensible objective in Cuba is to build the first mosque in Havana. But as Ken Chitwood argues, the main goal is to undermine the Sunni hegemony of Saudi Arabia and promote Turkey's version of Islam — which Chitwood describes as alter-Islamist politics — as 'a global brand made up of multiple cultures, languages, and histories'. It turns out that Cuba is as eager to oppose Turkish domination as it is to resist Saudi control, as it was to defy American authority. But Chitwood suggests that Turkey's alter-Islamist politics is an unfinished project with much life. It 'may or may not be relevant and appealing to the minority Muslim population in Cuba or in the rest of the LAC', but as 'a lived and felt political, social, and religious reality' it may change and evolve in a positive direction. Its strength lies in its ability to 'creates an environment of individual religious freedom over institutional religious structure' and the 'potential of creating spaces for interaction and interplay between multiple actors'.

A model space for interaction between a host of worldviews and outlooks, East and West, is Istanbul. As the 'bridge of civilisations', Istanbul is home to over 18 million people (unofficially). The majority of the population are Turks, with around 3–4 million Kurds, ironically making Istanbul the world's largest Kurdish city. During my stay in the city, I have witnessed the further rise of the Anatolian Muslim merchant and professional classes, although secularist ideology still maintains a dominant profile in Istanbul. But the rise of the 'Islamic bourgeoisie' has given the city a new vitality. As Aamer Hussein states in his short, evocative piece, Istanbul is one of those cities that 'aren't really ours as we aren't theirs, but we can love them and fit into them of our own volition, without compulsions or convictions or the pressure to belong'. I can say after Hussein, that 'Istanbul could take the place of home for a few days at a time because I laid no claims to it'. It is a Western cosmopolis; offers a 'version of the East that had confronted the paradoxes of modernity'; and serves as 'a microcosm that had made away with continental distinctions'.

But Istanbul is not Turkey per se. The vast majority of Turks reside in the smaller towns and villages of Anatolia. There are also major industrial cities with sizeable populations that have grown tremendously in the wake of the policies of industrialisation, liberalisation of finance and as a result of the social infrastructure created by the AKP. Many cities in Turkey highlight the intersections of vast civilisations, peoples and their cultures, making it one of the richest sources of pre-historical, archaeological and ancient civilisation artefacts. Wherever you travel in Turkey, you witness its rich and diverse history. I have been fortunate to visit the ancient city of Ephesus, with its near-perfect Roman ruins, and the remnants of a vast city that at one point was the fourth biggest in the Roman Empire. In Edirne, I saw an oil-wrestling competition, the Kirkpinar, which has been held annually at the same site, since 1346. The rock-cut churches of Cappadocia, with their beautiful frescoes, the brilliant white beaches of Fethiye, the Mausoleum at Helicarnassus – there is so much enthralling history and culture that it would take the 'halal tourists' from the Arabian Gulf states a lifetime to see it all. My Turkish friends tell me that I can visit and see them because the Europeans did not colonise the country, take away all of her cultural wealth, placing it in museums to demonstrate their historical status. They have a point; and, one must acknowledge, that Turkey has been reasonably good at preserving and conserving its cultural property.

However, there is a danger lucking over the horizon – forgetting. 'The past', writes Charles Allen Scarboro, 'is malleable and our memories live within the larger narratives of our contemporary society'. Scarboro takes us on a tour of Avcilar, his neighbourhood in Istanbul, and shows how little the Turks remember their multifaceted past. In Avcilar 'a short stretch of an older highway lies alongside the newer E-5, the six-lane divided highway leading out of Istanbul. This short stretch of older road is named Eski Edirne Asfalta (the old paved road to Edirne), echoing a slower time when Avcilar was a humble way station between Constantinople and the earlier Ottoman capital in Edirne. The E-5, in its cold and abstract name, sets our sights to a far faster and far more general connection between Istanbul and 'Europe and Turkey's participation in the economy and culture of Western Europe. Edirne fades into insignificance; it has become a kilometre marker'. The neighbourhood 'has also forgotten that the Eski Erdirne lies atop the Via Egnatia, a Roman road that tied Constantinople first to Adrianople, the earlier name for Edirne, and then on to the city of Rome. Those memories, however, are faint – eroded and replaced through the Ottoman then Republican policies of 'Turkifying' the old Roman and Byzantine realms, even to the level of the suburbs of Istanbul. Avcilar, itself, is named after the Sultans' hunting lodges located here and the name of the Greek village that long nestled here alongside the Sea of Marmara is forgotten'.

In the historical city of Hasankeyf it is not an expressway but a dam that threatens to wipe out the city and its memories. The neo-liberal economic policies of the AKP seek profit over the need to remember the past. Development knows no bounds. Hasankeyf, writes John Crofoot, is 'rich in Seljuk-era architecture and urban archaeology'. It is 'a treasure house of the cultural history of Eastern Anatolia from the twelfth to the fifteenth century and an invaluable source of insight into the complexities and nuances of Seljuk society'. It is one of the few places where we can 'acquire a comprehensive view of how cities were organised, the technologies that shaped everyday life, and the eclectic architectural tastes of Artukid, Ayyubid and Akkoyunlu patrons'. Yet, the city and its archaeological history could be drowned in a '10.4 billion cubic meter reservoir within a matter of a few years' – thanks to the Ilısu Dam project.

Fortunately, Konya faces no such dangers. But the city that gave us Rumi is a bit of anomaly as Sufi tariqas are still officially proscribed by the state. The Sufi mystic and poet, Jalāl ad-Dīn Muhammad Rūmi (1207–1273) is Turkey's greatest cultural export. His shrine in Konya, the home of his Mewlewi order and the Whirling Dervishes, attracts millions of visitors every year. Rumi's *Mathnawī*, composed in Konya, is regarded as one of the great glories of Islamic literature; and his spiritual, ethical and moral teachings continue to influence people all over the world on matters of human nature, cultural philosophy and religion. To be in Konya amongst the Whirling Dervishes, as I discovered, is to be moved into a parallel spiritual cosmos. But it is not just the Whirling Dervishes who leave a lasting impact on you. When Peter Clark comes face to face with the portal of the mosque in Konya, known as Ince Minare, he too is transformed. 'Its physical presence', he writes, 'moved me as I had never been aesthetically moved before'. The style and design of the portal 'lacked any possibility of further development. It embodied a kind of perfection'. Both the architectural and the spiritual manifestations 'eluded the kind of rational categorisation to which my education had conditioned me'. The experience profoundly changed Clark's life. It was a starting point for his career, an 'insatiable curiosity and quest for empathising' with the world of Islam.

Rumi's work is, without doubt, universal. But could one say the same about the noted Turkish novelists Ahmet Hamdi Tanpınar (1901–1962) and Orhan Pamuk? The political battles of the Ottoman-scorning secularists and Ottoman-loving conservatives, as well as Turkey's on-off lover affair with Europe, have naturally been replicated on the literary landscape. As Nagihan Haliloğlu points out, Tanpınar has been claimed by both secularists and conservatives. In his fiction and non-fiction, Tanpınar 'gives us a panorama of a modernising Turkey, as the country experiences all the possible pitfalls in the process'. He recognised the difference between 'our old life', the Ottoman way, and 'our new life', the way of the secular Republic. 'His old-new dichotomy', writes Haliloğlu, 'treats Ottoman and Republican cultures not so much as antithetical but as continuation of one another, with the possessive pronoun making sure that the reader knows that Tanpınar and his narrators have a sense of belonging to both'. Tanpınar's alleged Ottoman nostalgia found an echo with the conservatives and his A Mind of Peace has been hailed as a classic – to be read by all Turks after the Qur'an and Rumi's Mathnawi. But the publication of his diaries in 2008 revealed a different Tanpınar: one who thought conservatives yearning for the Ottoman Empire were 'ignorant and thick-headed (and much more besides)'. 'With the taint of being the go-to man of the pro-Ottomanists thus lifted, the new liberal brand of the secular establishment started to take to Tanpınar in the 1990s and the noughties, which culminated in Pamuk declaring him to be one of his influences'. However, Orhan Pamuk is himself quite problematic for many Turks who see him, in the words of Abdullah Yavuz Altun, as 'a pro-Western intellectual'. His Western readers, on the other hand, 'consider his works as coming from the periphery or East'. Pamuk may not be writing about universal love à la Rumi, but does that mean he is simply a local writer writing about 'Turkish love'? The answer depends on your inclination, but Altun suggests he certainly 'enjoys the paradoxical situation of being a modern novelist who outcasts himself from both intellectual fronts'.

There is little doubt that intellectual and political battles in Turkey are set to continue. In many ways, the story of its twenty-first century is the story of the rise and the fall of the AKP, its intellectual and cultural nostalgia for the Ottoman Empire, its attempt to tame the army, and its paradoxical relationship with secularism and Europe. Indeed, under AKP the country has come a long way in a short period of time. However, the need now is to move towards a civic nationalism model, one that effectively incorporates minorities and diversity into its legal, political, cultural, and economic systems. Consensus is important for stable democracies, but we should not forget the need for a critically engaged opposition. Only then can democracy be truly held accountable. It is the people of modern Turkey who provide us with a hope for the future – who maintain a legacy of a golden past, a revolutionary turn and a global perspective that sees them looking both east and west with confidence, poise and promise.

THE FALSE PROMISE

Ahmet T. Kuru

Since the collapse of the Ottoman Empire, most Turks preserved the belief, beyond a simple expectation, that one day they would have 'grandeur' again. In fact, this was largely shared by some Western observers who regarded Turkey as a potential model for the coexistence of Islam and democracy. Almost a century after the collapse of the Ottoman Empire, however, it would be fair to depict Turkey as a mediocre country, in terms of its military, economic, and socio-cultural capacities, and a competitive autocracy, regarding its political system. The promise of the Turkish case to combine the best parts of Islamic ethics and modern democratic institutions appeared to be false. What explains the failure of the idea of the 'Turkish model?'

To simplify a complex story, one could define the competing groups in Turkish politics until 2012 as Kemalists and their discontents. For the former, it was the religious and multi-ethnic characteristics of the Ottoman Empire that led to its demise. The Turkish Republic, in contrast, had to be assertive secularist, and Turkish nationalist, to avoid repeating the maladies of the Ottoman ancien régime. This project required radical reforms, including the replacement of the Arabic alphabet with Latin, and an authoritarian regime, since the majority of Turks were conservative Muslims, and Kurds resisted assimilation. A major problem of the Kemalist understanding of Westernisation was its extreme formalism, probably due to the fact that Kemalism was primarily represented by the military. According to this formalist perspective, dress code and way of life defined the level of Westernisation of a person. A modern Turk was supposed to drink alcohol, wear a swimsuit on the beach, and keep anything religious in the private sphere. Someone fulfilling such criteria, even if the person did not have a successful career and was very unproductive, proved to be a good citizen. The most infamous reflection of this formalism was the Hat Law, which made the omission by any man to wear a top hat punishable by imprisonment, and even death, as it was regarded as an insurgency in a dozen cases. Thus, unless someone fitted the formal requirements of being modern, the person's merits, achievements, and productions could be ignored.

Nevertheless, the Kemalists allowed democratic elections and power transition in 1950. They hoped that the conservative and Kurdish resistance would weaken after one party rule for three decades. To their surprise, the resistance continued. The centre-right Democratic Party led by Adnan Menderes ruled the country for a decade with popular support and some revisions in the Kemalist system. Authoritarian tendencies of Prime Minister Menderes solidified the Kemalist opposition against him. In 1960, the military staged a coup d'état, which started the vicious circle of the elections of non-Kemalist, right wing parties (1950, 1965, 1979, and 1995) and the military coups (1960, 1971, 1980, and 1997). Even beyond the coups, the Kemalist military and judiciary kept having 'tutelage' over the political system. A top item on their agenda was an exemplary obsession with formalism – to sustain the headscarf ban for university students. Another formalistic tendency of the Kemalists was to establish the personal cult of Mustafa Kemal Atatürk making him a semi-sacred figure.

A major Kemalist mistake in Turkish politics was the hanging of Menderes in 1961. This trauma consolidated right wing political activists, who, in fact, constituted a very broad spectrum from centre-right to Islamism. While the Kemalists had been blaming Islamic traditions as a barrier to modernism, the rightists began to blame Kemalism for most of the problems in Turkey. The so-called February 28 process provided an opportunity for the right to further popularise their criticisms of Kemalism. The process began with the soft coup against Islamist Prime Minister Necmettin Erbakan on 28 February 1997, and continued about six years. This period of time experienced military-led oppression, mass level of corruption, and two economic crises.

The Justice and Development Party (AKP) founded by Tayyip Erdoğan, Abdullah Gül, and Bülent Arınç, came to power in 2002 with the promise to undo the Kemalist mistakes. Erdoğan declared that the AKP politicians had dropped their Islamist past and would work to make Turkey a member of the European Union (EU). The AKP defined itself as a continuation of the centre-right trajectory, which was previously represented by Menderes, Süleyman Demirel, and Turgut Özal. In order to fight against the one-man rule in political parties, the AKP's by-law imposed the three-term limit for not only the party leader but also the parliamentarians.

Using the EU reforms as leverage, the AKP restricted the military's political power. Yet the institutional reform that eliminated several prerogatives of the military was not enough to stop the officers who planned coup d'états against the AKP. Several interventions were planned, especially in 2003-2004, and a failed e-coup attempt was staged in 2007 (when the military put an ultimatum onto its website). The failed closure case against the AKP in 2008 — the so-called judicial coup — was also supported by some generals.

During these tough times, the main ally of the AKP was the Hizmet movement led by Fethullah Gülen. The movement had opened dormitories and then schools in Turkey in the 1970s and 1980s; and in the 1990s, expanded its education, media, and business networks abroad. Due to the Kemalist military's pressure, Gülen migrated to Pennsylvania, United States, where he still lives. Currently, the movement has over 1,000 schools and about two dozen universities in nearly 160 countries. It also has several newspapers (including Zaman), magazines, and TV stations in various languages such as Turkish, English, and Arabic. Its business association, TUSKON, and charity organisation, Kimse Yok Mu, are internationally active.

In Turkish politics, the Hizmet movement was influential with not only its media network but also its sympathisers in various levels of the bureaucracy. The movement provided key support to the AKP in its struggle with numerous coup attempts. In a series of court cases, supported by both the AKP and Hizmet, hundreds of military officers were imprisoned due to various coup plans. The judicial processes during these cases were criticised on many grounds and several court decisions were later cancelled. The critics of these trials questioned the authenticity of documents recorded in DVDs, which were discovered in the military headquarters. The proponents of the trials, however, stressed the Council of State attack in 2006, the arsenals found out in various places, and documents leaked by military officers as convincing evidence; they also stressed that political assassinations ended following these prosecutions. Anyway, the main result of these cases was the consolidation of the AKP's power.

The AKP won the 2011 elections with half of the votes and the promise of drafting a new, liberal constitution. Erdoğan, however, blocked the new constitution project with his ambition to replace the parliamentarian regime with a presidential one and to make himself the ultra-powerful president for ten years (2014-2024). The three-term limit in the AKP's by-law could not contain Erdoğan's ambition while it helped him eliminate all other founders of the party, including Gül and Arınç. Erdoğan established a one-man rule in the AKP, and later in Turkey by fulfilling the power vacuum that had occurred due to the decline of the Kemalist military and judiciary. He tried to take various spheres of life under his control from soccer to judiciary, from religion to construction, and from media to education. His goal of dominating all spheres eventually conflicted with Hizmet; the old allies turned into enemies of each other.

Erdoğan also tried to extend his influence by leading the Arab Spring. His interventionist foreign policy towards the Middle East, however, turned into a failure. Rather than pursuing a well-crafted strategy toward the region, Erdoğan used foreign policy issues to energise and expand his domestic constituency with a populist rhetoric. While criticising the 2013 coup d'état in Egypt, for instance, he said that in Turkey's March 2014 local elections 'the ballot boxes will be empowered with the spirit of martyr Asma — the symbol of the Egyptian Revolution.' (Asma Al-Beltagi, the daughter of a Muslim Brotherhood leader, was killed by Egyptian security forces on 14 August 2013). Erdoğan's populist demagoguery removed any possibility for Turkey to play an intermediary role between Muslim Brothers and Egyptian generals. For similar reasons, Turkey currently does not have an ambassador in Egypt, Syria, Israel, Libya, and Yemen. Turkey's border with Syria is under the control of the Islamic State of Iraq and Syria (ISIS) and militias affiliated with the Kurdistan Workers Party (PKK). Due to the ISIS threat, Turkey evacuated its soldiers guarding the Süleyman Shah tomb, which was Turkish soil inside Syria. Turkey now has over two million Syrian refugees, who may stay for good. Erdoğan's populist rhetoric also fed anti-Western sentiments and thus damaged Turkey's relationships with Western countries. He even asked Vladimir Putin twice to take Turkey in to Shanghai Cooperation Organisation (that includes Russia, China, Kazakhstan, Kyrgyzstan, Tajikistan, and Uzbekistan), proposing it as an alternative to Turkey's EU membership bid.

Erdoğan's increasing level of authoritarianism coincided with his rising dosage of Islamism. He declared that his government would educate a 'pious generation'; for that purpose, he gave Islamic Imam-Hatip schools a pivotal role in the public education system. Instead of reforming the Directorate of Religious Affairs (Diyanet) as an autonomous body, Erdoğan began to use it as a political instrument. His antagonistic attitude towards the Alevi minority was also a part of his populist Islamist discourse. He further inflamed the secularists by defining anyone drinking alcohol as alcoholic and by declaring a plan to prevent male and female students from renting apartments together.

In order to establish his ultra-presidential regime, Erdoğan also decided to build a media network exclusively loyal to him and to establish patron-client relations with millions of poor voters. For this project, he needed substantial amount of money. Yet unlike Arab rentier states and Putin's Russia, Turkey did not have oil. Erdoğan, therefore, focused on construction projects and selling public lands in Istanbul. The Gezi protests occurred as a reaction to the combination of Erdoğan's authoritarian tendency, his insistence to rule until 2024, and passion for construction while ignoring environmental issues. Erdoğan declared that the Gezi Park in Istanbul's main square would be replaced by a rebuilding of an historic barrack to be used either as a mall or residency. In May 2013, the police and municipal officers began to bulldoze the park and started to evict the protester by using tear gas and burning their tents. This led to demonstrations that lasted two months and included millions of people. In order to motivate his religiously conservative followers against the protestors, Erdoğan claimed that the protestors attacked a headscarved woman and drank alcohol in a mosque; both were later revealed as false accusations. Erdoğan and his followers also defined the Gezi events as a Western conspiracy. Due to the police's brutal crackdown, 11 people died and about 8,000 were wounded. By revealing Erdoğan's authoritarian attitudes, the Gezi events discredited the idea of the 'Turkish model' of a functional combination of Islam and democracy in the international media.

The corruption probe, which began in December 2013, further questioned Erdoğan's regime. In the first 'wave' of the probe, prosecutors accused three cabinet ministers of receiving bribes from Iranian businessman Reza Zarrab. Several others, including a fourth minister, were accused of corruption on various issues such as government tenders and construction projects. Following the resignation of these ministers, the second 'wave' started with accusations against Erdoğan himself as well as his son, Bilal. Erdoğan defined the probe as a coup d'état staged by the 'parallel state' - an alias he used to imply the Hizmet movement. Erdoğan called Gülen 'a false prophet,' while calling the Hizmet movement's followers 'spies, collaborators of a US-based conspiracy, lovers of Israel, viruses, blood-seeking vampires, and assassins.' He declared an 'Independence War,' and has dubbed those who criticised his policies, including the main opposition CHP, Doğan media group, and Turkish Industrialists and Businessmen Associations, as 'traitors'.

But that was not enough. He also reassigned hundreds of prosecutors and tens of thousands of police officers, and ordered police chiefs to disobey prosecutors and judges in new corruption cases. Nevertheless, he could not stop the leakage of legal evidence, such as wiretapped phone conversations and indictments, to the Internet. The leaked conversations were about Erdoğan's villas acquired in exchange of doing favours for his cronies, his way of controlling media outlets, personal interference in governmental tenders, ambition to control judicial institutions, and interference in some court cases. Erdoğan confirmed some of these conversations, while denying others, such as the one in which Minister Egemen Bağış allegedly ridiculed the Qur'an. One particular recording had the biggest impact. Erdoğan rejected it as a 'montage,' but also said that his encrypted phone was tapped, which was perceived as an unintentional way of accepting the recording. The leader of CHP, Kemal Kılıçdaroğlu, defined the recording as authentic as Mount Ararat. Some expert reports have authenticated the recording, which allegedly included five phone calls between Erdoğan and his son (Bilal) on the day the corruption graft began. In the recording, Erdoğan allegedly asked his son to re-locate a large sum of money kept in houses of the family members. Bilal allegedly called his father back, toward the end of the day, reporting that he had handled most of the money but still had 30 million euros to dissolve. The recording emerged on Twitter, and watched about five million times in five days on YouTube. On 20 March 2014, Erdoğan said in his party's mass meeting: 'we will wipe out Twitter...I don't care what the international community says. They will see the Turkish republic's strength.' Few hours later access to Twitter was blocked for a day. Since then, the Turkish government has temporarily shut down Twitter, YouTube, and Facebook several times.

The AKP-controlled media produced a host of excuses for the corruption scandal, and claimed that money confiscated by the police was collected for Islamic services. For example, the police found $6 million hidden in shoeboxes in the house of the Chief Executive Officer of Halkbank, who allegedly received the money as a bribe from Zarrab. They claimed that the money was not a bribe, but a donation for an Imam-Hatip school. Erdoğan repeatedly defended their narrative, defining Zarrab as a 'philanthropist.' The debate was extended to a discussion of some fatwas that permitted the government to request companies to make donations to particular Islamic associations in exchange of governmental tenders. This triangular arrangement between government, companies, and pro-government Islamic associations created a major public debate in Turkey – not just about corruption, but also secularism, because it meant secular associations and dissenting Islamic associations were facing discrimination.

Despite the corruption scandal and Erdoğan's increasingly authoritarian one-man rule, the AKP maintained its dominant position in the March 2014 local elections with 43 per cent of the votes, and Erdoğan was elected as president in August 2014 with 52 per cent of the votes. The fact that the conservative voters were not too concerned about corruption or authoritarianism created a major debate in Turkey on the linkage between Muslim conservatism and public ethics. Moreover, Erdoğan declared a 'witch hunt' against the Hizmet movement. Hundreds of alleged members of the movement, including prosecutors, journalists, policemen, and military officers, were detained and held in prison for about a year without indictment. When two judges decided to release some detainees, Erdoğan's followers in the judiciary ignored the court's decision and even detained the two judges themselves. The media and the judiciary under his control criminalised the Hizmet movement by declaring it to be a 'terrorist organisation.' Erdoğan repeatedly targeted Bank Asya, which is affiliated with the movement. He declared that the bank was 'already sunk'; and when the Bank Asya did not sink, despite deliberate speculation, he got the bank confiscated. Erdoğan's regime also opened a case against the movement's charity arm, Kimse Yok Mu, defining it as a terrorist organisation. Thousands of bureaucrats lost their jobs, including 1,150 of Turkey's top 1,725 police chiefs, accused of being members of Hizmet. Erdoğan also closed Turkey's police academy and police high schools arguing that they were dominated by Hizmet's followers. Over 2,000 students of these institutions automatically lost their rights without any judicial process.

Since December 2013, when Erdoğan began his campaign against Hizmet, the media under his control has maligned Hizmet almost daily, including absurd assertions about Gülen himself: he is alleged to be a free-mason, his followers were Mossad spies, the Brookings Institute was under Hizmet's control, and Gülen personally ordered the assassination of Erdoğan's daughter. Hizmet is not the only group Erdoğan is demonising, but it has become Erdoğan's main target for the last two years, because it is perceived as the main barrier against Erdoğan's project to establish a personal hegemony over both the state and Islam.

The project faced a setback in the July 2015 parliamentary elections. The AKP received 41 per cent of the votes, a substantial decrease from its previous share (50 per cent) in 2011 elections. This decline becomes significant if seen in its specific context: the AKP, and Turkey's supposedly 'neutral' president, turned anything they could, including Islamic symbols, public institutions (except the armed forces), public funds, half of the TV channels and newspapers, and patron-client relations, as instruments in their electoral campaign. An AKP-controlled newspaper even declared the opposition as 'Crusaders'. Despite its declining popularity the AKP has stayed in power and pursued its two main objectives – to maintain the personal authority of Erdoğan and to conduct a witch hunt against Hizmet. Yet, the AKP is unlikely to make any progress in terms of re-establishing the rule of law, reviving democratic institutions, and re-emphasising Islamic ethics.

Only a few years ago, Turkey was hailed as an ideal prototype, a demonstration of the true compatibility of Islam and democracy – not least in the pages of *Critical Muslim*. Unfortunately this promise has turned out to be false, especially in the last two years. Erdoğan had pledged to make Turkey a member of the EU and to draft a new, liberal constitution. After a decade in power, what he has actually built is a 1500 room palace for himself at a cost of around $1 billion! Thanks to the presidential dreams of Erdoğan, the 'Turkish model' has failed.

There are, however, a few lessons to be learned from observing the Turkish experience:

First, Islamism is a powerful popular rhetoric with a strong appeal to the conservative masses but it does not have any serious policies to deal with social, economic, and political problems. Most modern political and economic institutions and principles, such as separation of power, have Western origins. Thus, Islamists' anti-Western stance and rhetoric become a barrier against effective institution building and deployment of liberal principles in countries where they come to power. The increasingly anti-Western rhetoric of Erdoğan coincided with his claim that Turkey should embrace an 'à la Turca presidentialism' in which there would be no checks and balances, and the president would control both legislature and judiciary.

Second, assertive secularists and Islamists in Turkey have a great deal in common. While they accuse each other, they are equally devoted to nepotism, illiberalism, and leader-centric politics. Conservative Muslims are as formalistic as assertive secularists. In Turkey, the Kemalist idea of defining modernity with drinking alcohol and wearing swimsuits is reflected by the AKP supporters' reduction which defines a true Muslim as not drinking alcohol and wearing headscarves. For dissenting groups, such as the Hizmet movement, the recent Turkish experience shows that an Islamist regime is as dangerous as an assertive secularist regime, in terms of restrictions over their freedoms of expression, association, and education, and even their property rights.

Third, ends should not justify means. The Machiavellian obsession to stay in power has been too costly for Turkish Islamists. Erdoğan became the most powerful leader of modern Turkey, only second to Atatürk. Yet in order to attain and maintain power, Islamists gave up most of their ethical principles – bringing conservative Islam itself into disrepute. In the post-Erdoğan era, Turkey may experience a new secularist wave in which conservative Muslims are blamed and held responsible for creating and maintaining an authoritarian regime.

THE AMBIGUITY OF TURKISH SECULARISM

Edip Asaf Bekaroğlu

Turkey defines itself, like most nations, as a miraculous and exceptional state. This uniqueness discourse inspires Turkish people to imagine themselves and their nation as superior and special compared with other nations of the Muslim world. Being a secular democracy is the first and foremost characteristic of this uniqueness; and this discourse cuts across all political and ideological divisions, and is shared alike by seculars, conservatives, liberals, nationalists, socialists and communists in Turkey. One of the most significant expressions of this discourse came from Recep Tayyip Erdoğan, then the prime minister of Turkey and the leader of the Justice and Development Party (AKP). After a trip to post-Arab Spring Egypt in September 2011, Erdoğan declared: 'in Turkey constitutional secularism is defined as the state remaining equidistant to all religions…I recommend a secular constitution for Egypt. Do not fear secularism because it does not mean being an enemy of religion. I hope the new regime in Egypt will be secular.'

Nevertheless, there have been ongoing debates about the degree of secularism in Turkey or the kinds of secularisms marking certain historical periods. It is common among liberals or religious Muslims to consider the Turkish experience as a replica of la laïcité en France in terms of not being tolerant to religion in the public sphere. Leftists and Alawis, on the other hand, accuse the Turkish state of having deficiencies in its model of secularism because of attaching a particular importance to Sunni Islam to define Turkish national identity. A broader question would be whether Turkish secularism is oriented more towards controlling religion for the sake of the state or separating it from the state for the sake of both. Lately, however, historical categorisations have been more popular. By taking the religiously conservative AKP government as a turning point, Turkish secularism is categorised into two periods: authoritarian (or republican) secularism close to the French model that marks the pre-2002 period and inclusive (or conservative) secularism in line with the Anglo-American model that has risen with AKP rule. Post-2002 Turkey is also regarded as a post-secular era, implying the end of authoritarian Turkish secularism.

I argue that Turkish secularism is too ambiguous to fit these conceptualisations, categorisations or models. This is not to say that they simplify the reality, but rather they distort it. Therefore, instead of contributing to fruitless debates where opposing arguments attempt to substantiate the importance of one of the mutually exclusive models, I argue that the general mood of state–religion interaction throughout the republic has been pragmatically changing while the radical exclusion of Islam has not been the general trend but rather a deviation limited to the 1930s and the late 1990s. I further argue that this pragmatic and continuously updated mode of state and religion relationship, or the pragmatic secular contract, is not particular to Turkey, but a common practice all over the world and throughout history.

Secular Contract

The pragmatic secular contract is pragmatic in the sense that each sovereign state since the Westphalia has drawn the limits of majority and minority religions in the public sphere according to the specific conditions it has faced. In that sense, there is no universal approach to organising the relationship between state and religion. On the contrary, each state has its own specific secular contract. What makes the pragmatic character of this contract more significant is that it is continuously updated according to the new conditions brought by changing power relations between state and religions, or within religions, or by the emergence of new religious groups demanding the same rights and privileges granted to the established majority religions. The practical secular contract also implies that there have never been strictly separated domains of state and religion, and 'neither societies nor states are completely secularised.' In other words, the strict separation of state and religion is only a myth even in Western democracies. There are established churches, publicly privileged majority religions, religious ceremonies at the state level, religious schools subsidised by governments, religious political parties, or exemptions granted to certain religious groups in all the European countries. Modernist expectations about the coming of secularised societies have never been realised either. In each secular experience, religion did not disappear from society but it was actually institutionalised in the private domains of the family or the public domains of education, health or social service. Even in France, known for its strict separation, there are ambiguous practices such as banning religious symbols (for example, Islamic headscarf) in some public institutions on the one hand while initiating the establishment of an Islamic umbrella organisation (le Conseil Français du Culte Musulman) to discuss the issues concerning its Muslim citizens on the other. In short, sovereign states have an authority to draw the limits of the public role of religions, but they feel obliged to take the demands of religious groups into consideration when outlining those limits. These limits are subject to change, as the contract is subject to update. And each sovereign state has its own terms and conditions regarding its relationship with majority and minority religions.

In France, Britain, the United States, Turkey, or anywhere else, secularism did not mean eradicating religion, but setting conditions for its existence in the public domain. In this respect, what differed from one country to another is how the borders of the public sphere and the limits of religious activities have been defined. However, the separation of public and private has never been complete or final. Neither did religion cease to play a role within the public domain in most European countries. Therefore, European secular democracies include a paradox, which consists of, on the one hand, freedom of worship for every confessional group, and on the other, a structured discrimination against minority (or non-Christian) religions because of having established, socially and culturally privileged churches.

Turkey's secular democracy has the same paradox. The ambiguity of Turkish secularism, however, goes further. To begin with, Turkish secularism fits neither republican secularism, where a strict separation removes religion from the public sphere and makes it a private matter, nor the constitutional conservative secularism where an official church is established and controlled by the state. While it is an ambitious experience in terms of removing religious symbols from some parts of the public sphere, especially in the areas of education, government, bureaucracy and military, Turkey, at the same time, gives priority to an orthodox version of Sunni Islam over other heterodox establishments, sects and non-Islamic religions. For example, the Directorate of Religious Affairs (DİB) is a governmental institution that is in charge of organising all Muslim religious activities; there are Vocational Religious High Schools (İmam-Hatip Liseleri) founded by the state to train enlightened religious personnel; and there are compulsory religious courses in elementary and secondary schools. All these activities promote orthodox Sunni Islam while directly or indirectly discriminating against non-orthodox Islamic sects and non-Muslims.

This ambiguity stems from Turkey's nation-building process. The Republic of Turkey was founded on the ruins of Ottoman Empire; yet, based its identity not on Ottoman past, but rather as a rupture from the ancien regime, which Dankwart A. Rustow defines as a 'cultural revolution' that aimed at creating 'a new Turk' and a secular nation. Some secular, modern and Western elements were already being inserted by the Ottoman reformers since the eighteenth century, first as the 'infiltration of new elements' to the Ottoman system, and later as systemic changes, with the realisation that there was 'something new and better outside of the traditional system.' However, applying secularisation as an ambitious top-down nation-building project with a new political entity was something quite unheard of. In this project, the founders of Turkey thought that Islam was a fundamental obstacle to progress, and that the first task was to break the influence of Islam en masse, so that progress would almost automatically follow. Nevertheless, Atatürk and his associates were well aware of the fact that Islam should not be left alone, but controlled. Furthermore, they thought that a particular version of Islam compatible with modernity would even be helpful. Therefore, they adopted a 'double discourse', without giving up the secularist/nationalist agenda, chose a friendly version of Islam as the partner, and through it, controlled the influence of religion on Turkish people. 'High' (orthodox) Islam was chosen, and put under state control because, compared to 'low' (heterodox) Islam, it could be state friendly, education friendly, order friendly and reliable. Unorthodox forms of Islam, on the other hand, were banned. This strategy of including Orthodox Islam in the national identity, both for feeding national identity with substance and controlling unwanted consequences of Islam, has made the Turkish secularist project even more ambiguous.

There are different answers to the question of whether this strategy has been successful. Scholars like Ernest Gellner and Dankwart Rustow, for example, approve this strategy by arguing that Turkey succeeded in building a nation and making the transition to democracy without a serious crisis. Indeed, 'high Islam' helped to legitimise the new national identity, and, in some degree, filled the emotional void caused by radical republican measures such as abolishing the caliphate and sultanate, outlawing heterodox orders (tarikat), sects and traditional religious schools (medrese), adopting the Latin alphabet, and imposing Western dress codes. The double discourse strategy was also successful in shaping the political discourse and strategies of centre-right parties, which, as players within the boundaries drawn by the strong state elite, also adopted a double discourse: play the religion card for popular support, but be careful not to provoke the state elite. In this way, Islam found a channel in joining the public and political discourse to some extent, and its radicalisation was prevented.

However, it is also true that this strategy overlooked the power and dynamism of 'low' Islam in establishing social relations, political choices, and identity discourse among the masses. It also dismissed the organic transformations (not necessarily through secularisation) that would take place in society during the modernisation process. Neither could it grasp the possibility of a hybrid culture that would be a form of intermarriage between the modern and the traditional. Moreover, exaggerating the autonomy of unorthodox Islam and its immunity from secularist reforms, and underestimating the consolidation of secularism in Turkey in spite of its top-down imposition, does not help in understanding the Turkish case fully.

Guardians of the Secular Establishment

After the transition to multi-party politics, the Kemalist state elite witnessed some of the failures of their strategy. Heterodox forms of religion were still there and continuing to influence society with every opportunity they had. Although it was the state elite who initiated the transition to democracy in 1946, what they had in mind was a type of multi-party politics where some enlightened, secular citizens could come together and, free from their short term interests, decide what would be best for the people. During the single-party rule of the Republican People's Party (CHP), this task was undertaken by the Turkish Grand National Assembly (TBMM), and the Presidency. Later, however, with multi-party politics, the new political elite started acting according to their short term interests and the demands of their constituencies. They made decisions that were 'irrational' and 'irresponsible' in the perceptions of the state elite. The TBMM lost its position as the 'locus of the state' and the Presidency, military and bureaucracy became the new loci of power, in other words, the guardians of the state. In time, the intellectual-bureaucratic elite fragmented as children of conservative Muslims became educated professionals and technocrats, and subsequently members of the new city-based middle classes. With this increasingly fragmented and polarised politics and bureaucracy, the presidency (directly) and the military (indirectly) became 'the loci of the state.'

The real tension between secular elites and conservative/Islamic segments started as the latter did not stay where they were supposed to be (that is, out of the bureaucracy, universities, and politics), pushing towards privileged domains of status. When the political parties of the National View, or Milli Gorus, led by Necmettin Erbakan, became the focus of this quest for upper mobility, secularist elites seized their spheres of influence; those which were supposed to have a Western and secular outlook, but were to be taken over by those with an Islamic outlook. This symbolic invasion was of great importance since the Turkish revolution was mostly 'about symbols rather than substance'. In the minds of the state elite, it not only damaged the 'modern' appearance of Turkey, but also constituted an assault on the privileges that they enjoyed for a long time. Having the power to decide what was best for the nation and future of the state was the most important privilege of course, but there were some other privileges, such as those related to status (holding the offices and posts) and those related to economics (dominating the means of production). By understanding democracy as a process among enlightened ones to decide what was best for the country free from the pressures of the masses and denying that ordinary people are competent to govern themselves, the Turkish state elite could not grasp the pluralising nature of democracy, the domesticating effect of playing the democratic game, and different and hybrid ways of being modern. Then, in every failure to limit the role of Islam (or any ideology perceived as a threat, such as communism or Kurdish nationalism) in society and politics, state elites acted as the guardians of the state and intervened in the political process in different ways (from putting pressure on politicians to military coups) to re-establish 'rational democracy.' After each intervention, state elites strengthened their positions by further empowering the autonomy of state institutions, and inserting some new tutelage institutions. The military's habit of equipping itself with more 'constitutional' powers after each intervention, in turn, generated a political system where the military monitored civilian politics thanks to the constitutional, legal-ideological and de facto power relations.

After the 1982 constitution, the guardians of the state had enough constitutional and legal mediums to intervene in politics without a military coup. In the 1990s, new elements were added to these means of intervention: the media and civil society. In spite of the arguments made by a lively and independent civil society, after the liberal openings of the 1980s, Turkey witnessed the construction of a widespread statist public culture, a civic religion, where the media was assigned as the messenger. In her ethnography of Istanbul just after the municipal elections of 1994, *Faces of the State: Secularism and Public Life in Turk*, Yale, Navaro-Yashin, challenged those who celebrated the rise of civil society and the contribution of political Islam to rational public debates. She basically argued that the realm of the so-called 'civil society' in contemporary Turkey is full of manifestations of increasingly popular civic religion, such as soldier's farewells, where ordinary conservative people send their boys to military service with great passion, sports games, where singing the national anthem with great respect in each match became a ritual, flag campaigns without any pressure from state officials, or the increasing popularity of the Republic Day celebrations in attracting more and more voluntary people than ever before. The flourishing of this civic religion and its rituals was a sign that the most important Atatürkist principles, which were pushed by top-down measures, now acquired a popular base. These principles are republicanism (giving priority to state rather than persons), nationalism (a secular entity of self-sacrifice for the state), and secularism (a new type of man with a positivist mentality). This new religion gained currency among the city-based middle classes in the post-1980 environment of de-politicisation, where neo-liberal policies were accepted by all the centre right and left parties, which did not present any 'imaginative thinking' or social project. Besides this popularisation of Turkey's civic religion, a new phenomenon was on the rise: Welfare Party, which emerged as an alternative in the eyes of those long ignored and marginalised by centre parties, those who could not wholeheartedly believe in the civic religion, the underdogs within big cities, and the new bourgeoisie, professionals and technocrats. In 1996, after its victory in the 1995 elections, the Welfare Party formed a coalition government with the True Path Party. It ended up failing to satisfy the demands made by the National Security Council meeting that took place on 28 February 1997. These demands were clear signs of retreat from the state elite's double-discourse strategy on Islam. After what became known as the 'postmodern military coup', the politics in Turkey is a story of slackening the strict secular regulations imposed by the military.

The February 28 Process

The state elite have refrained from showing hostility to Islam throughout the history of the Turkish republic. During the 1980s it cooperated with Islam to cope with communism and the anxieties caused by globalisation; or Milli Gorus (MG) leader Necmettin Erbakan's service as the deputy prime minister in three coalition governments between 1974-78 did not generate any reaction. So the question is why did the secular establishment not withstand the coalition government formed by the Welfare Party in 1996? First, the privileged state elite felt threatened by the upward mobility of the new conservative middle classes and the bourgeoisie who also challenged the secularly coloured symbolic baggage of the Republic. This tradition could not easily tolerate the occupation of the office of the prime minister by a leader of an Islamist party for the first time in Republican history. Second, the state elite thought that the centre parties were responsible for the rise of Welfare Party because of their irresponsible politics and unnecessary fragmentation and polarisation; they also helped the spread of Islamic symbols in the public sphere by using religious rhetoric for gains in popularity. Indeed, the state elite disliked democratic politics, which carried some popular demands that contradicted Republican values, and gave voice to the masses that challenged the domination of the state elite. Therefore, state elites led by military officers thought that a reconstruction of the political centre and a re-limiting of the use of Islam in politics were needed. Third, there was the change in the military's threat perception in a post-Cold War world. Since the threat coming from Soviet Russia and communism was eliminated, the military became more concerned with internal threats, namely Islamic 'reactionism' and Kurdish nationalism, which, in turn, transformed internal political, social, cultural and economic issues as security questions. This change in the concept is clearly stated both in the official papers of the Turkish Armed Forces (TSK) and in the statements of top commanders. The Ministry of National Defence's White Papers of 1998 and 2000 defined explicitly these threats to internal security as 'threats to Turkey's unitary state quality' and to 'the principle of secularism guaranteed in Articles 2 and 4 of the Constitution.' Another very clear expression of this was the deputy chief of general staff's statement in 2001: 'Countries that could not create a common value system are by definition in a state of conflict. Our common value is secular and democratic Turkey within the framework of Unitarianism and Atatürkist thought. All movements that do not meet with us on this common value are the enemies of the nation and country, and must be fought against'.

In this respect, from the very beginning, the military did not sympathise with Welfare Party's leading role in the formation of the government. Although the Welfare Party, as a legal political party, had given some signs of developing into a pro-system party with respect to the secular-democratic order in Turkey, its attempts were considered to be no more than hypocrisy. Yet, in spite of having strong suspicions about Welfare Party's secular as well as democratic credentials, the military officers adopted a strategy of wait-and-see. However, Welfare Party's rhetoric and moves, such as forming an economic and political unity of Muslim countries (known as D8), bringing up the idea of building large mosques in Taksim and Çankaya, two very symbolic centres of the modern Turkish Republic, inviting the leaders of religious sects to a Ramadan dinner at the official residence of the Prime Minister, and anti-secularist statements of some elected officials only exacerbated the military's suspicion.

The first explicit expression of this unrest was the National Security Council (MGK) meeting on 17 August 1996, noting that the activities of militant Islamists constituted a major threat to Turkey. By proposing that the MGK should look into this matter at its next meeting, they expected the government to understand the degree of seriousness of the military's sensitivity about any kind of anti-secular inclinations. However, the government could not satisfy the expectations of the military. At the MGK's 26 December 1996 meeting, the commanders noted that since August 1996, the Islamic threat had become greater, and retained their request that this matter be placed on the agenda of the MGK. At the same time, the commanders set up the so-called West Study Group (BÇG) in the General Staff headquarters to monitor the activities threatening the secular republic and plan appropriate measures against such threats. Also, a new organ called the Prime Ministerial Crisis Management Centre was formed within the MGK secretariat to observe and report on crises caused by Islamic 'reactionism' and formulate responses to this threat. With this organ, the General Secretary of the MGK was given the task of monitoring whether the MGK decisions were implemented by the government. The historical 28 February 1997 MGK meeting took place in such circumstances and it issued a list of measures to be implemented by the Welfare party-led coalition government 'to nullify the supposed Islamisation of Turkey and fortify the secular system.' These measures included raising the mandatory primary school education from five years to eight years and so abolishing the first three years of İmam-Hatip schools, hampering the graduates of İHL's from studying in universities other than theology departments, allowing Qur'an courses only in the summer vacation and only for the children older than thirteen. On 22 May, Erbakan stated that 'there were two options in front of the government. The first was not to accept the terms, and resign from the government. The second was to compromise and try to convince. We chose to compromise for the sake of the country and government.' At the same time, on 21 May, the Prosecutor's Office of the Court of Appeals opened a case against Welfare Party, arguing that it became 'the focus of anti-secular activities.' Not fulfilling the measures demanded by the MGK and under the pressure of the closure case, the Prime Minister Erbakan had to resign on 18 June 1997.

However, it would be a mistake to consider February 28 process as a military intervention where the military and political parties were the only players. The military, rather than directly talking to the government (except in the MGK meetings), initiated a campaign that included media, businessmen, labour representatives, judiciary, the president, the other political parties, and, therefore, a significant proportion of people to pressure the government to resign. This front seemed to be the grassroots of a political movement, where the TSK acted in the leadership position. In the end, this military campaign was able to bring the unwanted government down without actually leaving the barracks and using unconstitutional means thanks to the increasing popularity of the 'civic religion', the decreasing popularity of (and confidence in) politicians, and the legal mechanisms given to the TSK by the 1982 Constitution.

The goals of this intervention were of course in line with the reasons for not tolerating the Welfare Party-led government: lessening Islam from the public sphere and lessening the political. Although it can be argued that the events of February 28 were a rupture from the traditional state-Islam interactions because of its goal to cleanse Islam from the public sphere, it actually stood for a new mode of the Turkish state's tradition rather than a rupture. The architects of February 28 did not target Islam itself, but rather what they considered to be unwanted and harmful manifestations. In other words, the founders of the Republic, the state elite, the guardians of the regime, and the architects of February 28 were not against Islam as a spiritual belief, which could be exercised in the private sphere and mosques, but against socially and politically organised Islam, which, in the Turkish case, is crystallised in the Milli Görüş tradition. Perhaps, one of the most original objectives of the February 28 project was to force the Welfare Party, the most visible organisation of political Islam, to engage in the project of lessening Islam from the public sphere. In other words, pushing the Welfare Party towards political suicide.

The second and more sophisticated goal of the February 28 process, lessening the political, was twofold: restructuring the political centre and redrawing the limits of playing the democratic game. Always blaming the political parties that have used religious rhetoric for gaining popular support since 1950, pro-February 28 circles actually disliked democratic politics, which carried some popular demands that contradicted Republican values, and it gave voice to the masses that challenged the domination of the state elite. The TSK now questioned the logic and institutions of representative democracy because they thought that multi-party democracy had been used by Islamists to replace the secular nature of the Republic. Therefore, the military adopted a more critical stance against existing democratic institutions. Even secularist politicians were blamed for not adequately producing policies to fight against Islamic 'reactionism.' Indeed, the Welfare Party, during its government, could not find a reliable political interlocutor to negotiate on secularism, but the military.

After the February 28 events, the centre-left parties, CHP and Democratic Left Party (DSP), undertook the role of 'the agents and defenders of the reconsolidation of nation-state behind the totalising language of secularism,' while the centre-right parties, Motherland Party, (ANAP), True Path Party (DYP) and Nationalist Movement Party (MHP), 'gravitated towards a state-cantered discourse.' The outcomes of the very next elections in 1999 seemed to be a success for the February 28 process in terms of restructuring the political centre. The first and foremost winner of the 1999 elections was nationalism when considering the triumph of the MHP and the DSP, right-wing and left-wing nationalist parties respectively. Secularism was also another winner of the elections. A six-point-decrease in the votes of Welfare Party's successor, the Virtue Party, was one indicator of that. But a second indicator was more significant: the DSP, 'which was honoured as the representative of statist secularism by state elites,' received the highest percentage of the votes. These outcomes proved that an attempt to restructure politics was accomplished to a certain extent. It shows, moreover, that lessening the political dimension was also accomplished. The rise of the DSP and the MHP could not be attributed to any political accomplishment or the appeal of both parties. Furthermore, the most stable coalition government of the Turkish multiparty era, which was formed by these two parties plus ANAP, did not owe its durability to imaginative politics, but to 'a new version of the politics inertia;' in other words, it is a 'government by default'.

The popularity of Turkey's civic religion was further mobilised and consolidated by the February 28 process. By doing that, the officers hoped that the people would move without exhortation from the military when challenges to Kemalis or secularism appeared. Individuals were not only subjected to Kemalist state ideology, but were also the agents of its articulation and self-assigned inspectors and guardians. This mechanism of 'bio-political production', in Michael Hardt and Antonio Negri's term, was the 'exit guarantee' of this unique military intervention. The military coup of 12 September 1980, as a starting point of Turkey's neoliberal journey, also had a socio-economic agenda. However, none of the previous military interventions had such an ambitious micro-level restructuring as the February 28 process. Hence, if there was a change, it was not in the military's concept of secularism, but in its strategy. This time the military relied more on producing consent and support rather than invoking societal unrest and fear.

A Post-Secular Turkey?

In a meeting of MGK on 28 January 1999, Hüseyin Kıvrıkoğlu, then the chief of general staff, stated that 'If we take February 28 as a process, this was not started in February 28. It is a process started in the beginning of the Republic as reactionism has always been there. It implemented very well from time to time, but some other times, there have been deviations. By February 28, things were put back on the right track. And what is put on the right track should continue as long as there is reactionary threat. This may be ten years, twenty years, a hundred years or five hundred years. That is why we think that February 28 process should not end as long as reactionary threat continues'. Kıvrıkoğlu's target in this statement was Bülent Ecevit, then the prime minister of DSP-MHP-ANAP coalition, which was blamed by the TSK for not sufficiently implementing the February 28 decisions. Nevertheless, three years after this ambitious statement about the duration of the February 28 process, the 2002 elections brought an unexpected major realignment in the political landscape. The political parties that made up the 'government by default' lost most of their popular supporters; the Felicity Party (SP), the current Milli Görüş party, dropped to 2.5 per cent. The newly established Justice and Development Party (AKP), whose leadership emerged from the cadres of Milli Görüş, took advantage of the lack of confidence in current centrist parties, mobilised the groups hit psychologically by February 28 and hit physically by the 2001 economic crisis; and without having its first party congress or offering a detailed political agenda, it gained an unprecedented parliamentary majority of 67 per cent. Since then, politics in Turkey is a constant struggle between the AKP's attempts to stretch the secularist boundaries drawn by the state elites and the civil and military bureaucracy's resistance against its effort. The AKP has won two other parliamentary elections in July 2007 and June 2011, increasing its votes to 46.6 and 49.8 per cent respectively – although, in the June 2015 General Election AKP's vote dropped to 40.8 per cent and it lost its majority. Nevertheless, AKP's electoral victories and its ongoing efforts to stretch the aggressive secularist policies introduced during the February 28 process did not mean a 'post-secular' era as it is suggested by some scholars.

The post-secularism thesis argues that there is an unexpected trend towards a rise in the public influence and personal relevance of religion in secular societies. In other words, the post-secularism argument originally is not about secularism as the state condition but rather it assumes two mutually exclusive social conditions: secular society on the one hand and post-secular society on the other. In the Turkish case, however, post-secularism arguments refer to an end of the 'authoritarian feature' of state secularism and in this regard differ from the arguments in Western societies. Still, post-secularism arguments in Turkey also assume two mutually exclusive state practices about the religious-secular divide. While Turkey before 2000s had been dominated by 'the secular ideology' where Islamic communities 'lacked legitimacy,' post-secular Turkey with the religiously oriented AKP government 'devalued the secular ideology,' and articulated Islam and secular together, where these two are no more exclusionary but rather interact and create a new situation – 'in-betweenness.' In short, the post-secular Turkey arguments suggest a rupture in the practice of secularism with AKP governments. I, on the other hand, would argue that there is no such rupture in terms of the ambiguous nature of Turkish secularism. During the one-party rule, the Turkish state chose a friendly version of Islam as the partner, and through it, controlled the influence of religion on the Turkish people. And after the transition to multi-party politics, right-wing governments, which ruled Turkey in most of this period, have expanded the public domain through opening up some spaces for the previously excluded unorthodox Islamic sects and groups. Even the very initial post-February 28 government was not keen to implement the February 28 decisions, and was criticised by the chief of general staff Kıvrıkoğlu. Therefore, I argue that the mode of state-religion interaction throughout the republic has been pragmatically changing while the radical exclusion of Islam has not been the general trend, but rather a deviation limited to the 1930s and the late 1990s.

With high levels of autonomy from the social forces the Turkish state has always been the favoured side of the secular contract, especially considering the lack of a centralised and self-governing Islamic authority. Secular state elites supported by the urban middle classes have taken the advantage of this power and kept religious (and predominantly rural) masses away from domains where the latter could have accumulated economic, cultural, social or symbolic capital to challenge the former. Secularism has an 'instrumental role' in this struggle, and functions as an 'ideological justification of the existing power relations in society.' In this sense, if there was a rupture with AKP governments, it is not about the relationship between the state and Islam, but rather about the changing power relations between state elites and religiously conservative political elites. Still, the AKP's electoral victories themselves did not mean that the secularist civil-military bureaucracy automatically lost this struggle. The instrumental use of secularism had maintained its functionality for a much longer period. Whenever the AKP had pushed the limits, such as freeing the headscarf or removing the barriers for graduates of İmam-Hatip to enter any department in universities, the secular elites reacted aggressively and restated the red lines. In fact, the AKP has never been very insistent on crossing these lines. This was the lesson learned from the experience of the Welfare Party: be cool with the secular establishment if not cooperating. The AKP had continued this strategy until it managed to change the formations of higher bureaucracy, courts, and the TSK. The headscarf and İmam-Hatip graduates are two central issues to understand the struggle between the state elites and AKP.

When Abdullah Gül was announced as the nominee for the May 2007 presidential vote, the tension between the secular establishment and the AKP reached its peak. The guardians of the state could not accept a picture where a person with (a 'hidden') Islamist baggage and a wife with a headscarf could be the host of Turkey's presidential palace, one of the ultimate symbols of its modern, Western, secular identity. There were three significant reactions to this. First, the representatives of the secular establishment explicitly voiced their concerns. On 12 April 2007, the Chief of General Staff Yaşar Büyükanıt declared that the new president 'should adhere to basic principles of the republic and the ideal of secular, democratic state in deed as well as in word,' implying the hidden Islamist agenda of the AKP and its prospective candidate. The next day, President Ahmet Nejdet Sezer claimed that the Turkish secular system 'faced an unprecedented threat since the foundation of the Republic.' Second, just two days after Büyükanıt's statement, public demonstrations, the Republic Rallies as their organisers named it, started in big cities, gathering hundreds of thousands of people. Third, the TSK made its most explicit statement on the unrest at midnight on 27 April 2007. It posted a public declaration on its website, popularly called as the 'e-memorandum'. The army warned that 'some circles' were trying to disturb 'the fundamental values of the Republic of Turkey, especially secularism' and 'have turned into an open challenge against the state, do not refrain from exploiting holy religious feelings of our people, and they try to hide their real aims under the guise of religion.' The army, which initiated three coups in 1960, 1971, and 1980 and a 'postmodern' intervention in 1997, reminded everyone of its determination to preserve secularism and declared that it 'will display its attitude and action openly and clearly whenever it is necessary.' And finally, on 1 May, the Constitutional Court overruled Abdullah Gül's presidency. The AKP called for immediate elections which were held on 22 July 2007 wherein the major issue was whether a man with Islamist history and a wife with a headscarf would occupy the presidency. In the end the AKP increased its votes from 34.2 per cent to 46.5 per cent. And in the new parliament, Abdullah Gül was elected as the new president of Turkey with the support of the MHP.

Since then there have been two major incidents regarding secularism, and the Constitutional Court was involved in both of the cases: overruling the parliamentary vote on making a constitutional amendment to free the headscarf in universities, and the court decision on AKP's closure case. On 15 January 2008 in Madrid, Erdoğan argued: 'suppose that the headscarf is a political symbol. Could using it as a symbol be a crime? How could you ban symbols?' The Nationalist Action Party with its 71 seats declared that they would support AKP if it brings a draft bill or propose a constitutional amendment to free the headscarf. However, the constitutional amendment that was passed by a majority in the parliament was taken to the Constitutional Court by the CHP and it was overruled. This attempt was at the centre of the chief state prosecutor's indictment, which asked the Constitutional Court to close the AKP for being 'a focal point of efforts to change the secular nature of the Republic' on 14 March 2008. Five months later, the Court made its decision: 'no closure, but a "serious warning"' as one of the leading newspapers put it. According to ten out of eleven judges of the Court, the AKP was 'a focal point,' however, six judges voted against closing the party.

Although the AKP escaped the fate of many other political parties, its space for political manoeuvre was seriously restricted by this decision. As the AKP attempted to behave differently than the centre-right political parties, it was pushed towards the typical behaviour of the very centre it aspires to fill and transform. In the end, the AKP has lost most of its transformative power and reformist agenda. This became clear in the municipal elections of 29 March 2009. Erdoğan, who previously promised a better, more democratic and prosperous future, now confined himself to warning the electorate that the alternatives would bring a worse future if they do not vote for his party. Any reminder of the Islamist past has already dropped from the language during the foundation phase of the party. Indeed, taking their share of the lessons learned from the February 28 process, the AKP cadres, as Turkey's mainstream Islamic elite, have changed all their discourse, ideology and strategies. Concerning the discourse, the AKP, for example, clearly stated that the headscarf, the most significant component of Islamist politics in Turkey, was not a priority in the party's agenda. The AKP defined itself as 'conservative democrat' within the tradition of the centre-right, believing that it is political Islam itself that has damaged social and economic networks of conservative Muslims in Turkey. A strategic change is also apparent. For example, while risking a crisis to send Abdullah Gül and his wife to the presidential palace, the AKP has not insisted on making structural changes to the headscarf ban for ordinary people until managing to change the higher bureaucracy's and courts' formation. This strategy change does not only stand as a failure of Islamists to formulate more imaginative strategies to deal with the secular establishment, but also the success of the secular elite to limit the role Islam plays in Turkish politics. Moreover, secularism is no longer a lifestyle of elite circles but there exists a significant consolidated secular middle class. Furthermore, conservative segments too have adapted to capitalist society, the lifestyle it affords and modern society's secular logic, even if they continued the religious rituals in their personal lives and private spheres.

Indeed, this way of being Muslim is approved by the secular elite as well. The most recent manifestation of this approval is made by İlker Başbuğ, the current chief of general staff. In his annual speech in the War Academy on 14 April 2009, Başbuğ said that 'no one should have a problem with real religious people', who most commonly refer to the military as 'the Prophet's home'; and he argued that the military has never been against Islam as a faith, but against 'some of the religious-based communities' that abuse religion for personal and political interests. In his mild messages about Islam, Başbuğ, by making the difference between religion as a faith on the one hand and organised religion on the other hand, seems not to understand the complexity of the role religion plays in society. He also affirms the military's guardianship role by saying that the military would forever protect the republic's main pillars of secularism and democracy. The target here is clearly 'some communities' of organised Islam (for example, the Gülen movement) rather than the AKP itself. However, it seems that the military in 2009 still had an arbitrary power to decide which versions of organised Islam were 'harmful', and to take the necessary action to deal with them.

The TSK and judiciary have continued to be the supreme obstacles by using all legal means to limit the AKP government's efforts to untighten the February 28 policies. Just surviving a closure case, AKP has stayed very cautious about not offending the secular establishment while trying to keep its constituency motivated. Paradoxically, offending the secular establishment to some extent and receiving some nonlethal reaction have been motivating for the potential AKP electorate to equip the party with more power vis-à-vis civil and military bureaucracy. In the end, the AKP has continuously increased its proportion of votes, at least till the June 2015 election, while gradually changing the formation of high level courts and high ranking officers in TSK. The Ergenekon and Balyoz investigations, where some retired and commissioned officers were detained and/or arrested for initiating plots to topple the AKP government, helped in changing the top officers in the chain of command, replacing 'hawks' with officers tolerating civilian supremacy in political matters, or accepting civilians' 'right to be wrong.' Only after this, the legal regulations about headscarf and religious graduates could be made.

The Higher Education Board (YÖK) had attempted several times to abolish the regulations that complicated the graduates of vocational schools to enter higher education programmmes, yet they had been overruled consequently by the Council of State and Constitutional Court until 1 December 2011, when YÖK tried again believing that the member formation of the Council of State would not oppose its decision. Similarly, putting an end to the headscarf ban was a gradual process. After Abdullah Gül appointed Yusuf Ziya Özcan as the president of YÖK, a directive was sent to universities to stop headscarf bans for students in 2007. Most universities did not follow that direction for a few years. AKP proposed a constitutional amendment to free headscarf that ended up with a closure case at the Constitutional Court. Finally, on 1 October 2013, the headscarf ban was annulled by the parliament for public employees, except military and police officers, judges and public prosecutors.

AKP, while learning from the Milli Görüş experiences, has never been insistent on crossing the lines drawn by secular state elites, and continued this strategy until it managed to change the formations of higher bureaucracy, courts, and the TSK. In other words, the electoral victories of AKP did not mean a destabilisation of Turkish secularism or the collapse of the presumed wall between state and religion in Turkey. Rather, these victories have only equipped AKP to push the Turkish state to update its secular contract to accommodate the demands coming from religious masses. In other words, what has changed is the power relations between the state elites and religious political elite, not the secularity of the state or society. The secular contract has been slightly updated according to the new power relations by extending the place of religious symbols in the public sphere.

GAZI WARRIOR VS SUFI MYSTIC
TURKEY'S ERDOĞAN-GŰLEN BREAKUP

Sophia Pandya

Yesterday, they stabbed us in the back. Tomorrow, they will stab their current colleagues in the back if they get the chance. I call on those who are still silent in the face of this vile betrayal to reconsider their positions.

President Recep Tayyib Erdoğan, regarding the Hizmet movement.

There have been so many injustices, so many false allegations and slanders. The enmity is not mutual. We do not feel enmity towards anyone. We do not see them as the enemy.

Fethullah Gűlen, discussing the rift with Recep Tayyib Erdoğan

The two men with the most power in Turkey are President Recep Tayyib Erdoğan, and religious leader Fethullah Gűlen. The former is the founder and long-time former leader of the Justice and Development Party (AKP) and former Prime Minister. The latter, a Sufi theologian known reverentially as Hocaefendi (respected teacher) to his millions of followers, inspired a civil society humanitarian movement, called Hizmet, or service, which has founded thousands of educational centres and owns dozens of media institutions, in Turkey and abroad. They both recently appeared in the news, reflecting vastly different personalities and modes of masculinity. In a speech on 25 May 2015, Erdoğan angrily rebuked *The New York Times,* stating 'as a newspaper you should know your place!' after it published an article critical of his power-seeking authoritarianism. This article noted that an Ankara-based prosecutor (likely pressured by Erdoğan) just called for a ban on Gűlen-related media outlets, and that many journalists working for Hizmet have already been arrested. It went on to accuse him of 'brute manipulation of the political process,' and being 'increasingly hostile to truth-telling.'

Juxtaposed to this image of a livid Erdoğan, are recent news reports about Gűlen, honoured in Atlanta, Georgia, on April 9-10 2015, by the historically Black Morehouse College. Morehouse presented him with the 2015 Gandhi-King-Ikeda Peace Award, for his work towards global peacebuilding. A ceremony was held for him at the Martin Luther King Jr. International Chapel, and pictures of the three humanitarians, together with Gűlen, were prominently displayed in the lobby, to honour those whose life mission, like that of King, was to struggle towards positive social transformation. These contrasting representations of Erdoğan and Gűlen reflect their contesting visions of Turkey, but also their differing performances of masculinity, leadership, religion, and values regarding alterity.

Ironically, Gűlen and Erdoğan were allies for years, but experienced a ferocious fallout in 2013 after a series of events. Their alliance was based on their common traditional and religious inclinations, not to mention their shared political enemies. Their ultimate breakup was informed, in part, by their contesting forms of masculinity. It would be reductive to attempt to determine causality for their respective gendered identity performances: facets of identity are all dynamically interrelated. Nonetheless, an analysis of their gendered identities and behaviours sheds light on their feud, and on their greater religious and political landscapes. Cain and Abel offer historians of religion two examples of distinct biblical masculinity: Cain as the wild, unrestrained brother, and Abel, the disciplined, more diligent one; Erdoğan and Gűlen provide divergent contemporary models from the Islamic context. Erdoğan's macho demeanour, patterned after the archetype of the Anatolian Gazi Warrior, Ottoman Sultan, and the figure of Atatűrk, speaks to Turkish paranoia and desire for restored honour. Gűlen's masculinity, on the other hand, evokes that of Sufi sainthood – one less 'macho' than intellectual, less warrior than liminal mystic. While clearly 'mystics' and 'warriors/sultans' have at times had interdependent relationships, this one was unsustainable for a variety of reasons, including clashing agendas and a profound loss of trust on both sides.

Gender is not merely a subjective, individual construction or performance: it reflects personal agency and the sociopolitical, religious, and economic landscape; it is mediated, relational, in flux, and its analysis must be contextualised. Some in the contemporary Muslim community have conceptualised male gender roles in a narrow, hypermasculine way, especially idealised by political Islamic groups. However, as Amanullah de Sondy notes, multiple performances of masculinity are allowed by and reflected in the Qur'an and Hadith literature. Several other scholars of masculinity have theorised the connection between gender and politics. Lyndal Roper postulates that changing political environments shape masculinities; for example, in times of political conflict men are both allowed and pressured to behave more aggressively. 'After all', she writes, 'the city ultimately required brute fighting men to keep order and defend the town.' Mark Juergensmeyer argues that emasculated men ritualise and sacralise their aggression to restore honour. Hypermasculinity may be understood as a response to the emasculation of colonialism and volatile political realities. I also rely on Selin Akyüz's analysis of the 'gendered discourses' of Turkish political parties and their leaders and consider the power garnered by different modalities of being.

During numerous trips to Turkey between 2012 and 2015, I interviewed members of the Justice and Development Party (AKP) as well as members of Gülen's Hizmet movement in Istanbul, Gaziantep, Urfa, Diyarbakir, Izmir, Konya and Nigde, Şanlıurfa. I have observed Hizmet institutions (schools, universities, tutoring centres, cultural centres, hospitals) in ten different countries. And on 7 April 2015, I was able to briefly interview Fethullah Gülen, in his Pennsylvania residence. This analysis is based on these interviews and field work.

A 'Marriage' of Convenience

A Turkish journalist visiting California explained Erdoğan's appeal in Turkey: 'Erdoğan told us what we all wanted to hear. Our biggest trauma was the collapse of the Ottoman Empire and he created a dream to resurrect it'. Zeyneb Korkman and Salih Açıksöz note that the President's 'patriarchal authoritarian masculinity' has both lent him his 'charismatic popularity,' and also works against him.

'In the beginning', Gülen told me, 'the AKP, like us, also promoted Turkey's admission to the European Union, democracy and global ethical values. We always spoke highly of the other'. Other factors contributing to Gülen and Erdoğan alliance include common religious roots, inclinations towards the more traditional eastern Turkey, and valorisation of the Ottoman

Empire. More importantly, they both had a powerful foe: the ultranationalist Kemalist guard which controlled the military and had engineered a spate of coups in (1960, 1971, 1980, 1997, and attempted coup in 2003), ostensibly to protect the state from any threat to Atatűrk's model of an assertively secular state. An organisation comprised of Kemalist ultra-nationalist elite, likely trying to preserve their hold on Turkey, also carried out a number of secret activities to destabilise society. The group is called 'Ergenekon,' believed by many to be part of the 'deep state,' a clandestine wing of the military. On 21 September 2012, 330 military personnel were sentenced for 'Operation Sledgehammer,' in which the military planned to overthrow the government in 2003. They were allegedly planning to blow up a mosque in Istanbul and shoot down a Turkish plane over the Aegean Sea while blaming the Greeks, in order to provoke political unrest to justify the coup.

Graham Fuller mentions 'two essentially contradictory visions of what Turkey was and is. On the one hand, an ethnically and religiously diverse Turkey, steeped in Sufi piety and tradition, on the other a Turkey that is European in nature, secular, scientific, and "cleansed" of its religious and Middle Eastern heritage'. Both Gűlen and Erdoğan have opposed the aggressively secular, 'cleansed' vision promoted by ultranationalist Kemalists, a vision devoted to the legacy of Atatűrk, ethnic Turkish particularism and the repression of public forms of piety.

The history of secularism pre-dates Atatűrk's rule. Earlier forms were promoted in Turkey during the late Ottoman period, in part to resist Western colonialism through the strategic adoption of Western models. Atatűrk's model of repressive secularism arose from this paradigm – his insistence on new forms of Westernised masculinity and femininity in the Turkish Republic should be understood through this lens. His own militant, paternal, and virile image, ubiquitous in Turkey even today, was likely promoted to assuage Turkish emasculation anxieties after the Western invasion of Anatolia and the demise of the Ottoman Empire, and to provide a totem of militant manhood binding Turkish identity as secure despite external threats.

In 1996, for the first time since the rise of the Turkish Republic, an overtly practising Muslim came to power: Prime Minister Necmettin Erkaban through his Refah (Welfare) Party. This party was ousted through the 'soft coup' of 1997 carried out by the National Security Council (MGK), ostensibly because it was deemed Islamist, and thus unconstitutional—the constitution enshrined the secular nation of the state; an element considered 'unamendable.' Many public servants who were practicing Muslims were dismissed, and Qur'an schools were banned. Nine hundred military officers were fired for their religious activities after the soft coup, and Erkaban was banned from public office for five years.

Yet this was not the end of the Turkish Republic's new synthesis of politics and overt manifestations of piety. Erdoğan, who was sentenced to a ten year jail term for reciting a religiously militant poem by Ziya Gokalp in 1997, founded the AK Party in 2001. It swept the elections in 2002, a clear victory over the secular Kemalists and the ultra-nationalist Turkish Armed Forces. Abdullah Gűl served as Prime Minister from 2002-2003, and subsequently Erdoğan took over the post in 2003. Both Erdoğan's and Gűl's wives wear headscarves, a symbol of piety for the overtly Muslim community, but a sign of 'cobwebbed' backwardness for many secularists. In 2007 the General Chief of Staff issued a statement in which he warned of a conspiracy to change the very Kemalist nature of the nation and damage the military, and that those involved were growing in power every day. The military, he added, was the only protector against this threat. He was likely referring to the AKP and perhaps also to the Hizmet movement. While anti-AKP protests took place in 2007, those assembled addressed fears of the Islamisation of Turkey via Erdoğan and the AK party.

Erdoğan has not been able to convince the secular Kemalists that he does not have a panoply of secret agendas, such as Islamising Turkey or allowing the US, Israel, or Europe to control its policies. In fact, both Erdoğan and Gűlen have said they favour a secular state. Another widespread fear in Turkey is that the West is taking advantage of Turkey's form of moderate Islam, urging its use as a model for other Muslim states. By association, Hizmet has been accused of the same thing. Part of the problem both Erdoğan and Gűlen face is that collective paranoia and emasculation anxiety are part of the social tapestry in Turkey.

A journalist working in a Hizmet media outlet in Turkey, tells a story about his first experience with a military official when he was twelve. A colonel whipped out a map, and explained, 'Children, Turkey is a country surrounded on three sides with seas, and on four sides with enemies.' This terror of being surrounded by enemies stems from the fall of the Ottoman Empire, Turkey's geopolitical position, and is worsened by the contemporary turbulent and repressive political situation inside Turkey. On all sides of the political spectrum, people worry that their phones are tapped, or that if they admit their allegiances openly that they will be blacklisted. In one interview of an academician, my informant refused to be recorded and firmly shut the door during the interview, stating that he was afraid his views would be perceived as pro-Gülen, which might jeopardise his job. In 2013, *The New York Times* reported that for the second year in a row, Turkey jailed more journalists than any other country.

Other than working together against the secular Kemalists to support religious freedom in Turkey, another principal reason for the alliance has to do with the economy. TUSKON (Turkish Confederation of Businessmen and Industrialists) is a Hizmet-affiliated Turkish business association. In his book on the Gülen Movement, Hakan Yavuz argues that Gülen's emphasis on working hard and abstaining from idleness has boosted Turkey's economy, making it 'the sixteenth largest global economy.' TUSKON's financial power was a driving force behind the growing Turkish economy; it has strengthened the more traditional, less secular central and eastern Turkey. As the Turkish economy improved, Erdoğan and the AKP also benefited. However, leading up to the 2013 split, Hizmet became increasingly critical of Erdoğan's oppressive measures against journalists, intellectuals, Kurds, his neglect of the pursuit EU membership.

The Acrimonious Divorce

Although for about a decade, the AKP, the Hizmet Movement, and other religious groups benefited from the perks of a mutually beneficial alliance, such as more religious freedom, their coalition started to slowly unravel during the 2010s. In 2010, the chief of police, Hanefi Avcı accused Hizmet of infiltrating the judiciary and police, in the attempt to influence the Ergenekon trials. A further catalyst for the split was the allegation made by the Hizmet movement in 2012 against Hakan Fidan, chief of the MIT, the Turkish intelligence agency, and part of Erdoğan's inner circle. On 7 February 2012, special-authority prosecutor Sadrettin Sarikaya summoned Fidan, who was under suspicion for being linked to activities with the PKK. As Fidan is a member of Erdoğan's private circle, Erdoğan considered this charge a personal attack against his authority. After the MIT-judiciary crisis, the government abolished the special-authority courts and restructured the police force.

Three years later, the Gezi protests erupted during the summer of 2013, in which Erdoğan's heavy-handed response to demonstrators trying to save Gezi Park from development was widely criticised. Since the Gezi Park incidents, observers of Turkish politics began to describe Erdoğan's tone and demeanour as 'brash,' 'aggressive,' 'stubborn,' 'condescending,' 'authoritarian,' and 'intimidating.' Gülen and his supporters were among those that were critical of Erdoğan's handling of the Gezi protests and post-Gezi crackdown. They also began to speak out against the AKP's restrictions on press freedoms and Middle East policy. The Hizmet-affiliated think tank, The Journalists and Writers Foundation (GYV), released a statement accusing the AKP of spreading 'slander' on social media and for blaming the Gülen movement for the Gezi Park protests.

'Most of Hizmet didn't immediately get involved with the Gezi Park issue', a Hizmet supporter pointed out. 'Now I look at the tweets, newspaper columns, and people tell me there was an incident before, a spark here and there. People were naïve, but now being naïve has been transformed to guilt. Hizmet had "soft power", people ask us why didn't we pay attention. We were opening up schools, dealing with daily politics'. The conflict reached a tipping point, and in mid-November 2013, Erdoğan announced the closing of Turkey's dershanes, or prep schools; roughly a quarter of those institutions are affiliated with Hizmet. In a rare display of anger, Gülen stated in 2013, 'if people concerned with mundane interests in every realm are against you, if the Pharaoh is against you, if Croesus is against you, then you are walking on the right path'. However, more recently he has pointedly advocated forgiveness in his sermons.

Shortly thereafter the conflict reached its peak during the graft probe in December 2013, in which top Turkish ministers and their officials were accused of corruption and bribery, and of involvement in the Iran-Halkbank-gold triangle. Stacks of shoeboxes filled with millions of dollars, found in the home of Riza Sarraf, an Iranian-born Turkish citizen, were shown to the press. Sarraf reportedly had bribed Turkish ministers and officials, and was working with the sons of three ministers of the Turkish government, and was arrested for his part in a racketeering, money laundering, bribery, smuggling, and corruption scandal, although later released. Iran was barred from using international money transfer systems, such as LINK, due to international sanctions. Thus Iranian money passed through Turkey's Halkbank, returning to Iran as gold, ostensibly with Erdoğan's knowledge, allowing Turkey to indirectly pay for oil and gas purchased from Iran. Ministers were recorded discussing the deal on wiretaps and tapes of the recordings were released. The AKP accused those in the judiciary responsible for the wiretapping and release of the tapes, of doing so by command of the Hizmet movement, and of attempting to destroy the government. Gülen refutes this, stating 'I don't know one in 1000 of the people who executed the corruption investigations. But the whole world witnessed the proofs of bribery, thievery and illicit money'. Regardless, Erdoğan called the movement 'a state within a state,' or alternatively, 'a parallel state,' and accused it of infiltrating the judiciary to control the government; while Hizmet participants are employed in a range of fields including the judiciary, they deny this charge as a conspiracy theory.

Despite being embroiled in a corruption scandal, Erdoğan was elected as President in August 2014, earning the moniker 'Teflon Tayyip'. In October of the same year, the Gülen Movement was deemed a threat to national security by the National Security Council (MGK). In Gülen's view, Erdoğan has given up on full democracy complete with power sharing and freedom of speech. It is true that at different times he has cancelled Twitter, YouTube, Facebook and Google, and actively censors the press in other ways. Gülen expressed his frustration: 'all the AKP wanted was to basically bring every group in the country under their control. When this didn't happen, they became tyrants. The tyranny now is ten, fifteen, twenty times more than the coup eras of Turkey'.

In fact, the Kurdish community, who played a large role in bringing Erdoğan to power due to his promises to allow the Kurdish language to be taught at private schools and his investment in the Kurdish regions, is now turning away from the AKP. In 2015, Erdoğan unsuccessfully made every attempt to stop the Kurdish People's Democracy Party (HDP) from entering Parliament with the required ten per cent threshold of votes for the 7 June election. Fehim Taştekin writes that this party in turn is making efforts to spoil President Erdoğan's 'dream of becoming an omnipotent, executive president,' and that many Kurdish clans are leaving the AKP to join the HDP, because of the AKP's vacillating policies vis-à-vis the Kurdish issue.

Though the Hizmet Movement and the AKP are no longer allies, Gülen's recent proclamations suggest the enmity is not mutual nor set in stone, despite his vexation. Some Hizmet participants appear aware of the role the movement played earlier in creating its own image as secretive, a representation they now reject. A Hizmet-affiliated journalist in Turkey told me that some of the criticisms people have made against the movement are valid:

> We have made mistakes. One mistake is that at the earliest days of the move-ment, in order to create feelings of belonging, Hizmet members kept a low profile and led a secretive existence. They did not even tell their parents of their association with Hizmet, and they kept their distance from other religious movements. In my early days, jeans were forbidden. We were trying to create a sense of difference. We didn't consume margarine. We just said it was forbid-den. Any kind of secret movement gets people asking about the secret agenda of its participants. We knew this, but we chose to be something, even if it meant we would be criticised. By 1994, this stage of 'creating a sense of belonging' was over and members no longer needed to keep a low profile, but rather they needed to go out and establish organisations. The fact that Hizmet has been criticised for being secretive and having a secret agenda is our own fault. 'We did this,' he conceded.

While that might have been true in the past, Hizmet now would prefer to be seen as transparent. Because it is not a formal organisation— but rather a system of loosely-connected institutions—some still find it enigmatic, despite the plethora of scholarship detailing its activities. Clearly, image construction, as any form of 'knowledge,' reflects power at play and not necessarily reality. Similarly, constructions of masculinity portray issues of power and control.

Erdoğan as Divine Warrior

Masculinity is deeply embedded within the Turkish political structure. Under Ottoman rule, the Gazi Warrior archetype embodied the powerful, heroic male warrior, who fought to spread Islam. Yet, this archetype is 'a nationalist figure', notes Salih Açıksöz, 'which evokes imageries of legendary Muslim warriors, Ottoman sultans, medieval warrior dervishes, Atatürk, distinguished warships'. The tradition of hegemonic masculinity persisted during the early years of the Turkish Republic under the nation's founder, Mustafa Kemal Atatürk. The Grand National Assembly granted him the honoured title of Gazi for his accomplishments during the War of Independence, and under the Surname Law of 1934, he adopted the surname Atatürk, or Father of the Turks. He embodies the heroic warrior of the Ottoman past while simultaneously positioning himself as the patriarch of the modern republic.

In many ways, Erdoğan has also replicated Atatürk's model of masculinity: alternating between benevolent father and macho, authoritarian militant. Given that Turkey rates 125th out of 142 countries in the 2014 'Global Gender Gap Report,' it is worth noting Erdoğan's statements regarding women. He has stated that women are not equal to men, and that manual labour was unsuitable for their delicate natures. On 8 August 2013, he rebuked women protesting gender inequality in Istanbul, telling them their role is to bear at least three children. Erdoğan 'enacts the role of a husband who wants three kids, a father who forbids drinking at night, a brother who snitches on his sister for socialising with men. He is a man who dominates, forbids, orders, scolds, degrades, and threatens.' He is the archetypal Turkish tough uncle, or kabadayı.

Politicians often resort to hegemonic masculinity to justify their authority. The state has traditionally played a masculine role, working to fulfill masculinity expectations for Turkish males, and against emasculation anxieties. As Nil Mutluer explains, the 'nation is represented through an ideal father figure who is the head of the nation as well as the carrier of the ideal masculinity.' The refrain, 'every (male) Turk is born a soldier!' reflects the militarisation of Turkish masculinity. The legacy of a powerful military remains prevalent in Turkish society, as 'compulsory military service still operates as a key rite of passage for hegemonic masculinity.' Following his tenure as Istanbul Mayor, Erdoğan was imprisoned for 'inciting hatred based on religious differences' after he gave a speech in which he read Gokalp's poem. His verses, passionately rendered by Erdoğan – 'Our minarets are our bayonets, Our domes are our helmets, Our mosques are our barracks' – imbue Islamic symbols with militant masculinity.

Indeed, the militarisation of Turkish masculinity has even made use of the Kurdish conflict to increase national sentiment, although currently the 'dissident intellectual' has recently replaced Kurdish leader Öcalan as a scapegoat; frequently these intellectuals are charged with 'insulting Turkishness'. Even the noted author Orhan Pamuk was charged in 2005 by ultranationalist lawyers with insulting Turkishness, which seems to equal a castration of the state masculinity. Even the process to join the EU has also been seen as a threat to Turkish manhood. Not only is it illegal to insult 'Turkishness' under Article 301 of the Penal Code, but Article 299 makes it illegal to insult the Turkish President as well. Erdoğan regularly takes advantage of this law, and has detained a great number of activists, media professionals, and dissidents for speaking out against him. If Erdoğan embodies Turkey itself, an insult to him is an insult to the nation. This notion has extended to the way in which Erdoğan positions himself on a global scale. He often challenges, even scolds, leaders and institutions of other countries. In 2014, he furiously (and successfully) demanded an apology from US Vice President Biden over Biden's comment that Turkey had allowed ISIS fighters to pass through Turkey. His leadership style has grown progressively overbearing. Galip, a Hizmet participant in his forties told me, 'Erdoğan is turning inwards. He's saying, "I don't care what the rest of the world thinks. People elected me, they voted for me, so I don't care about everyone else". He's positioning himself as leader of the Muslim world'. But it is not only Hizmet activists who are concerned; the legions of journalists in prison testify to that. During the parliamentary election of June 2015, he actively campaigned for the AKP even though he is supposed to remain impartial as President.

As Juergensmeyer notes, extreme forms of 'warrior' masculinity or 'macho religiosity' is often being embedded in religiously-fuelled narratives of honour, and behaviours also intended to restore order and control in a world 'gone awry.' Erdoğan's comments about women can be seen as a response to what he perceives as social disorder, 'sex out of control', or women taking prominent public roles. He has alienated the secularists within Turkey, the Kurds, Alevis, and now the Hizmet movement. Restricting the press, banning media outlets, Twitter and YouTube, all work to shock and traumatise Turkish citizens, and thus may be understood as forms of 'symbolic expressions of violence,' or 'performance violence', intended to restore honour and power to the agent. In this case, while he might justify his actions in the name of 'protecting Turkey from internal enemies,' it is difficult to ignore that they increase his hold on power. This behaviour reflects his embodiment of 'warrior' masculinity, certainly witnessed in his feud with Gűlen.

Gűlen as Cerebral Dervish

Gűlen offers quite a different model of masculinity, a corporeal otherness that underlines his liminal status. He begins one of his books with the following words: 'love is the most essential element of every being, and it is the most radiant light, and it is the greatest power; able to resist and overcome all else.' Never married, he appears to represent the archetype of a celibate Sufi mystic whose strength is illustrated through his self-discipline, patience, and humility. A prominent Sufi theme is to strive to control one's worldly desires, and give up one's *nefis*, ego, or sense of self. Gűlen claims that struggling with one's 'inner world and carnal soul' is a Muslim's greater jihad. In fact, when I met him, he expressed anxiety that he would not live up to the image his followers had created, and credited Hizmet's successes to others. This model is likely influenced as much by Gűlen's profoundly pious, intellectual, and sensitive personality as by the legacy of Sufi masculinities.

In general, Sufism has often played a subversive, antinomian role to state-sanctioned and legalistic forms of Islam (although of course there have been legalist form of Sufism, and Sufism has at times enjoyed state support). Concepts that have typically been stereotyped as feminine, such as 'love, submission, and subservience,' are embodied by male Sufis as well. Male Sufis have also used gendered imagery in depicting their spiritual lives, describing themselves in feminine terms such as 'brides,' or as nursing babies, nourished by their male Sufi leaders, cast in the role of mother; however, Sufi practices, while often heterodox and diverse, have not rejected patriarchy. Even celibacy has been a hallmark of prominent Sufis, both male and female, such as Rabia al 'Adawiyya (d. 801), Ibrahim al-Khawwas (d. 904), and many others. Abu Talib al-Makki (d. 996) argued for Sufi celibacy during the Abbasid era, as did Ali ibn Usman Hujwiri (d. circa 1072). Celibacy is a requirement for the highest positions for the Turkish Bektaşi order. Thus, Fethullah Gűlen's celibacy, and that of a few of his students, must be understood in part as a drawing from the legacy of acceptable Sufi masculinity and behaviour.

Hizmet-affiliated schools and tutoring centres provide venues for male bonding and spaces where masculinity is shaped. So does the Abi (elder brother) system, whereby an older man mentors a younger one within the movement. Within these institutions, Hizmet males often carry out tasks antithetical to hypermasculinity, such as housecleaning and cooking. Smoking, aggression, physical confrontations and womanising are taboo. In Turkey, some men affiliated with the Movement carry 'Abi-purses,' small bags for storing a Qur'an, prayer beads, wallet and keys. At times these men have been teased for not living up to 'macho' ideals of Turkish masculinity, perhaps fuelled by gender stereotypes of men as authoritarians, shaped by Muslim theologians such as Syed Abul A'la Mawdudi, who believed that 'truly 'Islamic' piety for men was in their being superior and dominant' to women. Instead, Hizmet men weep together openly, following the example of Gülen, whose tears have been caught on camera many times. Ibrahim Karatop recalls his time in a Hizmet-inspired school, writing that his earliest memory was the 'comfort of crying collectively with men.'

Others also spoke of Gülen's influence on their gendered behaviours. Kaya, a thirty-eight-year-old Turkish educator now living in California, joined Hizmet in his teens in Turkey despite the fact that his extended family is composed chiefly of Marxists and Kemalists. He explained: 'I'm a little different from my father – I don't think he ever cried or cooked – but I have. I learned this in Hizmet circles. I never thought about this question, but yes, I might have been profoundly affected. Crying and cooking are rare in Turkish society for men, but common in Hizmet circles. My loyalty to my wife too – loyalty in my [extended] family is a problem!' He added, laughing, that actually his wife tells him that he is quite macho; when together, he does not let her drive, and believes it is his responsibility to lead the family.

Yet other Hizmet participants noted that their gendered behaviours were shaped by a variety of sources, refuting any assumption that Hizmet produces monolithic males. Pasha, a forty-three-year-old Hizmet official I spoke with in Huntington Beach, insisted that his own masculinity was influenced more by his upbringing in a Kurdish family, than by Hizmet, although he conceded that one reason Gülen has been speaking so frequently on the theme of forgiveness and compassion, is to encourage Hizmet participants to let go of their negative feelings regarding Erdoğan and members of the AKP, as he has, and to begin the healing process. Nonetheless, he emphasised his individuality, stating:

> Hizmet is a way of thinking or showing you things, but it doesn't affect all of life. Otherwise, if you are always following in someone's footsteps or way of living, how are you going to add to that community from your own thinking and learning and experiences? I don't want people to think that Hizmet is a factory, and that when people go into that factory they become like everyone else, as if it were a production line. I don't believe it is like that, and I'm not like that. Hizmet gives one values, but one applies them to one's personal life in one's own way. Islam has something to do with my masculinity, not Hizmet. Men are mostly the same in Sufi communities. It isn't Hizmet telling us to cry, the Prophet Muhammad cried, this is in the hadith literature. Maybe Hizmet brings that to light.

In fact, while Zahid, a thirty-eight-year-old artist and musician, spoke of desiring to pattern his identity after Gülen's model, he was quite critical of men in the movement, saying many really did not live up to that ideal, from his experience. He asserted:

> I like to be close to Gülen's style. As a person, I really like his style and the way he thinks. I have macho friends in the Hizmet movement, who yell at their wives. My observation is that there is not an enormous effect on the way Abis [brothers; Hizmet men] treat their wives. I am sometimes shocked that Abis treat their wives in ways that they do, ways that do not reflect Gülen's ideals. Maybe they would be harsher towards their wives, if they were not in the movement. Sometimes men in the movement cannot balance work and family. They help others, but when it comes to their families, they don't do a good job. Gülen always warns people to keep a better balance in this area, but many do not. When the wives ask them for something, they do not have time for their wives and children. They should spend time with their families as well.

Most men interviewed about this issue conveyed that their participation in the movement shaped them to be more patient, willing to carry out dialogue with others instead of being reactive, and to behave in ways that conveyed humility and respect. However, clearly the movement is not the only influence on their behaviour, gendered or otherwise, nor it is a panacea for marital harmony or constructing feminist men.

Indeed, patriarchy is reflected in many facets of Hizmet, and Gülen himself embodies paternal, charismatic religious authority, although his leadership style is that of a teacher, or hademe (servant), and not an authoritarian. Nonetheless, his statements regarding women contrast starkly with those of Erdoğan. Gülen was quoted in 2008 as saying that women should learn martial arts if needed, to defend themselves against abusive husbands. During Kaya's interview, he added that he enrolled his own young daughter in karate after hearing of Gülen's advice. Gülen also actively promotes women's career goals, and even asks husbands to consider adjusting their careers to facilitate that of their wives.

While also a patriarch like Erdoğan, Gülen's model of masculinity reflects Sufi ideals: humility, servanthood, patience. In his late seventies, Gülen is now quite reclusive, and in faltering health. However, Hizmet participants are asked to go forth and actively educate others, conduct peacebuilding through dialogue, and provide humanitarian service to anyone who needs it. He writes, 'we are only truly human if we learn, teach, and inspire others'.

Contesting Religious Expression

Gülen and Erdoğan both come from a Muslim background, of the Hanafi school of thought; the former's Sufism developed in part out of the Said Nursi (1878-1960) movement, the latter a pragmatic Islamist. However, they express their religiosity in very different ways, unsurprising given their respective roles as politician and religious leader. During the June 2015 general election, Erdoğan toured the country with a copy of the Qur'an in hand. Meanwhile, in his compound in Pennsylvania, Gülen led daily prayer circles, read Said Nursi's Risale-i-Nur with his students, wrote essays, and conversed with his numerous visitors. While Gülen openly discusses religion, history, philosophy, sociology, psychology, economics, and education, Sahih Yucel notes that the mystic often hesitates to respond to political questions. Thus, Erdoğan openly waves the Qur'an for political gain, while Gülen at least overtly avoids politics, focusing instead on piety. Yet both draw power (political and religious) from their behaviours.

Erdoğan's AKP has been described in recent years as possessing 'anti-Western and pan-Islamic' influences. In contrast, the Hizmet movement has hundreds of institutions in the West, it is non-partisan and promotes interfaith and intercultural dialogue. It has defined itself as apolitical (although it has political influence). Hizmet values piety, discipline, education, and a vision of Islamic morality focused on serving the other. Regarding education as a vehicle for service, Gűlen writes, 'now that we live in a global village, education is the best way to serve humanity and to establish a dialogue with other civilisations. I have encouraged people to serve the country in particular, and humanity in general, through education.' A Kurdish professor told me that other Muslim groups in Turkey have found Hizmet unacceptably apolitical, passive, and Western leaning. The Nurçus, the Naqşbandis, and the Islamists do not appreciate that Hizmet tries to dissolve boundaries between other religious and cultural groups, he added, and fear that the Hizmet practice of interfaith dialogue will result in a religious amalgam or synthesis of religion. He explained, 'they misunderstand Hizmet's interfaith dialogue activities, and they worry that getting together with other people to carry out interfaith dialogue will create a new form of Islam that will be a synthesis of the faiths of those involved in dialogue with Hizmet.'

Some Turkish Muslims were humiliated when Gűlen met with Pope John Paul II in 1998. They believe as Muslims that Hizmet participants should promote a religious state; Gűlen was criticised for 'talking less about an Islamic State than he does a fly'.

A Turkish political scientist, affiliated with Hizmet, explained that other Muslims do not like that Hizmet refuses to think of the West as an enemy, and stated, 'as Christians, Muslims and Jews we live in the same global village. Hizmet's enemy is not the West, we need to find our common enemies.' Hizmet is criticised for being too American, and for catering to Jews and non-Muslims. They are also jealous, he added, because as a powerful movement, Hizmet has created an international structure which provides its members with an expansive global network and opportunities.

Erdoğan, it may be argued, is not merely positioning himself as an Ottoman sultan or Middle Eastern dictator, but as Turkey's messianic saviour, if not a judgmental, angry, all-powerful deity to whom one should submit; decisively brandishing his *nefis* or ego. The eminent anthropologist Clifford Geertz notes that 'the mere fact that rulers and gods share certain properties, has, been recognised for some time.' Kings, moreover, go about 'stamping a territory with ritual signs of dominance' in order to establish the 'inherent sacredness of central authority'. The massive presidential palace Erdoğan is building for himself, replete with a mosque in the edifice, aptly illustrates this concept. Islam under Erdoğan is now an amalgam of religion, politics, nationalism, and conservatism - just as exclusivist as Kemalism. Given Erdoğan and Gűlen's clashing understandings of Islam, the role of Muslims, and of gender roles within an Islamic society, it is no surprise their relationship fell apart. While on a shallow level they share a common religion, in his role as politician, Erdoğan's Islam is nationalistic, chauvinistic, militant, exclusivist, and is a source for his authoritarian, patriarchal leadership style. Gűlen's understanding of Islam is inclusive, peaceful, contains universal values, and requires humility and service to others; ideals that few politicians have found easy to uphold.

Conclusion

Gűlen has preached that 'just as God showed His attribute of forgiveness through humanity, He also put the beauty of forgiveness into the human heart...the greatest gift that the generation of today can give their children and grandchildren is to teach them how to forgive — to forgive even confronted by the worst behaviour and the most disturbing events'. When I spoke with him, I asked about the rift between himself and Erdoğan, and if he envisioned a possible rapprochement. 'We didn't cause the illness', he replied, 'therefore we do not have a remedy to cure it. Since the source of trouble is not us, we can't do anything but pray.' However, he added that his door was always open to speak to Erdoğan. Given the severity of their falling out, it seems unlikely that reconciliation will take place any time soon. However, given the shifting political landscape in Turkey, one cannot rule it out. Despite Erdoğan's macho posturing, he might find it expedient at some point to open channels of communication again.

Erdoğan's Gazi Warrior hypermasculine behaviour responds to old feelings of humiliation and emasculation in the aftermath of the fall of the Empire, and to contemporary struggles for power in Turkey. It speaks to those anxious about both Turkey and Islam coming under attack from the West; his forceful aggressiveness a strategy to restore Turkey's honour and to keep it secure from the 'enemies on all sides.' Following Atatürk's footsteps, Turkey's new strong man has become repressive of religious and ethnic groups.

Ultimately, Gülen and the Hizmet movement have found it difficult to support him, while maintaining their Sufi ideals. Their collective power, success, and influence, reflected in the sheer number of Hizmet-affiliated members and institutions in Turkey and abroad, is inspired by Gülen's mystical theology and his particular embodiment of Sufism. Despite Gülen's mild-mannered approach, Hizmet's popularity appears to profoundly threaten Erdoğan's identity as ruling patriarch and sacred warrior.

THE HEADSCARF DEBATE
RECOGNITION AND CITIZENSHIP

Yusuf Sarfati

Turkish media called it an 'historic moment'. Four parliamentarians from the Justice and Development Party (AKP) entered the parliamentary session of the Grand National Assembly with their headscarves on 31 October 2013. This seemingly insignificant action was politically salient. Thirteen years ago, Merve Kavakçı, a member of parliament from the Virtue Party (VP), faced heavy protests when she entered parliament wearing a headscarf. In the aftermath of the incident, Kavakçı was stripped of her parliamentary seat, and the VP was closed down by the Constitutional Court. Similarly, political controversy ensued when the governing AKP, together with the Nationalist Action Party (NAP), passed two constitutional amendments in the Grand National Assembly on 9 February 2008. The aim of the changes made to paragraph 4 of article 10 and to paragraph 6 of article 42 of the Turkish Constitution was to allow veiled students to attend universities. The opposition Republican People's Party (RPP) took the amendments to the Constitutional Court arguing for their unconstitutionality on the grounds of Turkey's commitment to secularism. On 5 June 2008, the Court annulled the amendments, and later that year, found the AKP guilty of encouraging anti-secularist activities. As a result of this ruling, the AKP received a serious warning from the Court, and half of its public funding was cut.

As these incidents reveal, wearing the headscarf in higher education and other public institutions in Turkey has been politically contentious during the last three decades. After the 1980 coup, the veil's place in universities has been the focus of numerous legal battles between conservative parties and the higher judiciary. The first decision to ban the Islamic headscarf on university campuses was made by the Higher Education Council in 1984. Conservative centre-right parties then passed legislation to allow headscarf-wearing female students to enter universities. The Constitutional

Court's decisions in 1989, 1990, and 2008 thwarted each of these legal efforts. The debate around the headscarf became especially heated after the 28 February Decisions – which mark the ousting of the coalition government led by Erbakan's Welfare Party through pressure from the military – and the implementation of the ban was subsequently more strictly enforced. In September 2010, the president of the Higher Education Council sent a circular requesting universities to allow veiled students in campuses and classrooms, stressing that they could not be removed from class for being 'in violation of discipline regulations', although the instructor could make a note of the incident. Since then veiled students have been attending classes in universities, albeit a few still faced difficulties. On 30 September 2013, the amendment made on the dress code of public officials also allowed veiled women to serve in public service positions, except as policewoman, prosecutor, and judge. While these recent circulars appear to have provided a partial ad hoc solution to the decades-long headscarf ban in universities and government-run offices, the lack of a clear legislative or constitutional grounding to veiled women's rights to education and public office reveals their fragile status.

The legal and political struggle over the veil highlights a tension between different segments of Turkish society regarding the meaning of democratic citizenship and inclusion. Proponents of the ban apply the ideals of civic republicanism, and opponents employ difference-blind liberalism to support their positions. A strict interpretation of the republican ideal leads to political exclusion of veiled women and undermines their social rights. On the other hand, most scholars of Turkish politics maintain that implementation of liberal democracy would solve the headscarf controversy and lead to the inclusion of veiled women in the public sphere. While difference-blind liberalism does address the lack of political and social rights of the veiled women, it falls short of addressing the social stigmatisation of women wearing headscarves, the intersectional character of their subordination, and their lack of collective voice in the current public debate. By casting the headscarf debate solely a as right-based problem, liberalism neglects the significance of democratic principles, such as representation and voice. In order to overcome this, we need a positive argument and a politics of recognition approach that institutionally connects veiled women's collective voices to the public debate and decision-making structures and creates a more inclusive system in which veiled women can assert their subjective positions in the intersection of gender and religion, challenge the societal stigmatisation they face and be included as equal members of the polity.

Historical Background

When the republic of Turkey was founded in 1923, Republican elites adopted a secularist ideology that aimed to modernise Turkish society from top down. By abolishing the caliphate, religious courts, religious schools, and outlawing the religious orders, the ruling elite aimed to secularise the political sphere. For the republicans, modernity did not only entail embracing a secular homogenising nationalism and replacing religion with the guidance of science, but also meant adopting European cultural practices. Introduction of the Latin alphabet and Gregorian calendar in place of the Arabic alphabet and lunar calendar aimed to create a new Turkish nation with a European culture. During the one-party rule of the RPP (1923-1946), traditional culture and way of life were depicted as the main reason for the decline of the Ottoman Empire. Accordingly, many local cultural practices were debased, while Western cultural practices were depicted as superior.

The modernisation project also had significant effects on women's lives. In 1926, with the implementation of the Turkish Civil Code polygamy was outlawed, women were granted equal rights to divorce, and child custody rights were permitted to both parents. In 1934 women were granted suffrage. In addition to gaining social and political rights, women also played a crucial symbolic role. The regime actively encouraged the abandonment of veiling. In one of his speeches, Mustafa Kemal directly addressed the issue:

> I have seen women who put a piece of cloth or a towel or something like it over their heads to hide their faces, and who turn their backs or huddle themselves on the ground when a man passes by. What are the meaning and sense of this behaviour? Gentlemen, can the mothers and daughters of a civilised nation adopt this strange manner, this barbarous posture? It is a spectacle that makes the nation an object of ridicule. It must be remedied at once.

For the republican elites unveiling, as prominent sociologist Nilufer Gole notes, 'reinforced the movement towards Western civilisation in a Muslim society previously dependent upon the isolation of women'. Hence, the Kemalist regime constructed its 'civilised', Western image by displaying photographs of women unveiled, women athletes in sports uniforms, and men and women intermingling in tea salons and republican balls. As Jenny White states:

> Since the new Republican woman presented the modern, secular, Westernised state, she was expected to behave and dress in what the state defined as a modern, Western manner. Women who felt that their religious beliefs required them to dress modestly and cover their heads...were not accepted into this Republican sisterhood and were alternately reviled as the uncivilised primitive.

Despite the political hegemony of the RPP in the 1920s and 30s, the inculcation of the Kemalist ideals of secular nationalism, positivism, and cultural modernisation did not penetrate all of Turkish society. Vernacular Islam and religious symbolism survived in ordinary citizens' daily lives, especially in villages, and Islamic consciousness remained the foundation of communal identities among many. The reform of women's rights and lifestyle were effective only in urban centres. Accordingly a rift between the more religious, conservative masses residing in the villages and the secular, Westernised elites residing in the big cities was created. This centre-periphery cleavage would become one of the most durable divisions in Turkish social and political life.

After Turkey's transition to a multi-party democracy in 1946, the new government under the Democratic Party (1950-60) pursued a liberal economic policy. With the implementation of the Marshall Plan, mechanisation of agriculture became pervasive, prompting immigration from villages to cities. Rural-urban immigration, which characterised the movement of the periphery to the centre, accelerated significantly in the following decades. The percentage of total population residing in urban areas rose from 24.8 per cent in 1950 to 52.4 in 1985 and to 70.5 in 2010.

Yet most of the new rural immigrants did not integrate into the city life, instead living in shanties called *gecekondu*. Hence, even in the cities they remained on the periphery. In the 1980s, the number of *gecekondu* residents skyrocketed in the major cities of Istanbul, Izmir and Ankara, constituting the majority of the population. Nevertheless, in these cities rural immigrants and urban old-timers had more frequent contact, which led to the reinforcement of cultural hierarchies between the two social groups. In this context, for many secular urban dwellers the headscarf became the symbol of the negative change occurring in their cities. The veil signified for them the ruralisation of their cities and the threat political Islam posed to their secular life style. On the other hand, the headscarf became an important symbol of identity embraced by rural immigrant women to resist the homogenising secular republican life style imposed by the Turkish state. Yet this was not a rejection of modernity, as most of these women asserted their participation in the modern urban settings while donning the headscarf.

The form of veiling also changed significantly. Village women traditionally use a headscarf known as *başörtüsü* which is knotted under the chin and does not necessarily cover the shoulders, the neck, or all the hair. In contrast, the new headscarf, which is known as *tesettür* or *türban*, consists of two pieces of clothing. The scarf covers all the hair and is accompanied by a long gown or jacket covering the shoulders and the neck. Incidentally, the veiled women do not call their headscarf *türban*, which is a word imported from India. As Göle aptly mentions: 'in its contemporary form veiling conveys a political statement of Islamism in general and an affirmation of Muslim women's identity in particular. In this respect it is distinct from the traditional Muslim woman's use of the headscarf.'

Increasing literacy also contributed to the headscarf's visibility in public spaces. Female literacy in Turkey rose from 45.3 per cent in 1975 to 68.5 per cent in 1990. For some observant women the headscarf facilitated mobility in the public arena and provided easier access to education and work. According to Ayse Kadıoğlu, women who are donning this new form of headscarf, 'claim full citizenship and seek employment in competitive job markets. They show up in the urban cultural milieu such as art exhibitions, concerts, coffee houses and restaurants in their openly religious costumes.' They are particularly disliked by the urban elites for transgressing modern spaces with religious outfits deemed to represent backwardness.

The increasing visibility of the headscarf is also linked to the emergence of a Muslim middle class in Turkey, particularly with Turgut Özal's implementation of an export-oriented development strategy after the 1980 coup. In this period, the ratio of exports to the GNP rose from five per cent in 1980 to 14.4 per cent in 1989, while the ratio of industrial exports to total exports skyrocketed from six per cent in 1980 to 77.8 per cent in 1991. This new economic restructuring has led to a major boom in production and capital accumulation in small and medium enterprises (SMEs) in Anatolian cities, such as Konya, Yozgat, Denizli, and Gaziantep.

When these conservative businessmen – who were politically tied to the Islamist movement in Turkey – flourished economically, they synthesised their Islamic life style with their new middle-class positions and challenged the economic and cultural hegemony of the big industrialists. In this economic context, the Islamic headscarf, alongside other symbols of Muslim piety, started to represent the assertion of the cultural values of this rising Muslim middle class against the secular values of the industrial bourgeoisie. Numan Kurtulmuş, an influential Islamist politician, reveals the class basis of the debate:

> In the 70s, when I was young, in the Istanbul University there were a couple of students with headscarves. Yet, after the mid-70s girls in Anatolia started to get an education. Their families said that if you go [to school] like this [with a headscarf], I'll send you to school.... Yet, when these girls receive an education, they want to have a career, to attain a profession. They want to be doctors, lawyers, etc. Hence, the headscarf debate originated from this... Here, the main issue is the unseen contradiction between the political and economic elites and Anatolia. Hence, in the hospitals, when all the nurses, or the women who mopped the floors were wearing the headscarf, nobody said anything. But, when [the veiled women] said: 'We want to be doctors,' then this became a problem. Hence, in the high schools it was permitted to mop the floors, to bring tea [wearing a headscarf], yet when they said: 'I will come to the school as a teacher,' then the problem emerged.

The class dimension of the headscarf issue is also part of a new set of Islamic bourgeoisie habits, such as alcohol-free coffeehouses, headscarf fashion shows, and segregated vacation resorts that have become commonplace in the past two decades. While the new Muslim middle class sees these manifestations as a form of social and cultural recognition, the secularists interpret them as Islamisation of Turkey. The latter view underpins the resistance of secularist actors towards the wearing of the headscarf in public institutions.

Pro-Ban Arguments

Until recently, the pro-ban coalition consisted of various political actors including Kemalist segments of the RPP, presidents of several public universities, and certain members of the higher judiciary, including the Constitutional Court. The ban's supporters mostly utilise a certain interpretation of civic republican theory. Civic republicans see the body politic as the most important unit of democratic politics. Civic republican theory defines freedom on a collective level and associates it with the autonomy of the body politic. According to Benjamin Barber, a proponent of civic republicanism, democratic decisions should be based on the collective deliberations of citizens, and citizens need to transcend their particularities and adopt a general point of view in order to create a common will. The intention of civic republicans is to transcend the self-interest based politics of liberal democracies in which citizens are depoliticised and treated as consumers in the political arena. Yet, adopting a general point of view in order to create a civic community can be problematic as minorities are often seen as incapable of adopting the general point of view and the public debate is usually shaped by the values of the privileged.

In Turkey, the pro-ban coalition embraces a strict interpretation of civic republicanism and claims that one needs to embrace the secular values of the Turkish revolution in order to participate in the public arena. When applied to veiled women, this ideal amounts to demanding that they assimilate into the secular way of life by unveiling in the public sphere. Thus, the pro-ban coalition assumes a homogenous secular public sphere and perceives any assertion of 'difference' in public as a major threat to the assumed neutrality and homogeneity of the public sphere.

The arguments used to justify the headscarf ban are formulated in four different ways: i) wearing of the headscarf in public places would mean the Islamisation of the state; ii) the ban ensures the sustenance of national unity and social peace; iii) the ban is necessary for the emancipation of women; iv) allowing the headscarf in public offices and universities would undermine the rights of unveiled women in these institutions.

The first argument made by the ban's supporters can be summed up by the words of the RPP's previous leader, Deniz Baykal: 'What is wrong is to dress the state [with a veil, so to speak], to take it to the public sphere. Otherwise (meaning 'in other places'), a regular citizen can wear whatever she likes.' According to Baykal's statement, wearing the headscarf anywhere in the public sphere would mean a de facto Islamisation of the state. Therefore, the argument goes, there is a need to create a public sphere that is devoid of any religious signs and to relegate all religious signs to one's private life.

The 1989 and 2008 Constitutional Court decisions, both of which support maintaining the headscarf ban in universities, use a different argument. Both decisions posit that the veiling poses 'a threat to the public order'. This argument was used by the Constitutional Court and also informed the decision of the European Court of Human Rights (ECHR) in the case of Leyla Şahin vs. Turkey. Şahin, a fifth-year veiled university student in Cerrahpaşa Medical Faculty in Istanbul University sued the Turkish state in the ECHR after she was denied access to her lectures and examinations. The court decided, according to Paragraph 2 of Article 9 of the European Convention of Human Rights, that a state can interfere with religious freedoms of its citizens if the state deems that this interference is required to protect the public order in a democratic society. The court substantiated this decision by asserting that wearing of the headscarf in universities would undermine Turkey's long-standing commitment to the principle of secularism, especially in the light of increasing power of a religious political party that can potentially 'create a fully Islamic state in Turkey.' Both of these arguments show that those who support the ban in public spaces perceive the public sphere as a neutral and peaceful space as civic republican theories contend. The assertion of Islamic particularism in the veil is seen as an act that endangers this perceived neutrality and security of the public sphere.

The third argument used by the pro-ban coalition does not stem from civic republicanism, but has its roots in a long history of Orientalist representations, which depicts the practices found in a monolithically described 'Orient' as unenlightened, irrational, and oppressive. In most Orientalist representations, the veil is depicted as an oppressive tool of patriarchy and used to paint the image of the victimised Muslim woman.

The 1984 decision of the Higher Education Council utilises this type of argument to defend its headscarf ban: 'For those people (students who insist on attending universities veiled), (the) headscarf is no longer an innocent habit, but a symbol of a worldview that opposes women's liberty.' A female Kemalist activist criticises the headscarf of the current president's wife on similar grounds: how 'can the Turkish first lady at the doorstep of the EU display such an image of bigotry and backwardness? This is the twenty-first century not the dark ages.' Both positions associate the veil with the oppression of women in line with Orientalist discourse. This Orientalist gaze stems from the colonial experiences of Europe with the Muslim world in the early nineteenth century, when indigenous Islamic practices with respect to women formed the Western narrative of the 'otherness' and inferiority of Islam. Orientalism became a tool in justifying colonialist exploitation and the subjugation of the colonised. The assumption that Muslim women can only be emancipated when they uncover their heads is a product of this historical period of European colonialism. This Orientalist thesis and its emancipatory logic was borrowed by Turkey's republican elites and embedded in the Kemalist civilising mission.

A fourth formulation, which borrows from both the liberal and republican traditions, casts the headscarf ban as a necessary measure to protect the rights of unveiled women. According to this argument, if religious dress is not controlled by law, Islamist pressure to wear religious dress will affect all women and jeopardise the rights of the unveiled women in the public space. The 2008 decision states,

> Even though it is a personal choice and use of liberty, carrying the religious symbol in classrooms and labs, which are attended by all students, has the potential to turn into a tool of pressure on people with different life choices, political views, or faiths. The suggestion that it would not be permitted for the university administrations and public authorities to intervene, in case the carried religious symbol constitutes pressure on others, can lead to potential disruptions of education and disruption of public order, and can prevent everyone's right to receive education in an equal manner.

The Constitutional Court's decision on the unconstitutionality of the amendments to Article 10, which guarantees citizens equal treatment before the law, and to Article 42, which stipulates that the right to education cannot be restricted unless it is directly mentioned in the law, foregrounds the rights of unveiled women in its justification. Similar decisions of Turkey's Constitutional Court informed the decision of ECHR on the headscarf, specifically in the Dahlab vs Switzerland case. Lucia Dahlab, an elementary school teacher who was asked to remove her headscarf by the school authorities in Switzerland, filed a case in ECHR after she lost a case in the Swiss courts. The ECHR dismissed the application as inadmissible by claiming that the prohibition was necessary 'to protect others' freedom,' pointing to the vulnerability of the plaintiff's students to Dahlab's religious views. While ECHR's decision evaluated the relationship between an adult and minor as problematic and is substantively different from Turkish Constitutional Court's aforementioned decision focusing on the relationship between adults, it is important to note that both decisions cast the veil as a tool of religious coercion.

Anti-Ban Arguments

The political coalition that opposes the ban consists of centre-right, conservative, and Islamist parties as well as liberal intellectuals. Public opinion also overwhelmingly supports the lifting of the ban. Opponents of the ban mainly use liberal arguments. Unlike civic republicans who emphasise the primacy of community, liberals place the individual at the heart of a democratic society and define freedom on an individual level. According to liberalism, the state's primary role is to protect individual rights by implementing the law in a culture-blind manner. In the context of the Turkish headscarf debate, critics of the ban use three main arguments grounded in the liberal theory.

First, they claim that Turkish secularism, which is designed along the lines of the French principle of laïcité, is interpreted by the Turkish judiciary as an all-encompassing ideology. Rather than using this type of assertive secularism, Turkey needs to embrace passive secularism as it is implemented in the US. Unlike assertive secularism, which aims to create a secular public sphere by eradicating signs of religious particularism from the public space, passive secularism is tolerant of citizens' rights to manifest their religious beliefs in the public sphere, hence it is more liberal. Bülent Arınç, the deputy prime minister from the AKP, reflects this point of view: 'We would like Turkey to apply secularism as it is in the world, because secularism in America, Anglo-Saxon secularism in England, secularism in all European countries does not interfere with [people's] clothing.'

The second argument made for lifting the ban is closely related to demands to redefine secularism. Unlike pro-ban advocates, many politicians and social actors claim that veiled women do not attribute to their headscarf a political meaning, but don it as a result of their religious conviction. Therefore, the state should honour this practice and respect veiled women's right of religious conviction in the public sphere. The following statements of the then Prime Minister Erdoğan constitute a good example to this line of argument:

> How can [the headscarf] be a political symbol? Headscarf is one of the commandments of our religion. But ignorance is a bad thing. [The parliamentarian who construes headscarf as a political symbol] is ignorant to the point of not knowing that our religion has such a commandment.

Similarly, Mehmet Çiçek, a former AKP parliamentarian from Yozgat, casts the donning of the veil as a religious commandment and precludes any political meaning attributed to the Islamic veil:

> On the one hand, God says to cover your head and [on the other hand] the law says don't cover your head. If you [the law] say that those who cover their head due to God's commandment are permitted to wear the veil as they want [in the public], this is not [a legal] problem anymore, then the problem would be solved. This problem does not have anything to do with the state

By stating that veiling does not have anything to do the with the state, Çiçek contends that veiling does not have any political connotation.

Finally, those who favour the lifting of the headscarf ban in universities embrace a human rights discourse. They emphasise the fact that veiled women's right to education and to equal treatment is undermined by imposing a ban on the wearing of the headscarf in institutions of higher education in Turkey. This emphasis on human rights can be seen in the proposed constitutional changes to Articles 10 and 42. Veiled women, including Şenay Karaduman, Leyla Şahin, and Merve Kavakçı, sued the Turkish state in the ECHR, claiming that the headscarf ban violated their human rights. Hence liberal arguments that focus on civil rights are used not only in public and political discourse, but also in national and transnational legal forums.

Effect on Women

While the normative debate continues, the implementation of the ban in certain domains and the terms of the public debate have adverse material and psychological consequences for veiled women. Since political parties had not nominated any veiled candidates up until very recently, veiled women were stripped of their political rights and their views were rarely heard in formal politics. This creates a patriarchal atmosphere in which male politicians speak in the name of observant women even when it comes to the headscarf debate.

Moreover, the ban led to the social and economic exclusion of veiled women. Many students who were not permitted to attend classes effectively lost their right to receive higher education. The ban also affects veiled women's employment opportunities. According to one report, 5,000 public employees lost their jobs, and 10,000 were forced to resign between 1998 and 2002. Because of the linkages between the public and private sectors in Turkey, veiled women's lack of access to public jobs created discriminatory practices against them in private companies with regards to recruitment, promotion and wages, particularly in white professional jobs.

Further, many veiled women have undergone humiliating practices and endured emotional stress. Some university students had to wear wigs on their head while entering universities, because this was seen as an acceptable substitute to the headscarf by university administrations. In the immediate aftermath of the 28 February Decisions, students who insisted on attending universities while veiled were sometimes interrogated in the infamous 'persuasion rooms' erected next to the university gate. The veiled students were taken into the persuasion rooms alone in order to be persuaded to uncover their heads by several administrators. According to the accounts of students, young women who entered the persuasion rooms felt isolation, vulnerability and humiliation and sought psychological counselling to overcome these emotions. These rooms became 'an attempt to reign over body and the soul.'

In addition to this emotional stress, the decisions of the Constitutional Court and ECHR, which defined the presence of the veiled women in the public sphere as a 'threat to the public order,' stigmatise them in the eyes of the public by projecting them as a potential menace to the democratic order and the rights of others.

Finally, the current public debate on the headscarf leads to the trivialisation of women in the public discourse. During the AKP governments, the headscarf debate shifted from university students, who were seen as active citizens with political agency, to the wives of political figures, who are influential only because they are married to elected officials or state bureaucrats. For instance, the media extensively covered official receptions that deliberately excluded veiled women from the guest lists. This shift from protesting university students to politicians' wives reinforces the old sexist stereotypes of passive women and active men. Moreover, mainstream media and several politicians suggested different ways to tie the headscarf as a potential solution. According to these, the conflict over the veil could be resolved if women would wear the same kind of scarves worn by Western or Turkish celebrities, since these forms would be more acceptable to the public. These types of representations dilute the meaning and significance of the headscarf for its wearers by shifting the attention from identity claims to fashion and reveal a sexist subtext by giving the message that for women the most important thing is how they look.

Limitations

The pro-ban arguments based on republicanism have a democratic deficit as they assume that homogeneity is necessary for the neutrality and peacefulness of the public sphere. However, this assumed homogeneity does not reflect the sociopolitical reality in Turkey and excludes veiled women by limiting their civil, social, and political rights. Since the headscarf is framed as a threat to public order and the state's neutrality, an important stigma is also attached to veiled women. The republican argument of relegating ostentatious signs of one's religious identity to the private sphere undermines the very essence of democracy, namely respect for differences.

Opponents of the ban, including most Turkish scholars argue that liberal democracy can solve the headscarf debate and restore the rights of the veiled women in Turkey. For example, Yaşim Arat explicitly claims that she proposes 'a liberal solution to the problem' because the republican ban has the potential to alienate veiled women who are attached to secular-liberal ideals and radicalise those who are illiberal Islamists. Murat Akan claims that proponents of multiculturalism are wrong in blaming difference-blind liberalism for failing to accommodate diversity. After an examination of the headscarf question in France and Turkey, he concludes that it is state nationalism that 'threatens the free expression of culture...[while] difference-blind liberalism is theoretically well equipped to confront this threat.' Similarly Ahmet Kuru develops the concept of passive secularism, which reflects the liberal view of minimal state interference in religious affairs and tolerance of citizens' rights to manifest their religious beliefs in the public sphere in contradistinction to assertive secularism, which represents the republican view of state-led construction of a secular public sphere devoid of any religious expression. The conclusion drawn from these discussions is that there is no incompatibility between Islam and passive secularism's view of state-religion arrangements, and that this type of liberal secularism is desirable for Turkey in particular and for Muslim societies in general, as it imposes fewer restrictions on citizens' overt manifestations of piety.

Although it is accurate that difference-blind liberalism can better address the public and political exclusion of veiled women than do republican arguments, there are three potential problems in using the difference-blind liberalism as the sole framework to argue for veiled women's inclusion in the public space.

First, arguments grounded in difference-blind liberalism fail to address the stigmatisation and misrecognition veiled women have been facing in Turkey, simply because they maintain that veiled women need to be included on the same terms as other groups. Yet public discourse, administrative practices, and domestic and international court decisions have cast veiled women as a 'potential threat' to the public order.

Second, most liberal critiques of the ban in Turkey claim that women don the headscarf as a result of their religious conviction and not as a political symbol. They make this claim in order to counter pro-ban arguments that depict the veil as a symbol of Islamisation. According to this liberal argument, the public sphere can accommodate religious diversity, but not ideological particularism. I would argue that this is similar to what legal scholar Kenji Yoshino refers to as 'covering.' Yoshino claims that in the US, with its tradition of difference-blind liberalism, society pressures members of minority groups, such as homosexuals or Blacks, to fit into the mainstream by toning down their stigmatised identity expressions. According to Yoshino, oppressed minority groups, such as gays, are granted equal civil rights as long as they downplay their particularistic identity. For example, when a lesbian 'flaunts' her difference by engaging in pro-gay political activism, her civil rights, such as the right to employment or to have custody over her children, are jeopardised. Yoshino discusses numerous court cases to demonstrate how the US courts' interpretation of liberalism ties covering demands to granting of civil rights. Hence, minorities are not excluded categorically, but pressured to de-emphasise their differences and accept the interpretations of their identities favoured by the mainstream.

Liberal opponents of the ban in Turkey exert a similar pressure on veiled women by asking them to embrace one particular meaning of the headscarf; its meaning as a sign of piety. Yet the headscarf's meaning is neither uniform nor fixed in time, as it 'conflates in a single symbol both personal piousness and public assertion of Islamic difference,' and therefore its religious, cultural, and political meanings are intertwined. The meaning of the veil is also reconstructed in confrontations between the governing bodies and veiled women around the world. Therefore, it is important to accept the multiple meanings given to the veil by its wearers, and this requires adopting a position outside of liberalism. It is conceivable that in the absence of the current ban, discrimination in the form of covering demands (using Yoshino's terminology) might be directed toward veiled women who emphasise their political or ideological particularity by engaging in political activism in Islamist platforms, in contrast to those who see the veil solely as a symbol of personal piety. Insisting on the veil's meaning as an expression of 'religious piety' can lead to legal interpretations where legal bodies that protect freedom of religion can uphold one's right to wear the headscarf if it is seen as an expression of piety, whereas the very same courts can rule for a ban in cases where they believe the veil has political meaning.

Third, liberalism, which treats citizens primarily as individuals and not as members of certain identity groups, cannot provide satisfactory venues for democratic representation, because veiling involves the intersectionality of gender and religious identity categories. Intersectionality refers to 'the relationships among multiple dimensions and modalities of social relations and subject formations' and reveals the interwoven nature of systems of domination and exclusion. The Islamic headscarf constitutes an intersectional issue, because the wearing of the tesettür is religious in nature and its application is gender-specific. The veiled women in Turkey are disadvantaged due to the intersectionality of their gender and religious identities. Similarly to Black women in the US who assert their difference from the women's movement led by White middle class women on the one hand and the Black anti-racist movement led by Black men on the other, veiled Turkish women's experiences differ from Turkish secular women and from the Islamist Turkish men.

In Turkey, liberal anti-ban arguments are voiced by various groups, yet the collective voice of veiled women is scarcely heard in public debate. Secularist feminists are not in a position, nor willing, to articulate the discrimination veiled women face. The ideological gap between secularist feminists and veiled women surfaced during Abdullah Gül's presidential candidacy in 2007 when secularist feminists were at the forefront of mass protests against Gül's candidacy mainly because his wife donned the veil. Many argued that a veiled first lady would taint Turkey's secular and progressive image and hurt women's agenda. According to one secularist activist, veiled women 'were either brainwashed or forced by Islamist men to wear the headscarf and accepted it obediently.' In recent years, the conflict between pious women and secularist women has deepened considerably.

Despite this polarisation, it would be wrong to argue that secular women in Turkish women's rights movement always take a pro-ban stance. During the 28 February Process, initiated by the military's National Security Council, and during the 2008 constitutional amendment discussions, some liberal and leftist feminists writing in the feminist magazines, Pazartesi and

Amargi, declared their support for the wearing of the headscarf in public, while others supported the ban by presenting the headscarf as a tool of patriarchy. During the 2013 Gezi Park protests, dozens of unveiled women led by Nilüfer Göle, started a petition that demanded not only the removal of the headscarf ban in public offices, but also the end of implicit discrimination against veiled women in the workplace.

These voices are significant because they show that the views represented in the women's rights movement go beyond a simple secular-religious binary and represent contesting viewpoints on the headscarf. These dissenting secular voices are also critical attempts to create solidarity between the pro-secular and pro-religious women. However, it would be misleading to think that these voices could substitute for veiled women's political subjectivity as secular women do not experience the effects of the ban firsthand, and are usually not subjected to Turkish secularism's exclusionary practices due to their physical appearance in the public sphere. Moreover, it is important to note that secular women are overrepresented in the leadership positions of Turkey's feminist movement, and some female religious activists claim that their concerns are still not adequately addressed in Turkey's women's rights movement.

On the other hand, the Islamist movement, whose leadership is male-dominated, is also incapable of justly representing veiled women's point of view. As Fatma Akdokur, a veiled activist, explains:

If you are talking about women's rights, it is not difficult to be an Islamist feminist...We do fight against the domination of Muslim men, but we never receive the necessary support from (the secular feminists).

The split between religious men and women is vividly reflected in a debate prior to the 2011 parliamentary elections. On 18 March 2011, several prominent veiled women formed the 'We Want Veiled Members of Parliament Initiative.' In their 'No Veiled Candidate, No Vote Campaign,' the initiative called on all political parties to nominate veiled candidates in order to end the political discrimination veiled women face. They added that they would not cast their votes for any party that did not include veiled candidates in the candidate lists with a realistic chance of election. As a response, Ali Bulaç, one of the influential Islamist intellectuals in Turkey, criticised the initiative harshly. Bulaç, who has been an ardent opponent of the headscarf ban, claimed that the AKP should not nominate any veiled candidates for the upcoming elections, because this might be used as an excuse to close down the party. The then-PM Erdoğan reprimanded the women in the initiative and declared that he 'found No Veiled Candidate No Vote Campaign undemocratic.' When the candidate lists were announced, the AKP had nominated only one veiled candidate from Antalya to run for an unwinnable seat in the upcoming elections. Not surprisingly, she was not elected despite the AKP's landslide win.

In 2012, another disagreement surfaced between the AKP's male leadership and pious women, when Erdoğan hastily declared in a meeting of AKP's women-only branches that he sees abortion as murder and would prepare a legal proposal outlawing abortion. While this fait-accompli was supported by the AKP's mostly male leadership, it drew serious criticism from several Islamic women. Meryem İlyada Atlas, a veiled columnist, critiqued the religious public for adopting a paternalistic language and excluding religious women's voices when women's issues, such as abortion, are discussed, and added that she opposed both abortion and its outlawing. Similarly, Cihan Aktaş, another veiled columnist, criticised Erdoğan for bringing up the issue instrumentally in another context in order to distract attention from the Kurdish question. In her criticism, Nihal Bengisu Karaca adopted an Islamic feminist position which embraces a modernist reading of Islam that balances the right of the feotus with woman's empowerment and allows early abortions: 'Certainly, Islam is against abortion in principle. However, even the religious scholars have not acted as strictly as the prime minister. Some Islamic scholars permitted abortion if it is done in the first weeks of the pregnancy.' Karaca also substantiated her disagreement with outlawing abortion by maintaining that there would be an increase in women's deaths as many women would try to have illegal abortions in unsanitary conditions if a ban were to come into effect. While all the three veiled women criticised the AKP's top-down proposal to outlaw abortion, they also disagreed with secular feminists' claim that abortion is solely a woman's decision over her body.

More recently, six Muslim women with advanced degrees started an online site named Reçel blog, which discusses the day-to-day challenges pious women face in Turkey and the way they perceive societal issues. Among other things, the writings in the blog pose a sharp Islamic critique of the misogynist and patriarchal values voiced by Islamist public figures, such as presenting motherhood as the most important and defining role for women. Some of the writings also approached the headscarf issue from a different angle and criticised its instrumentalisation by male conservative political actors.

These developments reveal that veiled activists embrace political positions that challenge the patriarchy of religious men and secular feminists' claims on women's liberation. Therefore, it is critically important that their collective voice is heard clearly and loudly in the public arena.

Counterpublics

To achieve this, we need to move towards a politics of recognition approach, which goes beyond difference-blind liberalism and addresses the stigmatisation veiled women face by acknowledging their cultural marginalisation, and proposes positive institutional remedies to correct these identity-based cultural wrongs. The politics of recognition approach emerged as a critique of liberalism in dealing with difference in democratic politics. Theorists of this approach see stigmatisation, cultural marginalisation and the silencing of misrecognised groups as salient issues that democratic politics needs to address. As Charles Taylor explains:

> Our identity is partly shaped by recognition or its absence, often by the misrecognition of others, and so a person or group of people can suffer real damage, real distortion, if the people or society around them mirror back to them a confining or demeaning or contemptible picture of themselves.

According to this view, affirmative recognition of cultural identities and public respect of cultural traditions is required in order to remedy identity-based cultural harms. Hence, mere tolerance of culturally marginalised groups is not enough, because 'equal moral and political status, and hence democracy, cannot be achieved unless social institutions and sensibilities become more attentive to, and reflective of, cultural differences.' In order to address the adverse effects of cultural misrecognition and non-recognition, scholars, such as Charles Taylor and Will Kymlicka, proposed group-differentiated rights to cultural minorities as a potential remedy.

These rights can range from providing legal exemptions to group members, such as ultra-Orthodox Jewish men not serving in the Israeli army to preserve their religious life style, to granting autonomy to groups in certain legal domains, such as the Muslim community in India maintaining its own religious courts in matters of family law.

The politics of recognition approach has been criticised for two main reasons. Some of the earlier practitioners treat group identity as a fixed homogenous category and attribute a cultural essence to groups. Moreover, as Ayelet Shahar, Susan Moller Okin, and Seyla Benhabib show, group-differentiated rights can reinforce in-group hierarchies and harm vulnerable group members, such as women. This is particularly true, when group authorities who embrace patriarchal, authoritarian and exclusionary interpretations of their group's nomos are granted autonomy by the state and emerge as the de-facto leadership of the identity group.

While these criticisms address significant flaws with the earlier theories of politics of recognition, not all forms of recognition are necessarily susceptible to this line of critique. I would argue that a more nuanced interpretation and implementation of politics of recognition approach that takes into account the complexity of identity categories and their relation to material injustices can open a political space for culturally marginalised groups, such as veiled women in Turkey.

Nancy Fraser suggests that some forms of recognition politics represent genuine responses to serious injustices that cannot be remedied by other forms of politics. According to Fraser misrecognition should not be seen as 'a free-standing cultural harm' but as a denial of 'the status of a full partner in social interaction, as a consequence of institutionalised patterns of cultural value that constitute one as comparatively unworthy of respect or esteem.' The aim in addressing injustices stemming from misrecognition is therefore not valorising group identity, but creating channels to overcome the group's subordination and establishing it as equal partners in social and political life. The misrecognition of veiled women in Turkey is closely linked to material injustices, such as the undermining of group members' social, educational and economic opportunities, hence their social subordination. Many veiled women faced adversity when pursuing higher education, lost civil service jobs and face implicit discrimination in the private sector. Therefore, veiled women's misrecognition in Turkey fits into Fraser's characterisation of cultural harms that lead to social subordination.

Creating effective channels for differentiated group representation can play a significant role in overcoming the injuries from this type of misrecognition. Differentiated group representation aims to empower/ foreground marginalised subjects in democratic talk and decision-making. As Iris Marion Young states, a democratic republic 'should provide mechanisms for the effective representation and recognition of the distinct voices and perspectives of those of its constituent groups that are oppressed or disadvantaged within it.' One way to create this type of group differentiated representation for identity groups pushed to the margins is to form and institutionalise counterpublics as conceptualised by Nancy Fraser. Fraser defines counterpublics as 'parallel discursive arenas where members of subordinated so-called social groups invent and circulate counterdiscourses to formulate oppositional interpretations of their identities, interests, and needs.' I contend that it is conceivable to organise and institutionalise veiled women caucuses in workplaces, civil society organisations, or political movements. These caucuses can act as counterpublics, where organised groups of veiled women challenge the masculinist and secularist terms of the public debate. As Young aptly claims:

> Where some social groups have dominated political discussion and decision-making, these social perspectives have usually defined political priorities, the terms in which they are discussed, and the accounts of relations that frames the discussion. At the same time these perspectives are not experienced as only one way to look at the issues, but rather often taken as neutral and universal. Special representation of otherwise excluded social perspectives reveals the partiality and specificity of the perspectives already politically present...(and) bring to political discussion the situated knowledges (of these excluded groups).

In similar vein, the political discourse in Turkey excludes the experiences of observant women because it has been dominated by male and secular values, which are perceived as neutral and universal. The institutionalisation of veiled women's counterpublics is an attempt to undermine this implicit dominance and bring the situated perspectives of the veiled women, who have been heretofore marginalised, into the centre of politics. The aim is not to valorise any group identity, but destabilise the patriarchal and secular premises of the public debate and make it more attentive to social and political sensibilities of religious women.

Another aim of empowering counterpublics is to provide additional channels of representation for members of the polity who have less cultural capital than others due to social and historical processes of exclusion. In that regard, differentiated representation of historically excluded groups can encourage political and civic participation.

Opening channels for differentiated representation in forms of caucuses is different from top-down efforts of recognition, in which the state grants autonomy to religious groups and recognises a group authority as legitimate leadership thereby treating the group as a homogenous entity. By identifying veiling as an issue in the intersection of religion and gender, and therefore empowering religious women themselves rather than the Islamic community as such, the proposal escapes from blanket group recognition, which could lead to reinforcement of in-group hierarchies. The aim of institutionalising differentiated group representation for veiled women is to empower egalitarian, participatory grassroots formations and link them to the public debate.

One might argue that group representation obscures differences of class, cultural capital, and educational attainment among veiled women and therefore essentialises group identity. It is important to recognise that even if the headscarf ban is lifted in every public arena, and the stigma on veiling erodes in the future, veiled women from different classes and life situations will likely to continue to experience exclusion because of their class, gender, or ethnic position. The proposal of differentiated group representation does not address any of these issues. Yet, regardless of their socioeconomic differences veiled women share a similar social perspective, because they have been experiencing stigmatisation as religious women in the context of a republican emphasis of exclusionary Turkish secularism and the veil's presentation as an antagonist symbol in Turkey's national narrative. This similar social perspective emerges from experience, history and social knowledge that derive from veiled women's positioning in the secular republican history and the Islamist movement; yet people who have a similar social perspective often have different and conflicting interests. Thus, the veiled women counterpublics aim to create venues of representation for a shared social perspective, but do not claim to represent the interests or opinions of all veiled women, which are multiple and diverse.

Institutionalising veiled women counterpublics and directly linking them to opinion formation and decision-making bodies can also lead in articulating new strategies to combat the discrimination veiled women face. Legally, this might mean not presenting the headscarf ban solely as discrimination on basis of 'freedom of religion,' or 'gender discrimination,' but discrimination against 'religious women' emphasising the intersectional nature of the problem. 'We Want Veiled Members of Parliament Initiative' or the Reçel blog constitute important examples of this type of counterpublic, since they are organised by and claim to speak for women who don the headscarf. Although the former initiative could not be politically very effective in parliamentary elections, continuation of its activities at the local and national levels might be an important step to directly integrate the voices of veiled women into the public debate. Similarly, the establishment of parliamentary hearing committees or committees on local decision-making bodies that would incorporate veiled women caucuses or grassroots groups, such as Capital City Women's Platform, can transform the public debate and become a step in providing equality of status. The incorporation of these mechanisms can prevent the issue of veiling from being employed as a simple tool in the political conflict between the Islamists and the secularists and in the class struggle between the traditional secular middle class and the emerging Islamic bourgeoisie. Opening a space for group representation can aid in bringing the social perspectives of religious women into the centre of public debate and constituting them as subjects and not objects of politics. When women collectively and publicly articulate the meaning(s) of the veil, their social perspectives and political positions, they can effectively challenge the current public discourse that imposes on them a misrecognition and subsequently a subordinate sociopolitical position.

A politics of recognition approach, which emphasises group differentiated representation for misrecognised groups, goes beyond liberal toleration and foregrounds the meaning observant women themselves assign to their veil rather than ascribing a particular meaning to anyone's self-definition. It also challenges the presumed neutrality of the public debate, which privileges secular and male discourses by treating them as universal. In order to do this, the politics of recognition approach insists on instituting representative mechanisms for the direct inclusion of the voices of the excluded, marginalised or subordinated members of the polity. These mechanisms are necessary for democratic practice, because they can become significant discursive spaces where veiled women can challenge both the masculinist assumptions of the Islamic public sphere and the secularist assumptions of secular feminism on all issues – political, cultural, social and religious – that affect them directly.

MEMORY AND FORGETTING IN ISTANBUL

Charles Allen Scarboro

'I remember,' I say, thinking that memories belong to me as a person – after all – they are my memories. We act as if memories were unique, each of us collecting traces of events and feelings that belong to us alone. However, for more than one hundred years, sociologists have challenged this idea of memory and have worked to show that our memories are mostly not our own, but rather constructs that live only within social frameworks. Our personal memories take shape and are realised and expressed within networks of social, collective memories. First, a society remembers, then the actors create memories within a specific society which set limits and vistas within which ones memories are possible.

My memories are like one cobblestone that in combination with thousands of other cobblestones forms the streets that thread throughout Avcilar, a suburb of Istanbul where I live. The streets and the town itself provide the framework within which each single cobblestone makes sense. Further, a street is not just a bunch of cobblestones; a street is a higher pattern, a more inclusive ordering that determines where the cobblestones are placed. If the cobblestone is my memory, then the street, indeed all of Avcilar, is a collective memory. That collective memory arranges the individual cobblestones and, in fact, makes the individual cobblestone meaningful.

As we become more alert to the contexts of our own memories within the larger constellations of memories outside our own lives and groups, we can better hear the stories of others and, by hearing, find ways to live together where we are no longer strangers. By learning to participate in the memories of others, their stories also become our stories. Our memories grow to include an ever larger human family.

Much more than cobblestones or streets, monuments are conscious and intentional prompts to memory; further, monuments are locations for struggles over memory: what story and whose story does a monument tell and what rival stories are squashed? How does power shape what is memorialised? Whose story is being told? How do the viewers of monuments come to understand the history mounted in stone? How do people negotiate differing approaches to the monument?

The 2011 controversy over Mehmet Aksoy's 'Monument to Humanity' in Kars in eastern Turkey offers a telling example of the intentionality of and contentions over monuments. Aksoy constructed the monument both to commemorate the catastrophe that befell Armenians in the late Ottoman period and to offer a site where Armenians and the Turkish heirs of the Ottoman legacy could build a shared future. Then Turkish prime minister Recep Tayyip Erdoğan found the statue a 'monstrosity' and was the catalyst for monument's demolition. One wonders, what is 'monstrous' about memorialising 'humanity' – what story did the prime minister and his aesthetic supporters find unacceptable? What did the prime minister want to be forgotten? Whose story was hidden in the demolition? How did the controversy represent the use of political power to privilege one story while erasing a competing story? What is the story of the Turkish Republic that was challenged by the Kars monument? The case of this monument exemplifies how groups with different levels of power work to craft collective memories that set the winner's vision in stone.

On a level less intentional and conscious than monuments, the built environment also encapsulates and preserves complex stories and memories. Cities are more complex than monuments – they are more deeply layered – one set of memories overlies another, neighbourhoods laden with very different memories jostle shoulder-to-shoulder with one another, the process of accretion builds one set of experiences atop another, and the same sites can carry very disparate understandings. Neighbourhoods are different from monuments in two other ways as well: neighbourhoods are living spaces, shaped by daily life and by myriad individual decisions and practices as well as the lives of the cultures within which those lives unfold. Further, neighbourhoods are less likely to be locations shaped by conscious political power: neighbourhoods grow more in response to local decisions while official monuments or constructions reflect larger nexuses of power.

As a small example, in my Avcilar neighbourhood of Denizkoskler, a short stretch of an older highway lies alongside the newer E-5, the six-lane divided highway leading out of Istanbul. This short stretch of older road is named Eski Edirne Asfalta (the old paved road to Edirne), echoing a slower time when Avcilar was a humble way station between Constantinople and the earlier Ottoman capital in Edirne. The E-5, in its cold and abstract name, sets our sights to a far faster and far more general connection between Istanbul and 'E'urope and Turkey's participation in the economy and culture of Western Europe. Edirne fades into insignificance; it has become a kilometre marker.

Now, my neighbourhood is not on the way to anywhere, but is rather a sidelight in a faster, less personal panorama. Before expressways, themselves in many ways monuments, travellers paused and lingered in those places on the way to their destination but, on an expressway, the traveller focuses on the destination, on a place always in the future. The journey is defined by its end, not by the process of getting somewhere. My neighbourhood has also forgotten that the Eski Erdirne lies atop the Via Egnatia, a Roman road that tied Constantinople first to Adrianople, the earlier name for Edirne, and then on to the city of Rome. Those memories, however, are faint – eroded and replaced through the Ottoman then Republican policies of 'Turkifying' the old Roman and Byzantine realms, even to the level of the suburbs of Istanbul. Avcilar, itself, is named after the Sultans' hunting lodges located here and the name of the Greek village that long nestled here alongside the Sea of Marmara is forgotten.

The past is malleable and our memories live within the larger narratives of our contemporary society. Avcilar's pre-Republican past is forgotten and a new narrative ties the neighbourhood to a nationalistic story. When I first moved to Avcilar, I was surprised to note signs leading me to the Atatürk Evi (the Atatürk house). I was pleased to discover that I had moved into a neighborhood where the Founder of Modern Turkey had also once lived. Imagine my surprise to learn that the house in Avcilar was only a recreation and that Atatürk had no real connection to Avcilar – however, the Avcilar house relocates Atatürk from Thessalonika – now in Greece – to lovely Avcilar. A fictive collective memory detaches Avcilar and its neighbourhoods from connections to a more contested, less settled, more contentious past. The homes of the Greeks who lived here in the recent past and the church where they worshipped have been torn down – a mosque now occupies the spot where the church told its story. The neighbourhood and its landscape are now inescapably 'Turkish' — a much more diverse and less monolithic set of memories are submerged and elided into a more uniform story, a story leading our memories to Istanbul and Ankara rather than to a world of difference and variety.

Memory cannot exist without the simultaneous presence of forgetting. Memories, individual and collective, are always selective — not everything can be remembered. And, in many ways, memories are intentional — they are not neutral, but serve to support the person and the society we think we are in the present. We live, after all, not in the past but today and our memories exist not in the past but in the now. Sociologists argue that memory always entails the exercise of power — the powerful are heavily invested in what is remembered and what is forgotten. Collective memory is a framework wherein those in power legitimate and defend their right to exercise power. If history is the story of the winners, then collective memory helps us forget the vanquished by relegating them to the shadows.

For example, when I walk the streets of Sultanahmet, the historical center of Istanbul (and of Constantinople and of Byzantium), I am struck by the tension between memory and forgetting that grows out of the efforts of the Atatürk revolution to create a new Turkey. The Revolution attempted to build a new society, crafted in distinction to and separate from a past that the revolutionary leaders saw as an anchor slowing Turkey's move into modernity. While the buildings that stand throughout Sultanahmet speak of a glorious past that stretches far beyond the founding of the Turkish Republic, those buildings and monuments are strangely muted, their voices muffled. I note the gilt inscriptions flowing in Arabic letters on the buildings and I ask my Turkish companion, 'What does the inscription say? What building is this?' My companion replies, 'I cannot read the inscription — it is just an old building, maybe an Ottoman tomb. Who knows?' The alphabet revolution, with its shift of emphasis to Europe and 'modernity' guarantees that citizens in the new republic can know the past mostly through a set of lenses that highlight some meanings and obscure others.

We walk further and I notice an obviously Roman column. 'What it that?' I ask. 'Cemberlitas,' he replies. 'What does Cemberlitas mean?' I ask. 'Round stone. It is something old.' My guidebook names the edifice 'Constantine's Column,' a name that brings 2000 years of history present — something far more redolent than a round stone. The foreigner is opened to a past that is occluded for the native. We continue our stroll through the busy streets and come to what I think must be the most beautiful building in the world. I know the great stone structure as it strains to scratch heaven's foundations from art history courses I took in a small college in rural Ohio, thousands of miles from Sultanahmet Meydani. 'Hey,' I ask, 'I know this museum is called Ayasofya in Turkish. What does the name mean?' My companion maybe tires of my questions. 'Well, really nothing. Just a name.' Now a museum (a word from the Greek, a 'shrine of the Muses'; I ask my companion if he knows who the Muses are), Holy Wisdom and its soaring dome has stood for fifteen centuries for the aspirations of those who live in the Imperial City. Now, 'Just a name.'

Memory and forgetting can be paired with the notions of voice and silence. For sociologists, 'voice' refers to those who can speak for themselves, who can tell their own stories, who can participate in that great conversation which is society and culture. Voice comes from a position of potency and responsibility. With voice, persons and peoples can engage others, in dialogue, in argument, in assertions of their own needs and goals. Voicelessness, on the other hand, isolates people from public life and discourse; voicelessness disengages persons from negotiating and acting in their own interests. Silence characterises powerlessness. Silence marks those who have been devalued and disenfranchised. Memory then brings experience into voice. Forgetting is the location of experiences that are silenced. While some people choose silence (one thinks of hermits and mystics), most often silence is not chosen, but enforced, a product of the exercise of power. Since silence is usually not chosen by a person or a people, silence is also uncomfortable and uneasy. People seek avenues out of silence but those who do the silencing seek to maintain the silence of the disenfranchised. Thus silence is also the location of tension and conflict. Those in power craft stories that privilege the voice of the powerful. Sociologists call these stories of and by the powerful 'master narratives' – histories that highlight and justify the experience and the world of the powerful. In calling these stories master narratives, at least two meanings of the word master come to mind. First, these stories are the stories of the master, those in charge, those in control, those managing events. The names of the mosques that dominate the Istanbul skyline, after all, are named for rulers, not for ordinary people or for the virtues of common people.

Sultanahmet faces Wisdom. Second, master is also a verb: to master is to bring others into control, to take charge, to tame. Official histories work to define whose story is told and to eliminate competing stories.

Two recent events illustrate this tension between memory and forgetting, voice and silence. The 27 March 2011 Sunday's Zaman printed on its front page an illuminating article by Betul Akkaya Demirbas about Newroz, a spring festival associated with Kurds, widely celebrated in Turkey. She shows how this festival, with its antique roots and its message of hope, has become a site of conflict after political events in the 1980s. Kurdish people, in the republican Turkification program, were stripped of their names and their history and given a choice between being Turks or being silenced. Their story was to be discarded and their lives were to be absorbed into a nationalistic ethnic identity. The memories they were offered were designed by and intended to serve a national narrative. 'Mountain Turks,' after all is a very different sort of name than 'Kurd.' This renaming moved the people so-named into a story that felt alien to many of them. Newroz then became an avenue for voicing and remembering a story of diversity within modern Turkey. Demirbas, in her article, shows as well recent efforts, led largely by the current government, to bring Newroz into the larger Turkish story. For example, she noted that Culture and Tourism Minister Ertugrul Gunay has reframed Newroz not as a Kurdish festival but one 'celebrated by all humanity' and official reports name the festival Nevruz (the Turkish spelling of the holiday), dislocating it from its Kurdish to a more general location. This retelling of the story again negates a Kurdish claim of distinctiveness. A second recent event illustrating the tension between memory and silence was reported in Today's Zaman on 28 March 2011. The story reported the decision by the Supreme Court of Appeals' General Law Council that Nobel Prize winner Orhan Pamuk must pay several individuals whose honour required compensation for damage they claim Pamuk inflicted. How had Pamuk damaged these esteemed individuals? Pamuk, in an interview in Switzerland, had spoken of events from the 1920s that have long been silenced in official Turkey. Giving voice to silenced events and experiences can, it seems, cause harm to people who most likely were not even born when the event occurred. Silencing the past not only requires an on-going enterprise in the present, but that silencing also incurs costs and damages to those eager to maintain the silence.

Neither forgetting nor remembering is neutral: each involves intentionality and effort and collective action. A final example epitomises the struggle between memory and forgetting in contemporary Turkey. A diversion will help us see the logic of the process.

Charles Dodgson (1832–1898) was both a clergyman in the Church of England and a logician of note. He is, however, best known as the author of the Alice books: *Alice in Wonderland* and *Through the Looking-Glass*. Although I am not aware of any political science classes that assign his texts, Dodgson, better known as Lewis Carroll, is, I think, very helpful in understanding government and the exercise of power, voice and voicelessness. In both of Dodgson's well-known books, Alice encounters people, institutions, and situations that reveal the workings of the political mind. Her perplexity foreshadows our own as we move through a world built by politicians and their spokespersons. In many ways, Alice expresses Dodgson's own moral sense as well as his hope that clear thinking will help us make our way through the foggy realm of politicians trying to shape our reasoning, to make us believe that toadstools are thrones and that flamingos are croquet mallets.

Alice is especially helpful in thinking through the yearly fandango in Turkey each spring when minds turn to the Armenian 'catastrophe'. For example, in January 2012, the French Senate passed a bill criminalising denying that the 'catastrophe' was 'genocide'. For an American, the idea of criminalising speech seems bizarre – democracy depends, after all, on the 'marketplace of ideas'. But let's leave that issue aside for now. Rather, let us focus on the frantic response in Turkey to the French action. For twenty days, politicians danced around as if bitten by spiders. One denunciation followed another. The prime minister, in addition to recalling the Turkish ambassador to Paris, threatened and initiated a series of sanctions against the French. Politicians were joined by business groups, religious spokespersons, and amateurs of various sorts. Boycotts, hacking websites, threats to empty champagne bottles into the Bosphorus – symbolic gestures abounded.

One arena of great activity was in the media. I counted and found at least 99 articles and columns on the French action in Today's Zaman between 12 December 2011, days before the French legislators acted, and 23 January 2013, when the bill passed. Much of the media attention has consisted of finger-pointing ('the French have done bad things, too'), or accusations of a rising Islamophobia in Europe, or demands that 'outsiders leave us alone to deal with our own issues.' However, one prominent theme surfaces again and again: politicians, professional groups, and media pundits all called on a higher authority. To wit: it is not the job of the French to decide how to label the 'events' of 1915. Rather, that is the job of history.

This is disingenuous. To call for us to wait on history's verdict is to claim that historians have not studied these 'events' and have not come to a consensus. However, the record is clear: the 'events' have been studied by careful historians and their verdict is clear: let me quote Niall Ferguson, the Laurence A. Tisch Professor of History at Harvard University as well as a Senior Research Fellow of Jesus College, University of Oxford. In *The War of the World: Twentieth-Century Conflict and the Descent of the West*, he states, 'the murderous campaign launched against the Armenians from 1915 to 1918... is widely acknowledged to have been the first true genocide'. Now, Ferguson is a conservative historian but his conclusion is shared by scholars across the political and social spectrum. For example, another student of the Middle East, David Fromkin, comes to the same conclusion. In his *A Peace to End All Peace: The Fall of the Ottoman Empire* and the *Creation of the Modern Middle East*, Fromkin, a historian and Professor of International Relations at Boston University, identifies the events clearly as genocide. Further, Fromkin joins other historians in locating the instigation and execution of the genocide squarely in the official actions of Mehmed Talaat, Minister of the Interior, and Ismail Enver, War Minister, in the Ottoman government of Sultan Abdul Hamid II. The genocide was deliberate and had as its goal the eradication of a people perceived by government officials as a threat to their goals of a reinvigorated Ottoman Empire or of a 'Turkish' successor state.

Terrible events happen. In war and other times of crisis, terrible events are even more frequent and more awful than in other times. But what distinguishes 'genocide' from other terrible events or catastrophes? Raphael Lemkin, a Polish scholar, is credited with coining the term genocide. Tellingly, he proposed his definition of genocide before the terrible events of World War II. Lemkin defined genocide as 'a coordinated plan of different actions aiming at the destruction of essential foundations of the life of national groups, with the aim of annihilating the groups themselves.'

Lemkin's work later laid the groundwork for the establishment of the United Nation's definition of genocide as, 'following acts committed with intent to destroy, in whole or in part, a national, ethnical, racial or religious group'. Whether it is true that the Armenian genocide provided the model for the genocidal acts of the Nazi German regime is a matter in dispute. The 1939 Adolf Hitler quotation, 'Who after all speaks today of the annihilation of the Armenians?' is accepted by many historians while others doubt it and regard it as a propaganda product. True or not, the attributed quotation highlights that genocide is an act of government, an act with the goal of making a 'problem people' disappear into powerlessness, and that as a policy it often succeeds in reaching its goal. An annihilated people are a silent people.

Many of the comments by politicians in Ankara and much of the discussion of the actions of the French legislators served as diversionary tactics: smoke and mirrors to build nationalist frenzy or to derail attempts to reconcile the present with the past. As a telling example of the majority argument, let me quote Ekrem Dumanli who breezily declares that 'the issue is not about whether genocide was committed against the Armenians in 1915 (so offhandedly are as many as 1,500,000 deaths dismissed); the issue is all about the restriction of freedom of expression'. Alice's adventures come to mind once again.

In *Through the Looking-Glass*, Alice has a semiotic encounter with Humpty Dumpty. We listen in on the conversation:

> 'When I use a word,' Humpty Dumpty said in rather a scornful tone, 'it means just what I choose it to mean – neither more nor less.' 'The question is,' said Alice, 'whether you can make words mean so many different things.' 'The question is,' said Humpty Dumpty, 'which is to be master – that's all.'

The discussion about the Armenian events reveals a struggle for who will be master. Does history deliver us messages that help us find our way through the struggles of the present? Do we recognise that our past is in fact our past and that no measure of re-naming it can undo what was done? Or do we 'master' our past, contort it to frame whatever power games we are currently playing? Does it matter how we name our actions and our heritage? I think it does. And so does the prominent Turkish historian and sociologist, Taner Akcam. In his 2004 book, *From Empire to Republic: Turkish*

Nationalism and the Armenian Genocide, Akcam argues that the history surrounding the Armenian genocide occupies 'a perverse place in our mind' and that this perversity undercuts efforts to move towards a more just and a more democratic modern Turkey.

As I move through Istanbul, I listen hard. Some stories are easy to detect while others are faint echoes in the wind. However, the story of this city and its citizens is rich and full-flavoured. The buildings and streets and landscapes bring to my mind a panorama of diversity and multiplicity. The city reminds me of the Misir Carsisi, the Spice Bazaar – deeply textured, spicy and aromatic, crowded by people of all stripes and walks of life. That diversity is indeed what keeps the bazaar alive and astonishing. Those clamourous stories compete for the ear to save the bazaar from the fate of being still one more location to separate tourists from their money.

How dull it would be if only one spice were sold, if only one kind of *lokma* were offered, if only one kind of olive were vended in its stalls. How poor our memory would be if the Spice Bazaar were monochromatic.

EU AND TURKEY'S 'SELF' AND 'OTHER'

Melek Saral

Turkey's relations with the European Union (EU) have a long history. Almost from the establishment of the EU, Turkey has been interacting with the EU on several levels and to different degrees. It has pursued, over the last two hundred years, a policy of Westernisation; and EU membership has been generally seen as the final goal of this quest, the last step in bringing Turkey to Europe, where it belongs. Indeed, Turkey has experienced many positive changes in its economic, political and cultural life in the course of the EU membership process, changes that would be unimaginable without this relationship with the EU. However, Turkey's interactions with the EU have also had negative, unintended and counterproductive effects and shifted its definitions of 'self' and 'other' in opposing directions.

Within the framework of its relations with Turkey, the EU has not only questioned Turkey's self-definition as European, but has also given Turkey mixed signals regarding its acceptance into the EU. Historically, the 'Turk', or the 'Saracen', has been the dominant 'other', the darker side of Europe, because of the military might and physical proximity of the Ottoman Empire, combined with the strength of its religious tradition. It was also the relevant 'other' in the development of European identity. The European self was defined from the beginning in terms of what it was not. The non-European Turk as the 'other' of Europe played a decisive role in the evolution of the European identity. Based on this historically constructed image, Turkey has continued to be the ideal 'other' of the EU.

It would be an oversimplification to trace the change in Turkey's 'self' and 'other' definitions only to interactions with the EU institutions. Several internal and external developments, including changes in domestic conditions and international and regional developments, have contributed to the shift in Turkish national identity. However, the EU has been, till the deadlock of the relations, one of the most powerful factors shaping the political and public discourse in Turkey and the social environment of the country.

Social environment and social interactions have a decisive impact on the identity of individuals. States, like individuals, are affected by interactions with their social environment. Once they enter a social environment, or they interact with other actors, they are never the same. Although identity does not directly cause the action or behaviour, it indicates which behaviour is expected or legitimate in the pursuit of national identity. As the source of interest, it opens or closes the individual to different political discourses, makes them more or less predisposed to opposition and exclusion, more or less likely to pursue their interests aggressively or to anticipate the possibility of compromise. Thus, identity and the changes in identity involving the redefinition of 'self' and 'other' are of immense political significance.

Moreover, social identities are relational and collective. They are formed in relation to other actors such as states, nations, international organisations or institutions. According to the Norwegian political scientist, Iver B Neumann, 'collective identity is a relation between two human collectives, that is, it always resides in the nexus between the collective self and its others.' To confess a particular identity is also to belong to difference. Identity requires difference in order to be, and it converts difference into otherness to secure its own self-certainty. My personal identity is defined through the collective constituencies with which I identify or am identified by others; it is further specified by comparison to a variety of things I am not. Identity is unthinkable without such a difference. It would make no sense to say 'I am European' if this did not imply a difference from being 'Asian', 'African' or 'American'.

Turkey, a country that has experienced the collapse of an empire, still struggles for answers regarding its identity. It is torn between its Asian, Muslim and European identities. It does not share in the Judaeo-Christian cultural tradition, but neither does it belong to the predominantly Arab Islamic culture. It is usually described as a bridge between Europe and Asia, the West and the (Middle) East, or Western and Islamic civilisations. However, European civilisation has always been a very important factor in the formulation of Turkish identity – going back to the Ottoman Empire.

Modernisation, and to this end Westernisation, has not only been the major goal of the political elite in the modern Turkish Republic, it was also an objective of the Ottoman Empire. To be Western and European was regarded as a panacea for all the problems of the country; a path from underdevelopment to the civilised, modern world.

With the establishment of the new Turkish Republic, it became clear that the country's direction was toward Europe and the construction of national identity was characterised by Westernisation. The eagerness of Turkey to belong to the EU is closely linked to the perception of the membership as end point of Westernisation/modernisation of the country. For the founder of Republic, modernisation was equated to Westernisation, taking a place in the European civilisation and internalising all its cultural dimensions. The modernisation of the Turkish Republic included the isolation of the Turkish self from the Ottoman legacy, including the Arab countries. Despite the fact that the majority of the population of Turkey is Muslim, the country always stressed the differences between its 'self' and 'other' Muslim countries, and was allied with Western countries. While Turkey's approach to Middle Eastern countries became more multifaceted as a consequence of the Cold War and the 1960s Cyprus conflict, generally speaking Turkey was steadfast in its Western orientation. As a result of these 'self' and 'other' definitions, the interaction with the Middle East was kept to a minimum. It was reinforced by the negative images of the Arabs as untrustworthy people, who collaborated with the British against Turks during World War I, and uncivilised, backward states governed by Sharia law.

Turkey's strategic significance during the Cold War encouraged its identity as European and opened the door to several European and Western military, political and economic organisations including the OECD, the Council of Europe in 1948 and 1949, and NATO in 1952. The prospect of eventual membership of the EU was also offered to Turkey in the early 1960s. However, historical developments influenced Europe's approach to Turkey. In the 1970s, the EC's definition of Europeanness changed and democracy became the primary defining characteristic of a European state. Moreover, with the end of the Cold War, Turkey lost its strategic importance for Europe and, in turn, its Europeanness in the eyes of Western countries. Despite the decline of Turkey's importance for Europe,

Western values and the desire to become a European Union member only increased, particularly after the end of the Cold War.

But there were, and still are, mixed and conflicting perceptions of Europe. These go back to the war for the independence (1919-1923) of the Turkish Republic. While the West is associated with civilisation and modernisation, it is also seen as an imperialist power. Was Europe not determined to split Anatolia between the British, French, Greek and Italian regions in the 1920 Treaty of Sevres? Although it was never ratified and was replaced by the 1923 Treaty of Lausanne, the Sevres Treaty left a deep wound in the Turkish collective memory. Indeed, it has become a syndrome. The basic assumption underlying the Sevres Syndrome is that Europeans perceive the Turks as illegitimate invaders and occupiers of European-Christian lands and intend to restore those lands to their rightful owners – the Armenians and the Greeks in the past and now the Kurds. Today the Sevres Syndrome encompasses a broader meaning, including the fear of territorial dismemberment, mistrust of the outside world, a worldview based on conspiracy theories and other phobias. It is a filter through which the world is perceived; and used as a tool for manipulating public opinion and attitude towards the external world.

Several historical and political developments also galvanised the belief that the West wishes to divide Turkey, and strengthened the paranoia associated with the Sevres Syndrome. These include the on-going issue of Cyprus, the terrorist activities of Armenian ASALA and Kurdish PKK, as well as the establishment of a Kurdish federal state in North Iraq under US control. Turkey's EU membership process is also an important factor; the process is sometimes portrayed as a modern version of the Sevres Treaty. According to a 2006 National Public Opinion Survey, conducted by the International Republican Institute, 57 per cent of the participants stated that the EU requirements for the membership are similar to those required by the Sevres Treaty and 78 per cent stated that European states want to divide and break up Turkey like they broke up the Ottoman Empire.

Turkey was officially recognised as a candidate for full membership in the EU, without any preconditions and placed on an equal footing with the other candidate states, in December 1999 at the Helsinki Summit. After this recognition, the main strand of discourses emphasised Turkey's Europeanness and similarity to other EU countries, but also highlighted its differences. Turkish multidimensional identity was projected as beneficial for the EU. When the then Foreign Affairs Minister, Ismail Cem, evaluated the Helsinki Summit at a press conference, he stressed that Turkey's identity was different from any other EU member: 'We are not just any candidate. Turkey is contributing its unique identity and its historical experience. It is joining the EU with its East-West, Christian-Muslim syntheses'. This strand of discourses did not characterise the multidimensional character of Turkish identity as conflicting but as complementary. The eastern identity of Turkey was explained as strengthening and enriching the Europeanness of Turkey. Turkey was represented as European from geographical, historical and cultural perspectives but the Europeanness of Turkey was referred to sui generis and different than European Europeanness. As Prime Minister Bulent Ecevit explained in May 2000:

> The 'Europeanness' of Turks cannot be questioned from geographical, histori-
> cal or cultural aspects… It is an interesting example of lack of awareness in
> Europe that causes the European identity of Turkey to be questioned. However,
> we are not only European but also Middle Asian, Middle Eastern, Caucasian,
> Black Sea and East Mediterranean. This mixture of identity is not a defect in
> the Europeanness of Turkey but the richness of its European identity.

The emphasis on Turkey's multidimensional identity increased considerably after the 9/11 terrorist attacks. Now Turkey underlined, in addition to its 'Europeanness', its religious and secularist multidimensional identity more frequently in the framework of EU relations. It was a good card to play. It was believed that the religious and secularist characteristics of Turkey would help carry Turkey into the EU under the umbrella of multiculturalism. Particularly before the 2002 EU Copenhagen Summit, it was repeatedly underlined that Turkey's acceptance as a Muslim country would bring advantages to the EU and rescue it from being a Christian club. The emphasis was on being a role model for other Muslim countries and transmitting Western values to them. So the underlining of differences was mostly done, not to isolate Turkey from Europe, but to add value beyond its European identity. Differences and Europeanness were emphasised in tandem.

Another constant theme in support of Turkey's EU membership was the long history of Turkey's Europeanness and its attachment to Europe. Political actors constantly emphasised that Turkey's historical and cultural bonds with Europe went further back than the establishment of the Turkish Republic. Thus, to defend the reforms required to fulfil the EU criteria, Prime Minister Recep Tayyip Erdoğan argued that Turkey had been working on its modernisation and civilisation for well over a century:

The Ottoman Empire was, for centuries, a part of European history and played an important role. Since Atatürk's reforms, Turks have defined themselves as Europeans and Turkey is a member of all the political, economic and defence organisations in Europe. What makes Turkey European is that she adopted the principles represented by Europe, like democracy, pluralism, rule of law, human rights, secularism, freedom of speech and conscience…Turkey decided on the West at the establishment of the Republic.

Erdoğan represents Turkey's adjustment to Western values and principles as evidence of Turkey's Europeanness. The argument here is that Turkey's European identity derives not only from the historical roots but also from the adjustment to the common political and cultural principles of Europe. Thus, there are no separating lines between Turkish 'self' and Western 'other'.

Furthermore, the EU accession process was also seen as a joining civilisations project based on Turkey's Muslim identity. The will to join the EU was also on the necessity of uniting two very different civilisations – 'us' Muslim World and 'them' Christian World. Paradoxically, this argument of joining of civilisations negated Turkey's self-description as Western and European and drew the boundaries between 'self' and 'other' based on religious lines. As Prime Minister Erdoğan, explained:

We don't have an addiction to EU membership, but we believe in the necessity of our accession. We must separate these. Turkey wants to access the EU to make it the place for the alliance of civilisations. This is because we don't want the Islamic world and the Christian world to be against each other. We want them to show solidarity under one roof.

Parallel to increased use of civilisations project argument, the bridge metaphor referring to Turkey's role in connecting these two civilisations was used more frequently. In the bridge metaphor, which assumes two mutually exclusive worlds, Turkish 'self' is equated to a bridge linking two distinct worlds – Western and Eastern, European and Islamic – without belonging to either side. Politicians used the bridge metaphor to underline Turkey's importance as a link between the West and East, a perfect country to unite the two. For example, the then Foreign Minister Abdullah Gül, presented Turkey as 'being a model for other Muslim countries' and pointed to Turkey's ability to merge Islam and modernity: 'we showed the whole world that a country with 99 per cent Muslim habitants can be modern, can apply the same human rights standards as the most developed countries and offer its citizens democracy. In addition, we showed that leaders who are conservative and respect values and religion can do this.' The self was now also labelled as the representative of Islam and Muslim countries in the European community. 'With a great population and its relations with the Turkic Republics and Muslim countries, Turkey's membership will give these countries the feeling that they are represented in the EU.'

At the start of the negotiation process, the EU's Christian identity was also debated. The acceptance of Turkey, as a Muslim country, was regarded as the EU's choice to no longer remain a Christian club. Necmettin Erbakan, the leader of the Islamist Welfare Party, underlined the 'otherness' of Europe for Turkey and assumed that Europe would forgo acting as the 'other' of Turkey and become its 'self'. After the Helsinki Summit, he said, initially he was against EU membership. 'However, now I am for EU membership. But why do I now support membership? We didn't change, they changed. They didn't want us saying, "here is a Christian club". But now they respect our belief.' Similarly, the 2002 Copenhagen decision was not only perceived as authorisation of Turkey's Europeanness, but also as Europe's attempt to give up the idea of being a Christian club. The discourses were mainly indicating that the borders between 'us' and 'them' based on religious identity were diminished. The then prime minister, Abdullah Gül, pointed to the EU's decision at the Copenhagen Summit as proof that it is not a Christian Club. 'Some people say that the EU is a Christian Club, but it turned out that it is not...If Turkey joins the EU, it will be the success of a Muslim and democratic country.'

But there was also discord. Kurdish and Cyprus issues kept coming to the fore; indeed, they were always at the heart of Turkey-EU relations and heavily impacted Turkey's changing 'self' and 'other' definitions. Critics of EU-Turkey relations represented the EU in negative terms. For example, Minister of State, Sükrü Sina Gürel, responsible for the Cyprus issue, described the EU as a threatening presence: 'it is like somebody is threatening us from behind with a drawn knife. We don't know his purpose. If we suddenly turn, he might not be able to stab us. We are not going to cave in. At the same time, it hurts'. Like Gurel, many saw the EU as an enemy of Turkey, an unreliable, untrustworthy and unfriendly institution, and a supporter and spokesman of PKK. The letter, addressed to the President of the Republic, assembly speaker, prime minister, general staff and chiefs of foreign missions, of the Nationalist Movement Party's (MHP) Deputy, Sevket Bulent Yahnici, provides a good illustration of these sentiments:

> Government bows to the pressure from outside. If we would have said yes to everything, Turkey would not have been able to sign the Lausanne Treaty. It would have been bound by the Sevres Treaty... The most powerful countries in the world made us sign Sevres. Today's government says yes to everything because it cannot stand up to the EU. Some did not submit to the enemy... Turkey cannot submit to the defender of Sevres and is not going to do so.

The fact that the government was agreeing to some EU demands, particularly relating to the Kurdish issue, was problematic for Yahnici:

> The EU is re-imposing the Sevres Treaty and had decided to create a Kurdish nation...requirements regarding cultural rights and Kurdish television should be rejected... EU was acting as spokesman for the PKK and delivering their requirements to Turkey.

However, the relationship between the EU and Turkey were set to deteriorate further. In December 2006, only a year after the start of the negotiations, the EU suspended negotiations. The ostensible reason was that Turkey had not fully implemented the Additional Protocol to the 1963 Ankara Agreement, particularly in relation to the Republic of Cyprus. Although this suspension did not prevent Turkey from pursuing negotiations with the Union, it signalled mistrust between the parties and caused a slowdown in the negotiations. There were signs of revival in 2009 with Erdoğan's first visit to Brussels to discuss the accession process. This visit strengthened expectations that the government was determined to bring the EU issue back onto its agenda. However, the hope for a new start for EU-Turkey relations did not last long, because Angela Merkel and Nicolas Sarkozy insisted that Turkey should be accorded 'privileged partnership' without becoming a full member of the Union.

Following the suspension of negotiations, Turkey's emphasis on 'self', not only as part of Western civilisation, but something different and more special, namely as Muslim, democratic and secular at the same time, increased. It should be stressed that not only conservative and Islamic-oriented actors but also left-leaning, secular actors stressed Turkey's unique identity and defined the 'self' as Muslim. For example, the then leader of Republican People's Party (CHP), Deniz Baykal, declared: 'the EU has to realise the importance of access of a Muslim country that is also secular and democratic. It has to see the potential positive impact and importance of this membership for its interests.'

The emphasis once again shifted to Turkey's multidimensional identity. The civilisations project argument continued to be applied by some politicians, the strong advocates of Turkey's EU membership. However, Turkey was now seen not so much as a bridge between two civilisations but as the active actor of a distinct civilisation. Turkey's Muslim, secular and democratic identity was underlined; and the Turkish self was represented as more distinct and powerful because of its special identity.

After the suspension of the negotiations many Turks saw Turkey's membership of the EU as a dream going nowhere. The enthusiasm for EU membership was replaced by indifference. The financial crisis of 2008, the problems with Greece and other internal problems in the EU further eroded the attraction of the Union. The government searched for other potential relations and looked eastward. Some saw the eastward shift of Turkey as a pragmatic avoidance of the excessive concessions required by the EU. Others considered this shift a result of the ideological and emotional motivations of the ruling Justice and Development Party (AKP). Many scholars pointed to the Foreign Minister, Ahmet Davutoglu, as the person behind the new orientation. Now the stress on European identity was weakened, if not totally abandoned. The continuing arguments and debates on Turkey's multidimensional identity also made Turkey aware of its potential as an international actor and made it more self-aware and conscious of its eastern identity.

The new active regional policy was explained on the basis of Turkey's multidimensional identity stemming from its historical and geographical position. Davutoglu claimed that Turkey's new regional policy is to accept its regional responsibility and work to solve the problems and crises in its region. However, to play a dominant role in the region required a European vision as strong as Turkey's Muslim identity. Without a European vision, Turkey could not become a global power. So Turkey, Davutoglu suggested, still aimed to be inside the EU. In a Spiegel interview, Davutoglu emphasised the EU's strategic relevance for Turkey, but at the same time reminded the EU of the significance of Turkey's multidimensional identity for the Union. Davutoglu echoed the sentiments and words of former Prime Minister, Bulent Ecevit:

> Turkey's EU membership is our most important strategic aim and it will remain so. We have pointed toward Europe since the Ottoman Empire's reform policies in the nineteenth century. Turkey is not only a European country. It is, at the same time, an Asian, Black Sea, Mediterranean, Caucasian, and Middle East country. It is a multidimensional country. This is not a problem for the EU; on the contrary, it will help the EU.

The components of Turkish identity have been systematically reordered and rearranged based on political expediency and developments. However, the redefinition of Turkey's 'self' and 'other' has never led to a total rejection of Western identity. But it is clear that in the course of this re-definition, the underlining multidimensional character of its identity has come to the fore, and its Muslim identity now has priority. Although Turkey has not entirely walked away from Europe, it has positioned itself closer to the Islamic countries. The EU is no longer regarded as Turkey's destiny, but as a strategic political union. The once popular metaphor of Turkey as the 'bridge between two worlds' has almost disappeared. The country now seeks to play a more active role in the region and in the international arena.

SAVING HASANKEYF

John Crofoot

From the edge of town, the footpath climbs gently toward Zih Canyon, tracing a line between the Sâlihiyya Gardens and the cliff of Ra's Tibbah, the mount that forms the southern boundary of Hasankeyf. Here the villa of an Artukid prince, there a sheikh's tomb stand among the rows of fig, pomegranate, and mulberry trees that divide the gardens into a patchwork of uneven plots. A little farther uphill, one pauses at the mouth of the canyon to survey 12,000 years of urban history: the Neolithic mound on the far side of the Tigris River contains the earliest evidence of organised human settlement ever found. Towards the left, the lower city of Hasankeyf, marked by two Ayyubid minarets, lies in the shadow of the storied Hisn Kayfa (The Citadel of the Rock) – atop the sheer cliff that towers a hundred metres above the Tigris River.

Particularly rich in Seljuk-era architecture and urban archaeology, Hasankeyf provides us with a broad and comprehensive view of how cities were organised, the technologies that shaped everyday life, and the eclectic architectural tastes of Artukid, Ayyubid and Akkoyunlu patrons. Hasankeyf is a treasure house of the cultural history of Eastern Anatolia from the twelfth to the fifteenth centuries and an invaluable source of insight into the complexities and nuances of Seljuk society. The eclectic architectural repertoire of Hasankeyf underscores the well-documented Seljuk blending of Turkish and Persian, so intricately interwoven as to render useless any attempt to think of one without the other. In 1978, Turkey's Ministry of Culture declared Hasankeyf a first-degree archaeological site and its General Directorate of Antiquities and Museums placed the site under protection. Ironically, Hasankeyf is not a UNESCO World Heritage site, even though it meets nine of ten UNESCO criteria. Worse still, the immeasurable cultural heritage of Hasankeyf and the Tigris Valley are now under serious threat by a controversial mega-dam nearing completion at Ilısu, a village sixty kilometres downstream from Hasankeyf.

Geographically, Hasankeyf lies in the 'Diyar Bakr', as the Arabs designated the northern region of Upper Mesopotamia and the city's cultural heritage is a product of its turbulent history. In the eleventh century, the Kurdish Marwanids ruled this region, serving as a buffer between the two great empires of the day. To the east, the Great Seljuk Turks ruled a vast territory from their capital, Isfahan; to the west, the Byzantine Empire controlled most of Anatolia from Constantinople. In the late-eleventh century, however, the balance changed substantially in favour of the Great Seljuk Empire, which extended its territory into Anatolia at the expense of the both the Byzantines and the Marwanids. But in the twelfth century, internal strife among the Great Seljuks allowed for the emergence of several successor states, the most important of these being the Seljuks of Anatolia (with their capital first at Iznik, then Konya), the Zangids (at Mosul, Aleppo and Damascus), the Inalids (who controlled Amid, the modern-day city of Diyarbakır) and the Artukids (Hisn Kayfa, Mardin and Mayyafariqin, modern-day Silvan). As a small potentate living under constant threat of attack by larger neighbours, the Artukids of Hasankeyf sought to improve their position and formed alliances with Nur al-Din (1118–1174), the Zangid ruler of Aleppo, and later with Salahaddin (1137/8–1193), founder of the Ayyubid dynasty, and joined the fight against the Crusaders. Thanks to his alliance with the Ayyubids, Artukid rulers of Hasankeyf were awarded Amid as a fief in 1183.

By 1232, however, the tables had turned against the Artukids of Hasankeyf due to their alliance with Khwarazm Shahs, who ruled large parts of Greater Iran and challenged Ayyubid holdings in eastern Anatolia. After a joint Ayyubid-Seljuk counter-offensive forced Khwarazm Shah to retreat, the Ayyubids punished the Artukids, terminating their rule and taking control of Amid and Hasankeyf. They established a line of Ayyubid rule that endured in Hasankeyf for nearly three centuries. Elsewhere, the Ayyubid Empire disappeared rather abruptly, overthrown in Egypt by the Mamluks in 1250, and wiped out of Syria and the Jazira in 1260 by the Mongols. By contrast, the Ayyubids in Hasankeyf evaded the wrath of the Mongols and also survived the campaigns of Timur in the late-fourteenth century and the ongoing contest between two Turkmen tribal confederations, the Kara Koyunlu (Black Sheep – Shi'i) and Akkoyunlu (White Sheep – Sunni) in the fifteenth century.

This long period of fragmented rule and territorial contests was also a time of heightened prosperity in Upper Mesopotamia, and Hasankeyf was one of several cities that flourished economically and culturally in the twelfth and fifteenth centuries. The cities of the region hummed with power and activity. In addition to remarkable engineering accomplishments, such as the twelfth-century bridges at Hasankeyf, Cizre and Malabadi (near the present-day city of Batman), the sophistication and diversity of architectural achievements within a small territory provide clear evidence of prosperity and far-reaching trade relationships: some of the finest examples of expert workmanship blending Arab and Persian influences include the Great Mosques of Mayyafariqin (1152–57) and Dunaysir (now Kızıltepe, 1204), and in Mardin the Sultan Isa Madrasah (1385) and the Madrasah of Kasim Pasha (late fifteenth to early sixteenth century).

Unfortunately, there are only limited textual sources available to elucidate the role that Hasankeyf played in the economic and cultural flourishing of the Jazira at this time. The historian Ibn al-Munshi chronicled Ayyubid rule in Hasankeyf, covering the thirteenth and fourteenth centuries, but practically no other sources provide detailed accounts of the city's history. The twelfth century Syrian memoirist ibn Munqidh makes passing references to Hasankeyf, where he lived for ten years; the thirteenth century topographical historians Yakut and ibn Shaddad provide brief descriptions of the citadel and lower city. These partial glimpses offer nothing like the detailed and sustained view provided in contexts where foundation deeds and other documents add to the historical record, and it is important to examine closely both the urban structure and the distinctive architectural monuments of the medieval city.

Urban Structure

While superficial differences in architectural design help to distinguish one city from the next, the basic layout of Seljuk cities was broadly consistent across Iran and Anatolia, and comprised four major areas: citadel (seat of the sovereign), the lower city outside the citadel, suburbs, and irrigated hinterlands. These four broad divisions of the urban landscape formed an integral whole, often without clear boundaries to distinguish one division from another.

The Citadel Mount of Hasankeyf comprises an area of some 2,300 square metres, guarded on all sides by steep cliffs. The principle structures within the citadel precinct include the palace, the foundations of which date to fourth century, and the Great Mosque, thought to date to the twelfth century Artukid period. Water from the hinterlands was pumped to the citadel, where it was stored in the *maksem*, an underground storage facility from which, similar to the function of the eighteenth-century facility at Taksim in Istanbul, water was redirected to the different quarters of the citadel, including fields where grains were cultivated. In case the water supply was cut, for example, during a siege, a hidden staircase cut into the cliff allowed access to the river.

The archaeological remains of the lower city represent the various sectors of medieval urban economy, from trade and light manufactures to religion and education. The major monuments here are the twelfth-century Artukid Bridge, the Koç Mosque whose date of construction is uncertain, the late-fourteenth century Sultan Süleyman Funerary Complex and the Rizk Mosque built in 1409. The remains of several churches have been discovered as well. Fragments of the walls thought to have surrounded the lower city are visible at intermittent locations, and just beyond these walls lies a small ceramics factory, including numerous kilns, cooling pools, and areas for painting and storage. As the first ceramic production site unearthed in eastern Anatolia, this site attests not only to the commercial importance of Hasankeyf, but also provides an extraordinary in situ display of medieval manufacturing facilities. The extent of these ceramics workshops, which are arguably the most important kiln remains in Anatolia, suggest that ceramics production in Hasankeyf was comparable to that of Iznik.

Halfway between the kilns and the river, a Seljuk-era water purification system was recently excavated. Nestled between the rocky slopes of the Tur Abdin Plateau and the Tigris River, Hasankeyf is fed by a network of streams and artificial canals. Local residents describe underground cisterns and channels that are much more extensive than what is visible to the casual observer, suggesting that further excavation may well reveal additional examples of medieval water distribution and technology, such as the Seljuk-era refrigeration system discovered in Konya.

Hasankeyf Lower City: Koç Mosque (foreground), the Sultan Süleyman Funerary Complex (centre), and minaret of the Rizk Mosque (left)

Sâlihiyya Gardens

The Sâlihiyya Gardens are located just east of the kilns outside the city walls. There are various explanations for the name of these gardens. Today, the name is sometimes written as 'Salhiye', following local pronunciation. Some speculate that the name 'Salahiyye' may have been given by immigrants from Syria, who recognised its resemblance to the Salahiyye district of Damascus. Ibn al-Munshi writes that 'al-Malik al-Sâlih' ordered the rebuilding of the gardens in the late thirteenth century and refers to the district as 'al-Sâlihiyya'. Fragments of Artukid and Ayyubid villas, mosques and madrasahs stand among small plots where local Hasankeyf residents still cultivate fruits and vegetables. In its location and distinctly 'suburban' atmosphere, the Sâlihiyya district recalls the City of the Dead in Cairo (where the wealthy retreated to family mausoleums for holidays and in summer), the Salahiyya district of tombs and dervish lodges on the edge of Damascus, and the cemeteries and gardens on either side of the defence walls of Istanbul. Whereas modern urban sprawl has engulfed and dwarfed the old fields and gardens in most cities of the region, in Hasankeyf the proportions of the Sâlihiyya district, lower city and citadel are much closer to what they would have been nine hundred years ago, when the Artukids made their capital here.

One of the better-preserved sites in the Sâlihiyya Gardens is the Haydar Baba funerary complex, comprising a small mosque, study rooms, some graves and the monumental tomb of the sheikh, all centred on a small pool. These gardens also hold traces of residential architecture, including the *eyvan* and pool of the 'Artukid villa'. The *eyvan* is a distinctive architectural form, typically described as vaulted porch or veranda with 'walls on three sides and completely open on the fourth'. The three walls of this *eyvan* still stand, but the vaulted ceiling is gone. Ibn al-Munshi' writes that Sultan al-Malik al-Adil spent the summer of 1348 at the 'Sâlihiyya Pavilion,' where he 'enjoyed the pleasures of youth,' sitting most mornings 'at the *eyvan* with his deputies and commanders attending to the affairs of the people and the business of government' and 'summoning court entertainers' and his princely guests in the afternoons. The sultan's guests would likely have gathered in various chambers of the pavilion or in the courtyard, those of the highest status taking in the scene from the shade of *eyvan*. Following Artukid tradition, the innermost wall of the *eyvan* would have been ornamented with a fountain from which water emptied into a shallow channel in the floor, cooling the air as it flowed to the pool in the courtyard.

Most of the pools that can be seen in the gardens today are square in shape, but ibn al-Munshi' notes the placement of an octagonal pool before an *eyvan* constructed in 1317. A pool might also be used as a stage for displaying ingenious devices to delight and entertain guests. In his *Book of Knowledge of Ingenious Mechanical Devices*, the polymath and inventor al-Jazari (1136-1206), who served the Artukid ruler of Hasankeyf and Diyarbakir, provides detailed plans for fountains shooting water in varying patterns, such as jet, arc, tent and fan. In addition to automated pitchers to be used at drinking parties and dispensers to assist with hand-washing, al-Jazari also outlines detailed specifications for a model boat bearing dancing figures and musicians powered by a concealed system of tanks and axels in the hull of the boat.

Garden districts were an integral part of medieval cities in Seljuk lands and across the Islamic world. The gardens of Merum, which stood outside the city walls of Konya, were, in the words of Redford, 'famed in Seljuk and Ottoman times for their lushness and beauty'. These gardens are completely lost today. Medieval Islamic texts –poetry, epic, travel narrative and scientific treatises – are replete with illustrations depicting gardens and the accompanying pavilions as an alternative place to conduct business and entertain guests, with activities ranging from theological discussions to drinking parties. Further archaeological excavation of the Sâlihiyya Gardens of Hasankeyf would significantly enhance historical scholarship on landscape design in medieval Iran and Anatolia. Similarly, the physical infrastructure and overall urban fabric visible today in Hasankeyf can shed new light on the cultural history of the entire region, where many cities boast important Seljuk-era monuments but have lost the streets and water distribution networks that formed the fabric of the city.

Pool and *eyvan* of the 'Artukid pavilion'

The Artukid Bridge

Built in 1145, the Artukid Bridge, the remains of which stand with graceful majesty at a slight angle to the sheer cliff of the Citadel, is one of the most striking visual elements of the city. The seven massive pylons trace the route by which travellers would have traversed the 250-metre bridge, entering the lower city next to the Rizk Mosque. The Arab historian Yakut, who visited Hasankeyf in the thirteenth century, described this bridge as the largest and most beautiful of its day, and even in its current state of ruin, it is a compelling monument to the robust trade and technical ingenuity of Upper Mesopotamia in the twelfth century.

The remaining pylons also hold Turkey's most extensive collection of in situ human figural relief carvings from the Seljuk era. Originally the pylons would likely have displayed eight, possibly twelve, relief carvings depicting royal court pages. Five have survived. These extremely rare and curious figures have prompted a wide range of speculation as to their origin. Oluş Arık suggests that they may represent symbols of the zodiac. In his book *Voyages archéologiques dans la Turquie Orientale*, Albert Gabriel

One of five relief carvings, thought to represent court pages, displayed on the pylons of the Artukid Bridge at Hasankeyf

speculated that the carvings may have been recycled from a Parthian structure. According to Adnan Çevik, these reliefs reflect a tradition of Central Asian Turkish ancestors, and Estelle Whelan argues that these images of court pages (*khassaqiyyah*) were installed as symbols of sovereign power, noting that figural representation of the sovereign was not acceptable but that no restriction applied to depicting figures closely associated with the sovereign.

The history of pictorial representation in Islamic civilisations is rich and complex, ranging from textual illumination to ceramics, metalwork, and architectural ornamentation. Among the Umayyads in Syria and the Seljuks in Iran and Anatolia, for example, the display of human figurative representation, including sculpture in the round as well as relief carvings, was particularly widespread. Unfortunately, countless examples of these relief carvings have been lost along with the secular buildings that held them; in some cases, they may have been replaced by more conventional abstract floral and geometric ornaments and inscriptions. The surviving examples are far and few between. Relief carvings showing human figures appear on the twelfth-century bridge at Cizre, on the Syrian side of the border. Of the two reliefs remaining from the Konya Citadel, one is in the Konya İnce Minareli Medrese Museum and the other is in the Staatliche Museum in Berlin. The relief carvings of the Hasankeyf bridge further augment the historical value of the bridge.

Hasankeyf mosques

The mosques constructed in Anatolia during the Seljuk era are predominantly hypostyle in form, having an interior of many pillars supporting the ceiling, which is done in vaults or consecutive bays finished in small domes or transverse arches. There is usually a larger dome or cupola above the area in front of the *mihrab*, designating the *maqsura*, or space reserved for the sultan. In the harsh climate of both the Anatolian Plateau and Upper Mesopotamia, the thick masonry walls insulate the interior space from extreme winter cold and the scorching heat of summer. The exterior surfaces are typically long and flat, meeting at right angles, with only limited ornamentation around small windows. The entrance is often understated – of modest size and decorated with simple engraving (for example, at Mayyafariqin and Dunaysir) or moderate use of honeycomb *muqarnas* (as in Huant Hatun Mosque in Kayseri).

Great Mosque of the Hasankeyf Citadel (before restoration)

Individual variations on this style make for a rich diversity in spatial layout and architectural ornamentation, no less in Hasankeyf than in Divriği. The elaborate ornamentation on the exterior of the hospital and mosque at Divriği is an obvious exception to the general Seljuk tendency toward measured use of ornamentation on exterior walls. In Hasankeyf, the simple exterior lines and well-insulated interior of the Koç Mosque and Great Mosque fit the general model, even if these mosques are not technically 'hypostyle' in form: the long, narrow wings on either side of the *maqsura* comprise a single vaulted corridor resting on exterior walls (without pillars). But what truly distinguishes these mosques from all others in Turkey is the insertion of a grand vaulted entryway or *eyvan*. In place of the understated entryway typical of most Seljuk-era mosques in Anatolia, the vaulted portico lengthens the moment of transition from exterior courtyard to interior prayer space. This is a direct borrowing from the Great Seljuk architectural tradition, and it alters one's experience of the mosque.

The *eyvan* has a long history in Mesopotamia, where it was employed as early as the first century BC in Seleucia-on-the-Tigris. By the eleventh century, it had become an integral part of mosque architecture in Iran, achieving new equilibrium in scale and symmetry in the Friday Mosque in Isfahan. From this time forward, the *eyvan* has been the single most salient feature of mosque design in Iran and Central Asia, just as the central dome has defined an Ottoman mosque since the sixteenth century. In Syria and Anatolia, by contrast, the *eyvan* was used almost exclusively in madrasahs and residential buildings, with three exceptions. First, in the Great Mosque of Malatya, built in 1224, an *eyvan* with a high arch precedes the domed area, but this entryway, for all its elegance, is too short in length to provide the accustomed space of transition. In addition, the visual impact of this *eyvan* is diminished, as it can only be viewed at close distance from the small interior courtyard, which was enclosed when the mosque was enlarged. Second, the Great Mosque of Hasankeyf, where the *eyvan* provides an extended portico but has unfortunately lost considerable value as an archaeological record of Artukid and Ayyubid stone masonry due to an aggressive rebuilding effort completed in 2012. Third, the Koç Mosque, despite its extreme state of deterioration, is arguably one of the most

The vaulted prayer space, central dome and *eyvan* of the Koç Mosque

important monuments in Hasankeyf and by all counts a highly original
model of mosque design in Turkey. The walls of the *eyvan* are standing, but
the vaulted ceiling has collapsed, as has part of the dome above the *maqsura*.
In addition, the stucco relief carving around the *mihrab* is an excellent
specimen of Seljuk workmanship. In its day, the *eyvan*-and-dome
combination, framed at ample distance by the cliffs at the southwest corner
of the lower city, must have made for a compelling visual and physical
experience, not only for its distinctive monumental design but also for the
sense of ceremony it afforded to those who entered.

How did Hasankeyf come to boast two of the three mosques in Turkey
to be adorned by an *eyvan*? In his discussion of the Koç Mosque, former
head of archaeological excavations at Hasankeyf Oluş Arık calls attention
to the unconventional use of the *eyvan*. But he does not venture an
explanation as to why builders in Hasankeyf might have chosen to break
with well-established regional models. In his analysis of the Great Mosque
of the citadel, Arık notes that the dates on the minaret (1327), the *eyvan*
(1394) and the *minbar* (1396) probably refer to Ayyubid-era repairs and
renovations to a structure originally built by the Artukids. It is important
to question further to what extent does the use of the *eyvan* in Hasankeyf's
mosques depend on the presence of craftsmen who trained in the east, and
did they come to Hasankeyf by invitation or by chance? But is it not also
possible that the Ayyubids added the *eyvan* to this mosque after having built
the Koç Mosque? Might the Ayyubids, whose monuments are very similar
in style to Artukid buildings in Mardin and elsewhere, have opted for a
different use of the *eyvan* in order to distance themselves from Artukid
conventions? And looking broadly at the contrast between Great Seljuk and
Anatolian Seljuk architectural practices, what reasons inhibited widespread
adoption of the *eyvan* in the design of mosques in the west when this was
such a common practice in the east?

Zeynel Bey Tomb

The architectural repertoire of Hasankeyf continued to expand under the
Akkoyunlu ('White Sheep') tribal confederation, which ruled in eastern
Anatolia in the fifteenth century. Not only did the Akkoyunlu contribute to

the upkeep of existing monuments, such as the tomb and lodge of Imam Abdullah, but they also gave the city its most exquisite monument: the tomb of Zeynel Bey, the Akkoyunlu prince who fell in the Battle of Otlukbeli in 1473.

The Zeynel Bey Tomb sits on the left bank the Tigris River across from the Citadel of Hasankeyf

The Zeynel Bey Tomb is a unique example of Timurid architecture in Anatolia, with cylindrical exterior and octagonal interior, topped by an onion dome. The large Arabic calligraphy in blue tiles, with the names Allah-Muhummad-Ahmad-Ali, are fine examples of Timurid glazed brickwork, and the overall effect is a highly Persian work, the colours and shape of the building resonating strongly with the mountains on either side of the Tigris River. This tomb is a memorial to the all-important contest between the Akkoyunlu, led by Uzun Hasan, the father of Zeynel Bey, and the Ottomans, led by Mehmed the Conqueror (1432–1481). To appreciate the geopolitical context of this monument, it is useful to recall that Timur (c.1336–1405) and his allies the Akkoyunlu posed serious and successive threats to Ottoman rulers throughout the fifteenth century. Timur's campaigns (1398–1402) in Anatolia culminated in the capture of Sultan

Beyazid I (1360–1403) during the Battle of Ankara in 1402, reducing Ottoman territory drastically and launching a crisis from which the empire recovered slowly. In return for their assistance against the Ottomans, Timur gave the Akkoyunlu control of Diyarbakir.

Three generations later, the Akkoyunlu had become a world power: their rule extended to Iraq and Iran, Tabriz was their capital, and the Pope and Venice had become their allies against the Ottomans. Mehmet the Conqueror considered the threat posed by the Akkoyunlu forces so significant that he left the western frontiers of the empire largely undefended in order to focus on the challenge from the east. Despite the Ottomans' concentrated effort, the battle of Otlukbeli in 1473 was indecisive. Nevertheless, the Akkoyunlu weakened steadily, and the Ottomans took control of eastern Anatolia, Syria, Egypt and Iraq in the early years of the sixteenth century. Looking back over the centuries it is perhaps tempting to assume that Ottoman hegemony was always a matter of destiny. But the Zeynel Bey Tomb is a strong, visually engaging reminder that Ottoman power in eastern Anatolia was steeled in the struggle with rivals combining formidable military power and strategic acumen. This Timurid-style monument in territory that subsequently remained in Ottoman hands for five hundred years is a reminder that the history of this area might have been very different, were it not for the gradual decline of the Akkoyunlu and the steady consolidation of power by the Ottomans. Persians had ruled Anatolia several times throughout

The large Kufic calligraphy on the exterior of the Zeynel Bey Tomb

history, and there was no reason to dismiss the possibility that the Akkoyunlu might not push the Ottomans out of western Anatolia. These were the stakes that justified Mehmet the Conqueror's decision to divert resources from Europe for the defence of the eastern boundaries of the empire just seventy years after Timur's devastating campaign. The fact that the Zeynel Bey Tomb today appears exotic in its Anatolian context is a tribute to Ottoman achievements.

The Ilısu Controversy

While its history is rich with unique architectural monuments, the future of Hasankeyf is less assured. If the Ilısu Dam and hydro-electric project is implemented fully, more than 80 per cent of Hasankeyf's archaeological and natural treasure will be immersed beneath the waters of a 10.4 billion cubic meter reservoir within a matter of years. Thousands of years of history would be lost and tens of thousands of people displaced from affected areas.

The Ilısu project is part of a comprehensive development programme, known as the Southeast Anatolia Project (GAP), which has invested $32 billion in the region, primarily in the construction of 22 dams (19 of which have been completed), to expand agricultural production by 1.8 million hectares and meet a quarter of Turkey's electricity demand with hydro power. The Ilısu Dam project, costing 1.5 billion USD, is expected to return 400 million USD in direct revenue each year from the generation of 3800 GWh, approximately 1.5 per cent of total electricity consumption in Turkey. In addition to helping to reduce Turkey's reliance on imported fossil fuels, the Ilısu Dam project includes investment in almost every aspect of social life, from transportation to education, housing and welfare.

Despite these far-reaching investments, the Ilısu Dam project has become one of the world's most controversial dam projects, prompting vigorous opposition by local, national and international groups. At the centre of this controversy is Turkey's failure to produce an internationally recognised environmental impact report (EIR). In 2009 several European countries took the unprecedented step of withdrawing financial support for the Ilısu project when Turkey failed to respond to 150 conditions related to environmental impact and resettlement plans. In 2013 Turkey's Council of State (Danıştay) ordered the halt of construction of the dam, again on the grounds that the government failed to follow laws requiring an EIR. The government revised the rules and continued with construction. The Ilısu Dam project also figures in the ongoing Turkish-Kurdish conflict, with leaders of the pro-Kurdish Peoples' Democratic Party repeatedly protesting the dam's impact on the environment, culture heritage and human rights. In addition, the project is causing considerable concern in Iraq, where experts argue the Ilısu project, including a related irrigation reservoir at Cizre, will reduce Iraq's water income by nearly 50 per cent.

Most nations face painful choices as they weigh the value of environmental and cultural treasure against the demands of economic growth. The challenge to planners and policy-makers is especially acute in Turkey, where the accretions of previous civilisations are particularly dense. However, the special status of Hasankeyf, which according to Michael Meinecke holds 'some of the most extraordinary monuments within the borders of Turkey', suggests that it could become one of the major destinations in Anatolia and serve as an anchor for tourism in the southeast. However, if Hasankeyf is to survive on the basis of its potential to outperform the Ilisu Dam project in economic terms, it must attract at least two million tourists (the number of visitors to Ephesus in 2014), primarily during the spring and early fall, and generate tourism-related revenue of $600.00 million each year (a benchmark surpassed in Cappadocia at the cost of considerable degrading of cultural heritage). It is practically impossible for the central districts of the historic city of Hasankeyf to accommodate this many visitors without suffering irreparable damage to the archaeological ruins and natural beauty that form the basis of the city's economic potential.

The solution lies in an alternative approach: establishment of a large nature and culture preserve, managed according to a diversified strategy for sustainable tourism. Within an area of at least 500 square kilometres, tourism, recreational and educational activities could be organised into zones or categories defined by their level of environmental impact. For example, the central zone (Citadel, Lower City, Gardens) would be focused on archaeological excavation and carefully regulated visits. In zone

2, comprising the Tigris River and villages of the hinterland, high-margin offerings (for example, 'slow food' tours, village home stays, horseback riding, rafting and other 'adventure type' activities) could be balanced with activities suited to a broader clientele (such as picnicking, hiking, camping). Education and exhibition facilities are already under construction in the new Hasankeyf settlement area, providing a setting for conferences, seminars and field-study programmes ('Zone 3'). The preserve could be expanded to include a fourth, highly protected nature zone, providing the setting for a prestigious retreat designed according to the latest standards of sustainability in order to minimise environmental impact. More environmentally intensive offerings (multi-storey hotels, shopping centres, entertainment, etc.) could be concentrated on the periphery of the preserve, for example in Gercüş and the eastern reaches of the city of Batman.

This alternative approach would balance the demands of archaeological and environmental conservation with the need to promote economic growth. International pressure, court rulings and political opposition against the Ilısu Dam project have so far failed to secure the future of Hasankeyf, and closer consideration of ways to boost commercial income may lead toward a compromise solution. Should Hasankeyf be spared from flooding, its accumulation of medieval urban archaeology promises to give scholars and visitors new insights into Seljuk society.

Picture credits: John Crofoot, Hasankeyf Matters

OUR MAN IN HAVANA

Ken Chitwood

As relations between the US and Cuba are improving, and economic and political bulwarks are beginning to disintegrate, there has been talk of renewed religious liberties in the Caribbean country. Reports surfaced earlier in 2015 that Cuba's first Catholic church to be built since 1959 is set to break ground soon in the rural town of Sandino. Would this perhaps preclude the expansion of religious liberties to other groups? Might this presage the construction of Cuba's first mosque?

Over the years, various investors from Qatar, Libya, and private organisations such as the Muslim World League have attempted to supply funding to the Cuban government with the attendant promise to build a public mosque. However, no attempt has been successful. This includes the latest effort by Turkey's Presidency of Religious Affairs (Diyanet İşleri Başkanlığı) in contestation with another bid from Saudi Arabia. Working with local Cuban Muslim community leader Pedro Lazo Torres (aka Imam Yahya) and said to have backing from President Recep Tayyip Erdoğan, this plan too has failed.

However, Turkey's relationship with Latin America and the Caribbean (LAC) dates back to the nineteenth century, when there were several waves of migration from the Ottoman Empire between the 1860s and the end of World War I. In the 1990s, the LAC region came to be considered a source of potential partnership for Turkish politicians and elite actors. Yet, it was in 2006 that links took a giant leap forward with the launching of the regions 'Latin America Action Plan' – a proposed roadmap for political and economic relations. Turkey gave priority to high level visits, increased economic trade, military exchanges, bilateral cultural interchanges, mutual cooperation agreements, strengthened diplomatic presence, established business councils, and initiated cultural and academic interaction, specifically with the establishment of The Latin America Research Centre in

Ankara University and the proposed Turkish History and Cultural Centre at Havana University.

As part of the cultural exchange, Erdoğan hosted a first summit of Latin American Muslim leaders in Istanbul in November 2014. Under the banner, 'Building Our Traditions and Our Future', the Diyanet invited and hosted 76 religious leaders from 40 different countries – including Brazil, Venezuela, Argentina, Chile, Mexico, Suriname, Uruguay, Paraguay, Nicaragua, Panama, Colombia, Bolivia, the Dominican Republic, Guyana, Ecuador, Jamaica and Haiti – under the directorship of Mehmet Gormez. The five-day summit aimed to merge Turkish and LAC Muslim projects and consider religious education, publications, problems, and proposals for solutions in light of the 'vilification' of Islam in the global imagination. Gormez hoped that LAC Muslim leaders might learn from the Diyanet's claim of extensive experience and global leadership. In essence, this meeting was meant to wrest the narrative of Islam away from the 'wrong' people and towards Diyanet's own vision of, and for, global Islam.

Some representatives from the LAC region voiced disquiet, saying they felt they were being propped up as tools for the Turkish government to further its own agenda. Claudio Santos, a Brazilian Muslim who attended the conference, told the Cihan News Agency that Turkish government plans to collaborate with the heads of Muslim communities in the LAC were solely designed to further its Islamist agenda in the region. This perspective, coupled with the fact that only certain Islamic organisations were invited from the LAC, and Erdoğan's dubious claims concerning the Muslim 'discovery' of the Americas, created some coolness when Erdoğan visited the LAC in February 2015.

Erdoğan's visit to Cuba included an audience with President Raul Castro and discussion about the Diyanet's proposal to build the Caribbean nation's first place of prayer near the site where Erdoğan claims Columbus sighted a mosque in the fifteenth century. Certainly, Cuba's Muslim population would welcome the construction of such a facility as there is a pertinent need. Some Muslims in Havana can visit the Casa de los Árabes (aka 'The Arab House'). Owned by a wealthy Arab immigrant who has lived in Cuba since the 1940s, it includes a museum, restaurant, and a place used by Muslim diplomats for prayers. However, it is off-limits to Muslim converts in Cuba. Outside of the Arab House, private homes are the sole places where Muslims can gather for prayers in Cuba. Many gather at Imam Yahya's house to pray and study the Qur'an. Imam Yahya hoped that with Turkish backing, and promises to significantly fund the project, the mosque might come to serve the estimated 1,500–4,000 Muslims in the country.

To provide a historical justification for the project, Erdoğan told the Latin American Muslim Religious Leaders Summit that 'America was discovered prior to 1492', claiming that Muslim sailors reached the Americas in 1178. He asserted that Columbus included the sighting of a mosque off the coast of Cuba in his memoirs. 'We spoke about this with my Cuban brothers. And a mosque will suit that peak very nicely', he said. While historians, anthropologists, and scientists overwhelmingly challenged, or even refuted, Erdoğan's claim, the Turkish President insisted that a careful re-reading of history would show the contribution of the Middle East, and specifically Islam, to American civilisation. This emblematic intimation is strengthened by the fact that the proposed project would be modelled after Istanbul's Ortakoy mosque, which has long symbolised the bridge between 'East' and 'West' as the edifice faces the geographical dividing line of the Bosphorus.

Erdoğan explicitly expressed that part of the project in the LAC was to assert the superior character of his country's civilisation. Still, he has a long way to go to confidently maintain this dominance, especially in Cuba. While economic and political ties between the LAC and Turkey seemed to be strengthened by Erdoğan's visit, his religious intentions were met with cool reservation and rejected. Cuba turned down his offer and no mosque is set to be built in Havana any time soon. The only consolation is that the contract was not given, in Erdoğan's words, to 'other people', specifically Saudi Arabia who also put forward a proposal to build a mosque in Cuba's capital. The Saudi proposal was also rejected.

It could be said that Erdoğan's and the Diyanet's attempt to build a mosque in Cuba and to rally LAC Muslim leaders around their brand of Islam is an attempt to buttress the AKP's own 'post-Islamist' politics. By supporting, and seeking to shape Islam in the LAC and offering funds to build mosques in places such as Cuba, Erdoğan might be attempting to present Turkey's Islam and what I will call alter-Islamist politics as a global brand made up of multiple cultures, languages, and histories.

Turkey's 'Alter-Islamism'

Over the course of the twentieth century the public face of Islam in Turkey has undergone a multivariable transformation due to the variegated ebbs and flows of state power dynamics. This ever-shifting metamorphosis has involved a diacritical exchange between public and popular expressions, with both mutually affecting one another. Official expressions are shaped by, and likewise influence, daily discourse and popular practices in Turkey, which today are shaped by the official 'post-Islamism' or 'alter-Islamism' of current President Erdoğan and the AKP.

'Post-Islamism' differentiates itself from 'Islamism'. Essentially conceived, Islamism is a political and social imaginary in which religion (Islam) is the holistic and totalising source for the inextricably intertwined realms of daily life and political establishment. The effort of Islamists throughout the twentieth century was not only to emulate caliphates of the past, but to attempt to establish Islamic polity in the context of modern nation-states. The forebears of the AKP certainly imagined this would be the case, though it must be said that at various times and through multiple interlocutors, Islamism has had diverse and varying levels of construction, application, and means of enforcement and advancement. In a word, not all who call for political change in the name of Islam are Islamists, and not all who are Islamists call for a complete overhaul of society based on any particular reading of the Shari'a.

What Asaf Bayat and others now call 'post-Islamism' is an attitude and a political strategy that emerges out of, and reacts against, this stream of thought and attempts to fuse Islamism with universal conceptions of human rights, individual faith and piety, liberty, freedom of religion (a la notions of 'pluralism'), and democracy. Through the efforts of the AKP, Islamism was slowly normalised, nationalised, and privatised so that politics were given precedence over religion in the name of religion itself, and the emerging Turkish middle-class sought to reform the self rather than society. This offered individuals and institutions ways of being authentically and passionately Muslim within a secular state and provided a way to navigate the dilemma of coming to grips with an established secular principle in a country where people are still stridently religious, but diversely so. Although there is still tension between multiple actors, post-Islamism offers a middle path for secularists, Islamists, and other actors. Thus, it proved politically powerful as the AKP quickly gained influence and eventually power at the local, regional, and national levels.

But 'post-Islamism' as a concept is not without its problems. As Cihan Tugal has noted, post-Islamism can be imagined as the 'retrenchment of Turkish conservatism'. Tugal makes the case by citing that Turkish conservatism has long been the banner of what is being witnessed in Turkey's popular and public realms today as conglomeration of development, democracy, patriotism, and personal piety. Thus, while the term 'post-Islamism' signals a critical departure from what came before perhaps what it attempts to signify is not so much marked by rupture and difference as continuity with pre-existent Turkish ideals, norms, and modes of being and precursors and simultaneity with various movements and multiple actors.

Instead of 'post-Islamism', I prefer to use the term 'alter-Islamism', which is helpful in trying to simultaneously identify the change and appreciate its antecedents in the past. This is due to two factors: not only does 'post-Islamism' presume a non-existent historical moment, it is, as condition or project, also a departure into untested terrain and, as of now, proves a woefully unfinished project. Just as alter-globalisation, as a movement, is seeking to merge global interaction and cooperation with environmental, indigenous, economic, and labour rights in addition to advocating peace and civil liberties without extreme forms of anti-globalisation or socialism, so too 'alter-Islamism' seeks to merge the ideal of an Islamic state with the mechanism of democracy and the advocacy for individual rights, human rights, and other aspects of 'Western' culture deemed beneficial. While both camps reject the tout blanc implementation of globalisation, socialism, and/or violent anti-globalisation activism on the one hand and Islamism, secularism, and/or jihadism on the other, they are seeking a merger of worlds and ideas to achieve a common goal. For alter-globalisation activists it is compassionate globalisation, for alter-Islamists, Islam is still the solution, but in a democratic, individualised, form. Both have yet to materialise as coherent systems, but are burgeoning movements involved in constant contestation of what it means to undergo a sea change in antithesis to what has failed in the past.

Alter-Islamism is still emerging. Its vision is one that is simultaneously defined by multiform expressions due to an inherent emphasis on the individual and the heightened role of the imagination as it emerges in a globalised context. Instead of a top-down assignment of norms and practices, alter-Islamism has to lead to a knowledge network of expressions and disintegrated religious, institutions, and authorities founded in 'imagined identities' more than in official policies or hierarchical religious institutions. Amidst this blossoming of religious ideas and practices, individuals are re-appropriating Islamic symbols, arguments, rhetoric, and norms under the banner of alter-Islamism and its passive form of state secularism and concomitant emphasis on religion as vital to the identity and politics of Turkey and its citizens.

Such a process is not only occurring at an individual or parochial level, but at a national and global level as well. In addition to the transformations of lived popular Islam that alter-Islamism has furnished a causeway for, it is also providing a pathway for cultural and political elites to imagine a future golden age of Islam not only on a national, but also global stage. Indeed, Turkey's liminal geographic and imagined location betwixt and between 'East' and 'West', and its re-emergence on the political and economic global stage, as well as AKP's consolidation and transformation of its Islamist heritage and secular statecraft in the 1990s and its ascension to power at the turn of the millennium, not only nationalised Islamism, but also began to globalise it in the form of alter-Islamism. This is yet another reason why the concept of 'post-Islamism' is insufficient to analyse contemporary currents in Turkish Islam (and elsewhere). So far, explorations of 'post-Islamism' have been provincial at best. Due to its very nature, this shift's relationship with democracy, voting rights, pluralism, and universal human rights can only be investigated from a global, rather than regional/national, perspective. Thus, just as alter-globalisation must be localised to make sense of its implications, the study of alter-Islamism must be globalised to tease out its repercussions on both local and global stages.

As a case in point, in seeking to build a future golden age of Islam while simultaneously utilising symbols and idea(l)s from the past, the leaders of alter-Islamism in Turkey (principally Erdoğan, the Diyanet, and the AKP) seem to be mapping their imagined Islam on the globe and in direct confrontation with other global actors. Of course, this alter-Islamist imagination of Turkey's leaders is as much a product of, as it is a driving force behind, the globalisation of Turkey's culture, politics, and economy. Indeed, it was the flowering of Turkey's political and economic climate in the 1980s and 1990s which provided the fertile ground for a rising middle-class of social, political, and economic elites and intellectuals who were as dedicated to Turkey's Islamic past as they were to its secular present. Thus, looking toward the future it seems they have re-imagined 'Turkish Islam' as one that merges Western ideals with Islamist symbols, forms, and practices, and one that seeks to foster new relationships and allies both in their region and further abroad. Thus, Turkey's hopes for entrance into the EU, its increased ties with regions such as the LAC, and its contestation over Sunni hegemony with Saudi Arabia can be viewed as both a base and a by-product of the alter-Islamist turn. The two go hand-in-hand as alter-Islamism has led to, coincided with, and emerged out of Turkey's irreversible trend towards globalisation.

Therefore, Erdoğan's attempts to influence LAC Muslim leaders and build a mosque in Cuba can be interpreted as part-and-parcel of this project and process. While contexts such as Syria, Iraq, Egypt, and Yemen may be observed as prime loci for the 'war within a war' between the state ideologies, locales such as Cuba and the LAC cannot be overlooked. For it is here too that the 'cold war for Sunni hegemony' is being played out. Although such a statement is speculative and the two contexts differ in terms of how Turkey and Saudi Arabia are active, we cannot dismiss the relevance of seemingly peripheral contexts in considering the contest between global Muslim political powers.

While the Arab world and its peninsular premiers at first welcomed Turkey's re-emergence as a political and economic force as a potential counterweight to Tehran's power in the wake of the Arab Spring, an ever-deepening rift can be readily observed between Saudi Arabia and Turkey. Sparked by Saudi Arabia's disapproval of Erdoğan's tacit, and sometimes explicit, support of the Muslim Brotherhood in Egypt and its goals to install a pro-Istanbul power in the wake of Assad's regime, the contest between the two nations to hold sway over the politics of Sunni Islam has spilled beyond the Middle East and North Africa to include other regions as well. In this contest, controlling religious interpretation is just as important as political power and economic prowess. Thus, the competition over building Cuba's first mosque cannot be viewed as a mere, petty, skirmish. Instead, it is a flashpoint wherein the two nation's forms of Islamic governance and religious expression meet head-to-head. Of course, this current conflict reaches back to the past to not only the relations between Saudi Arabia and the Ottoman Empire, but also to the multiple juxtapositions of Saudi Arabia with Egypt, Iran, Pakistan, and non-national entities such as al-Qaeda, the 'Islamic State' of ISIS, and shadow (f)actors such as the US, the former USSR, the European Union, and China. Certainly, this contest cannot be analysed in a silo, but as part of a multipolar global game.

Erdoğan, as the embodiment of the hopes and dreams of the alter-Islamist ideal in Turkey and abroad, becomes vitally important in this context. Indeed, just as he and the AKP utilised Turkey's coming ever closer to EU membership as a way to carve out a territory for themselves in Turkish politics in the 1990s and early 2000s, so too Erdoğan could perhaps now be flexing Turkey's alter-Islamist might in regions such as the LAC in order to directly oppose both internal, and regional, competitors. However, in doing so, Erdoğan is facing the dilemma of deterritorialisation – the separation of social, political or cultural norms from the place of their origins. Just as King Faisal and the Saudi government sought to re-inscribe foreign locales with Saudi symbolism and import in an effort to reterritorialise and monopolise their Wahhabi ideals and expressions (for example, the Faisal Mosque and Islamic University in Islamabad), so too Erdoğan could be viewed as seeking to wield transnational influence with a globalising Muslim mission constructed, and re-imagined, from Turkish discourse and symbols.

Mapping Turkey on Cuba

Alter-Islamism's goal is not to make institutions more Islamic, instead it is to reform the piety of individual citizens. This is seen not only as the key to successfully navigating domestic issues, but also the telos for global goals. Eschewing the traditional Islamist objectives of restyling educational, federal, economic, political, and social institutions according to Islam, alter-Islamists in Turkey instead focus on the preservation of Islamic and Turkish culture through the mobilisation of Islamic individuals, ideologies, and icons.

For example, when Erdoğan became mayor of Istanbul he was confronted with the decades-long shift in Turkey's population from rural to urban centres and the legacy of Islamists who imagined an 'ideal Muslim city'. To navigate between the godless landscape of a secular city and the Islamised vision of his forebears, he began to co-opt Istanbul's symbolic religious heritage as a means for not only inviting foreign investment and tourism, but also to mobilise the masses around the re-conceptualised ideal of the Turkish national imaginaire. Rather than simply relying on the vestiges of Turkey's Ottoman past, Erdoğan and the AKP went on a campaign to replace ancient buildings with new, or sufficiently refurbished, pastiche versions that merge the modern and what the AKP and the alter-Islamists see as démodé. This hybrid architectural move utilises symbols such as the illuminated Bosphorus Bridge to craft a fusion of consumer culture and Muslim *umma*. The material aspects of the alter-Islamist vision pervade the beliefs and begin to inform the habitus of the citizens. Without ever reforming an institution, Erdoğan and the AKP are able to transform society by altering its architecture, space, and landscape.

This brief snapshot of Erdoğan's project to Islamise Istanbul in alter-Islamist style illustrates how materiality might also go hand-in-hand with the global imagination of alter-Islamism. Indeed, Erdoğan and the alter-Islamists of the AKP and other parties and constituencies have realised that in order to maintain their vision for Turkey they must not only inscribe their own landscape with the symbolic and spatial icons of their imagination, but also other locations throughout the globe. This can be seen in the efforts Erdoğan has put into cultural projects and centres that promulgate the alter-Islamist's version of Turkish ethnohistory in the European Turkish diaspora in countries such as Germany, France, and the Netherlands.

In trying to frame alter-Islamism as more amenable to the West and its influence, Erdoğan and his compatriots are moving beyond attracting allies, tourists, and 'protectors' in erasing their historical animosity toward the West, but are repositioning Turkey as central to the West's own project. Thus, in attempting to simultaneously situate Turkey and Islam as a bridge between 'East' and 'West', Erdoğan's statements concerning, presence in, and proposed projects for Cuba and the LAC exemplify how he is attempting to reterritorialise Turkish Islam in the West by re-imagining history and mapping the alter-Islamist vision of Turkey onto the Cuban landscape. Three specific aspects of his proposal and statements regarding the project are illustrative of this contention.

First, Cuba, like Turkey, is a symbol of liminality and hybridity. While admitting that boundaries and geography are imagined and constructed, it can be said that both Turkey and Cuba are situated along conceptualised borderlands where new hybrid identities are forged between 'East' and 'West' and 'North' and 'South' respectively. Although 'hybridity' has come to mean all sorts of things concerning the mixing and combinative forces occurring in the moment of cultural exchange, it can be said to be that 'in-between' which refers to the 'third-space' as a space of cultural separation and merging. It is the place where 'transculturation' takes place, which involves the acquiring of limited aspects of a new culture, the loss of some elements of an older one, and the creation of a new, hybrid-but-coherent body of old and new amalgamated together. In this instance, the 'third space' is represented by geographical locations, two nations socially constructed – Turkey and Cuba. Thus, their geographies act as 'borderlands' and 'third spaces' where processes of 'glocalisation' and the dialectic of deterritorialisation and reterritorialisation can play themselves out. They become the locales where Turkish alter-Islamists can navigate their proposed identity and attempt to merge the multiple cultures living inside them.

This is somewhat parallel to the projects of the USA and the USSR to inscribe their own visions of 'nationhood' on Cuba in the 1950s and 60s during the Cold War. Today, Cuba serves as a tableau upon which Turkish alter-Islamists are attempting to illustrate that their brand of Islam is the better solution than Saudi Arabia's in terms of salvation, self-esteem, and economic and political success for a nation re-emerging after decades under Fidel Castro. In trying to strengthen economic, political, cultural and religious ties between the two nations, Erdoğan is attempting to do so along the lines of the Turkish brand of alter-Islamism, which emphasises impartiality and the equal treatment of all religions by the state, which is not currently enjoyed in Cuba (nor really in Turkey, one could argue). Thus, it can be said that in his recent expressions of fidelity between the two nations, Erdoğan is trying to make Cuba into a prime locus for alter-Islamist experimentation in a country where Muslims are the minority, therein intimating that if the project can be successful in Cuba, it can be successful throughout the 'West'. Indeed, in some ways Cuba may even act as a heterotopia, in the Foucaultian sense, that challenges Western and Saudi Arabian hegemonies in a form of post-colonial solidarity between Cuba and Turkey.

Second, Erdoğan's efforts to re-imagine history to re-conceive 'Columbus' as a Muslim, the Muslim world as Catholic Spain. Although met with scepticism and critique from cultural and academic historians, Erdoğan made the bold claim that Muslims, not Catholic Spaniards, discovered the Americas. Citing the works of Youssef Mroueh from the neo-conservative 'Sufi' As-Sunnah Foundation of America and tele-evangelist Abdullah Hakim Quick, Erdoğan points to Columbus' travel journals where he claims the explorer mentioned the existence of a mosque on a hill on the Cuban coast. Regardless of their veracity (it is argued that these words written by famed friar Bartoloms de las Casas and not Columbus were metaphorical and not literal, that the hill 'looked like a mosque'), Erdoğan's invocation of the faded glories of the past are no doubt part of his political aims in the region. In re-imagining Cuba as Muslim before it was touched by 'Western' influence, Erdoğan is playing a game of origins. He is using imagination to re-write history in a way that creates a 'community of sentiment' – a group that begins to imagine and feel together beyond national borders that challenges the forced dichotomy between 'East' and 'West', central and peripheral, hegemonic and marginalised. Furthermore, this re-imagined narrative is one that corresponds with, and connects to, the imaginary of many Muslim reverts in the Americas who utilise the powers of the imagination to envisage themselves as part of a global *umma* via 'dreams of al-Andalus' and other means of conceiving 'Islam in Spanish' as 'authentically' Muslim as much as it is 'authoritatively' Hispanic and/or American in the hemispheric sense.

Third, to establish a bridge between the imagined and 'the real', Erdoğan's proposal includes a symbolic material aspect as well. Like his work in Istanbul, Erdoğan hopes to create a structural and geographic symbol of this imagined solidarity between Cuba and Turkey. Thus, not only does Erdoğan want to build the mosque upon the hill once metaphorically seen as 'a mosque', but he wants to fashion the structure of this building after the Ortakoy mosque in Istanbul and its incipient symbolism. Built in the 1850s as the Ottoman empire was passing its peak and a new Turkish nationalism was beginning to stir, the Ortakoy mosque's location on the Bosphorus with the physical bridge in the background still symbolises the idea that Turkey is a link between the 'West' and the 'East'. Just as Erdoğan erected ersatz versions of ancient symbols infused with new modernistic ideals when he was mayor of the city, so too the Ortakoy mosque's potential Cuban cousin would stand as a symbol of the merger between 'East' and 'West', Turkey and Cuba, Islam and Latin America.

'Those who command space', David Harvey has written, 'can always control the politics of place'; and thus the building of a Turkish style mosque, with its concomitant alter-Islamist symbolism, is an attempt to command Cuban and American space not only religiously, but also, economically, politically, and socially. Furthermore, integrating Cuba into the imagination, perception, and experience of the Turkish imagination thus (re)defines what it means to be Turkish and Muslim in a global age in contradistinction to other imaginaires being produced by interlocutors such as Saudi Arabia or 'Islamophobes' in the Western world.

Even so, Erdoğan's and the alter-Islamist's conception of Turkish Islam is but one of many imaginaries of Islam in Turkey. It may be the state-supported and funded version, but it is not the sole idea competing for space and recognition. This is even more evident as Turkey competes with other forms of Islam throughout the *umma*.

An Unfinished Project

While the vast majority of the Turkish population is Muslim, there is enormous heterogeneity within this demographic with the presence and vivacity of various Shi'a and Sufi populations and different schools of Sunni thought, all with varying opinions on the mix of Islam and politics that Erdoğan and his constituents have brought to the table. Some of Erdoğan's religious rivalries are well-known and vocal, most notably his feud with Fethullah Gülen and his popular, cosmopolitan, modern, and mobile Hizmet movement. Furthermore, there are more robustly pious communities in Turkey who find alter-Islamists too secular and, on the other end of the spectrum, Islamic intellectuals who are calling for a unique brand of Turkish Islam and state policies that try 'to create a new community and state that is neither East or West', but distinctly Turkish. Indeed, Erdoğan and the alter-Islamists face multiple internal challenges, as the 2015 general elections made clear. Outside of Turkey, Erdoğan and the alter-Islamists face the affront of

Wahhabism from Saudi Arabia, Kurdish conflict within their borders and in neighbouring Syria and Iraq, and the rising threat of the 'Islamic State' of ISIS. Not only do these opponents offer geo-political confrontation, but also contrasting Islamic visions of global politics.

We must not assume that Cuba is simply a canvas to be drawn upon by global actors on their cold war over Sunni hegemony. Cuba possesses its own distinct agency and has its own specific history regarding religion. Although Cuba's constitution guarantees religious freedom, the government regularly restricts religious activity. The Cuban Communist Party's Office of Religious Affairs is responsible for regulating religion in the island nation and retains the power to officially recognise religious groups and grant building permits for houses of worship. Beyond this control, they also can approve or deny religious visitors, imports of religious literature, and public performance of religious services. Even though the activities of all religious groups are limited, the Roman Catholic Church has been awarded extra freedoms in the past and as Cuba blooms into a new epoch of relations with the US and other global powers the Catholic Church has seen the most benefits – principally due to Pope Francis' involvement in negotiations between Presidents Barack Obama and Raul Castro. Jews, Muslims, Santeria, and other religionists are limited from producing their own periodicals, worshiping as they please or in public, and maintaining websites. Thus, the rejection of both Saudi Arabia and Turkey's plans to build a mosque in Havana must not be seen as a repudiation of any type of Islamic governance or position, but a totalising opposition to religious incursions into Cuba at the present moment.

Furthermore, it must be said that Turkey's alter-Islamism may or may not be relevant and appealing to the minority Muslim population in Cuba or in the rest of the LAC. Although Imam Yahya and other Muslim leaders in Cuba and the LAC may welcome external funding to augment their practice of piety, some of the grander aims of alter-Islamism do not match the lived realities of a minority Muslim population in the LAC. Islamism's historically slothful record on social justice initiatives and meeting the needs of the poor may preclude a certain reticence from LAC Muslim leaders who are keen to respond to the needs of the people in their nations and region. Furthermore, it can be said that modern democracy, a religion-neutral state, freedom of thought, and other human rights and dignities can come via many religious and political projects, not necessarily alter-Islamist ones. Thus, Muslim minorities in Cuba and the LAC may not look to Turkey and its brand for assistance to achieve the religious freedom and recognition they desire.

This brings us to consider that other actors are still active in the region as well. Turkey and Saudi Arabia are not alone in seeking to influence Cuba's future. The US, China, Russia, European powers, and regional entities all want an opportunity to direct Cuba's future. Turkey and its alter-Islamist leaders must remain mindful of this and recognise that they cannot control the process on a global stage with a plurality of interlocutors.

Alter-Islamism is an unfinished project. It is a process as much as it is a lived and felt political, social, and religious reality. Thus, it may change its direction at any given time. Local electoral dynamics, regional fluctuations in power structures and conflicts, or global shifts may all cause alter-Islamism in Turkey to alter its own course or abandon its project in favour of either a more, or less, conservative line in the years to come. What is evident is that Erdoğan and the alter-Islamists have lost some of their clout abroad given his recent comments and strong-handed efforts to influence Islam in the LAC. This might give his opponents at home more ammunition in national and local elections. Already, the Republican People's Party (CHP) and the Nationalist Movement Party (MHP) have voiced their desire to drive deeper dividing lines between politics and religion. These structural discussions are not ethereal, but bear out deep ramifications for those practicing Islam day-by-day in the city streets of Istanbul, Ankara, Izmir, and elsewhere. However, if the project were to meet with success and deeper ties were made between LAC, Islamic leaders and Turkish Muslim authorities, a feedback loop might be created wherein Muslims in minority populations could be influenced by, and simultaneously exert some effect on, their global partners. Due to the fact that alter-Islamism creates an environment of individual religious freedom over institutional religious structure, it has the potential of creating spaces for interaction and interplay between multiple actors.

DOĞUBAYAZIT, ONE JUNE DAY

Rebecca Soble

On Saturday 7 June 2014, two Kurdish youths were killed in a clash with Turkish police during protests in the town of Lice in the Kurdish region of Turkey. The Turkish government had planned to build new military outposts there, which was seen as a threat to the Turkish-Kurdish peace process. In the following days, further clashes erupted in many more places around Turkey. On that same weekend, I was in the midst of a solo tour through Eastern Turkey. This is the story of my Monday 9 June in Doğubayazıt.

I

There are things you first need to know. This is not the land of Turks; this is the land of Kurds. They have Turkish citizenship, but they hold tightly to their own culture and language. These are people whose language was made illegal so that even using the letters q and x represents rebellion. These are people who logically celebrate the Nevroz New Year with the spring equinox by jumping over bonfires with crazy abandon. These people also treat strangers like family, or better.

II

It was a short visit sandwiched between fortresses in Van and Kars and scenic rides through wildflower fields. Stepping off the early morning bus, I was immediately in the midst of young men hurriedly wrapping their heads in makeshift scarves and pushing past me towards the central square. Only some nervously giggling young women, with heads wrapped in floral scarves, and a few older men remained near the bus stop. The girls and I walked and chatted for a short distance until they turned into a side street. Ten more metres forward, I stepped into the square and into a standoff between Kurdish youth and Turkish police. I wasn't overly scared, because I had seen plenty of these riot-gear-encrusted police in Istanbul during and following the Gezi Park protests, but I was noticed by some locals and I was not left alone. They came to me, asked where I was going, and I was guided through. I was a guest.

I was staying at the local öğretmenevi, a residence for teachers. These places exist all over Turkey for teachers who go to work in a region for a few years as payment to the government for their free education. If there is space, they also offer beds for visitors. In Doğubayazit, I shared a room with a teacher from Denizli, in Western Turkey, who had been there for two years. She worked in a very rural school, and had few polite things to say about her students and her time there. She was anxious for the school year to end to return to her familiar Aegean surroundings.

As I was led from the square to the öğretmenevi, I saw that all of the shops had their metal security shutters closed, even though it was definitely time for them to be open. It was explained that all the shops were shuttered in protest, which left me a bit shocked and concerned. This meant no snacks, no bottled water, no restaurant meals. Without the security of being able to buy my needs, I would have to rely on the abundance of human kindness.

III

In Doğubayazit, they jokingly say there are three seasons: mud, dust, and ice. I arrived for dust. Dust on the ground when walking, dust in my shoes and cuffs, dust in my scalp and fingernails. At one point, I encountered a startling cloud of it billowing down the street, and escaped only by a hasty duck into an open doorway. It wasn't my quick thinking that saved me, but that of a local man, who thoughtfully pulled me into the doorway with him. Together, we watched the dust blow by just a few metres in front of us.

Even if the town itself is not especially attractive, the surrounding countryside is magnificent, and Mount Ararat is the prime attraction. Ararat is a permanently snow-capped dormant volcano, a hiking destination only for experienced mountaineers. Surrounding Ararat are up-tilted sandstone ridges with green hanging valleys, functioning as salad bowls for the many grazing sheep. Hundreds of sheep, watched by shepherds with vigilant Kangal dogs, add up to a family's annual income when sold in cities for the sacrifice holiday.

Besides Mount Ararat, another reason to visit Doğubayazit is the Ishak Pasha Palace, in the foothills above town. The advice from the taxi driver who took me up there was not to wander where there were no people, likely because of the Kangals. I was left at the historic palace, at which point I realised that because it was Monday, it was also closed. Sigh; lots of time, not much to do. I eyed the couples, families, and groups of young men wandering around on the trails above and decided the locals felt the same. I stood in one spot for a long time.

IV

They appeared unexpectedly, two men scrambling up the steep rubble at my feet. They had come from around the corner of the palace, from a direction where I would not have expected anyone to be. I paused, and then plunged, asking an opening question to get their attention.

I knew I would be a startling sight for them; I had gotten used to that reaction during this trip East. I was a foreign uncovered female. I was travelling alone. I could speak and understand Turkish. But despite their certain surprise, when I asked, not in their native language nor in mine, what they had been doing ('Pardon, orada neyi bakıyordunuz, acaba?'), it was as if questioning a stranger's activities was as natural as asking the time. Without hesitation, a hand was put out and I was helped back down the rocky slope to see some wooden sculptures that were built into walls of the palace. We stood in a narrow strip of shade granted by the palace wall discussing the sculpture, my visit, our names, and their family. In the space of ten minutes, complete solitariness transformed to steadfast companionship.

V

Often-heard advice for travelling in the East: be open to what strangers offer. I had already experienced it in small ways. But this day took the biscuit; countless childhood safety rules were broken. After leaving the palace, we three jumped in their rickety van for a short ride up to the trails. While climbing through a tricky spot, one offered to take my backpack, and gallantly insisted on carrying it from then on. They are cousins, Fırat in his twenties and Baran looks to be in his forties, but he is undoubtedly younger. At any rate, he can climb like a billygoat. We climb to the highest lookouts, where no others are hiking, where they know I will have the best views of Ararat and the surrounding mountains. On the way, we share knowledge about the rocks and the plants on the path, and there are always four hands ready to help me balance or a knee to offer a boost. Constant encouragement and smiles; at the top, we stop for a rest and pictures, and they smoke their cigarettes.

I wonder why they are hiking in the hills on a Monday. Fırat works at the Iranian border about 30 kilometres from Doğubayazit, and they are closed for three days because of the protests. Baran also says that he works at the border, but they laugh about it, and I finally understand that he smuggles cigarettes and other tax-free products across the border from Iran. Now I understand his climbing skills better. They test my knowledge of Kurdish (rudimentary) and I test their knowledge of English (equally rudimentary), and we settle back into Turkish. I hear family stories and tell some of my own. We take pictures with arms around shoulders. Later, we hike back down the trail and settle in for tea and more cigarettes at a dingy but friendly café near the parking area. Families are all around; children kicking at balls, young men in groups laughing at their own jokes, old men tossing crumbs to the sparrows.

VI

Going back to town, we all realise at the same time that there will be no restaurants open for dinner. I see other tourists wandering around with lost looks, probably also searching for a meal. I'm secretly hoping my companions will know a place to go, perhaps a friend of a friend who has a restaurant that is only open for locals, but they say we'll have to eat at home, in their apartment. They worry that there is almost no food at their house – some bread, some cheese, perhaps some eggs. Definitely tea. So walking around a bit, we find a small old man pulling a produce cart through the streets and buy some tomatoes and a melon to round out the meal. Walking into a dilapidated building and up dim and dirty stairs triggers another recollection of childhood safety rules, but inside the apartment, it is tidy and homely, with family photos on the walls and doilies on the backs of the sofa and chairs. Fırat's mother and sister have been here to decorate and clean, even though they are spending the summer on the family farm on the far side of Mount Ararat. So here I am, and all is fine. We are eating our makeshift feast cross-legged on the floor in front of the television, discussing politics and culture as best we can with our shared language. Better than fine, because, even stuck inside a shut-down town, we have the sharing of home-cooked food for sustenance and glass after glass of tea for friendship.

MY ISTANBUL

Aamer Hussein

My first chance to visit Istanbul came suddenly, in the spring of 2004. I'd be spending my forty-ninth birthday where continents converged, in a city which contained both east and west: just where life had placed me and so many others like me. A city with a body of water that was both river and sea. When we arrived, I was as anxious as a lover: or more appropriately as someone meeting an unknown partner for the first time after an arranged marriage.

On the way from the airport my eyes began to respond to hazy colours: blue and coral and pale gold, of skies and walls and water. A few hours later, in the blue mosque, where people prayed while tourists looked on, I found that odd sense of tranquillity I'd often experienced in places of worship, though I didn't say the ritual prayer. In contrast to the interior, the architecture of the outside was more stern than I, accustomed to the mosques of Delhi and Lahore, was used to: grander, perhaps, but more austere. Everywhere in the city, I found the architecture both familiar and unfamiliar, resplendent but intimidating.

After we'd visited the mosque, my travelling companion suggested that we take a boat trip across the Bosphorus, to Uskudar. We'd be setting foot on Asian ground. We would be stepping on the edge of our own continent: an illusory encounter, perhaps, but romantic. The April sky was very dark when we stepped off the boat and so was the water. For a moment we imagined that the stars in Asia were shining with a certain different light.

On the way back, walking back to our family-run hotel, we heard music in the shadow of the mosque's dome: it came from a café in the wall. We sat down on a pavement table: I asked for Turkish coffee and my friend ordered a *raki*. The very courteous waiter smiled and responded that they didn't serve alcohol, because the café was on the precincts of the mosque. For a moment I faced a familiar double-edged dilemma: though we're used to enjoying ourselves without alcohol, we find ourselves in awkward situations with those who don't. But my friend decided on tea, and I could see that she was fascinated by the spectacle of young people clapping and revelling as they listened to traditional music in the space where people who may have been their relatives had been praying just a little while before. We sat facing the square and looking at the dark outline of trees and towers against the night sky.

My friend had filled each waking hour with plans for sightseeing. We were there five nights, and every day we visited mosques and monuments, markets and malls. On a Friday evening, in the walls of a railway station by the Bosphorus, we watched dervishes, some of them women, dance to the verses of Rumi's *Masnavi*, and I, who grew up with Rumi's words in my ears, felt I understood the Turkish translations.

In an old house in the Sultan Ahmet neighbourhood we met a man on the street outside the shop where he sold quaint hats: he told my friend she was silly to buy one. He was an architect who had opened his curio shop as a diversion. His mother spoke Laz, which he could barely understand. He took us to the roof of the old house which belonged to him: we saw the neighbourhood spread around like a peacock fan. But when he offered us tea, my friend refused and we left an unfinished conversation.

We cruised down the straits again – in daylight, this time – and saw the pastel colours of the villas on the Asian shore. Neither of us had any Turkish, but the few words we acquired helped us find our way everywhere: the old men of the city, seeing us lost, would approach us and point us in the right direction. All too often I'd be taken for an expat Turk; how strange it felt, to be taken for a native, and yet to feel so foreign. And feeling foreign was a consequence of my frustration at being unable to communicate, though the language seemed so familiar that at night I'd dream I was speaking it. I vowed that the next time I was here I would walk around with someone who spoke in Turkish.

And I did. Three years after I visited Istanbul, I received a note from an editor in Turkey, asking me to write an essay for a collection of essays entitled 'Istanbul in the Eyes of Asian Writers'. I hadn't kept a diary on the trip: I wasn't going to try to list the epochs and eras and dynasties that seemed to coexist in Istanbul, as if analysis or reportage would take away the colours.

And the launch of the book took me back in the summer. I was on the other side of town, very near Taksim, in a street that had none of the charm of Sultan Ahmet, in a luxury hotel that could be anywhere. At midnight I was taken to a TV studio, where I was to give a live broadcast, with the editor of the volume and an interpreter, on my relationship with Istanbul. I don't remember what I said, but I do have in front of me the essay I wrote for the volume. Interwoven with the memories of the city I'd reconstructed were some reflections on my oblique relationship with Turkey.

This time I saw Istanbul through Turkish eyes, in gardens and pavilions, cafes by the waterfront, listening to traditional songs in ancient churches, and eating grilled fish on boats on the Bosphorus. Our two interpreters, a young woman and a young man, called me 'older brother' and became my good friends. They represented two different facets of contemporary Turkish culture: she'd been born in a Kemalist milieu, but was sympathetic to those young women who wore the headscarf and struggled to be allowed to attend university in Islamic dress; she was attracted to Arabic and to Sufism, though she smoked and drank in public, and wore the latest Paris fashions. He said his prayers as often as he could, didn't drink alcohol, fasted throughout Ramadan, and was fascinated by the Ottoman past, but also played Western classical music, which was his passion, on the piano. Both of them would stop in front of Ottoman inscriptions and ask us to read them out, as they couldn't read the script, and laugh in delight when they understood what we recited.

I began to feel a transient sense of homecoming. Though I was born and brought up a few miles away from the sea, I have always loved rivers, cities through which they pass. But the lashing blue Bosphorus isn't a river, it's a strait, which divides the city in two like a river would. There are cities that aren't really ours as we aren't theirs, but we can love them and fit into them of our own volition, without compulsions or convictions or the pressure to belong. Istanbul could take the place of home for a few days at a time because I laid no claims to it.

Mostly I'd felt on my first trip that I was in the East, but in this version of the East that had confronted the paradoxes of modernity. Or, more accurately, in a microcosm that had made away with continental distinctions. Away from Istanbul, conservatism or tradition may persist, but there in the city I felt I was in a cosmopolis which was, at the same time, firmly located on the edge of Asia. More than once, however, in a bar near Taksim Square, surrounded by young men and women dressed in the latest styles drinking beer, I thought I was in Berlin or Barcelona. But the illusion passed when, on a stall in the street, I saw a Karagoz shadow puppet play. And I was back on the western shore of the great body of water that lies between Europe and Asia, and closes the distance between. I'll be back, I vowed, before too long.

For several days I was on television every day, and on stage for the launch of the book. The gist of the questions was often the same: was Istanbul an Eastern or a Western city, or a city with a unique and multicultural identity? My position among the other writers who had arrived for the launch of the book was anomalous: they were Arabic speakers from Lebanon and Iraq, and had ancestral memories of the Ottoman Empire that braided historical insights with deep and possibly imaginary nostalgia, of Turkey as the once and future centre of a civilisation that questioned Eurocentric hegemonies. I came from a country and a region that had its own imperial heritage – the Mughals, who had left their imprint of every aspect of culture I could recall. And its legacy of an entirely different kind of colonialism.

KONYA CHANGED MY LIFE

Peter Clark

'We have created you male and female, and have made you nations and tribes
that ye may know one another.'

The Qur'an 49:13

'A diversification among human communities is essential for the provision of
the incentive and material for the Odyssey of the human spirit. Other nations
of different habits are not enemies; they are godsends. Men require of their
neighbours something sufficiently akin to be understood, something
sufficiently different to provoke attention, and something great enough to
command admiration.'

A N Whitehead

'I do not advise you to go to Ankara to teach Mathematics,' the University
Careers Adviser told me. 'You have a promising academic future, and could
make something of Whig history. In Ankara are likely to meet a lot of
academic spivs who will pull your standards down. You have been an outspo-
ken student politician here and you would have to be much more careful what
you say and to whom. Turkey is an unstable place, coups, military take-overs
and violence in the streets. It is not a place for you.'

The year was 1962. I was in my last year at university. I had come to the
University of Keele after seven outstandingly mediocre years at Southend
High School. Keele was the first of the British post-war universities and
had several pioneering features. The aim of its founder, A D Lindsay, was
to undermine the exclusiveness of specialists. Biochemists and historians
should be able to communicate with each other and with the rest of the
world. No subject should be in tightly sealed boxes. All students did a
common Foundation Year with lectures on all subjects, and in the following
three years the student should do two principal subjects and two

subsidiaries. Of those four subjects one should be a science, one an arts subject and one a social science. I did History and Politics as principals, and Latin and Mathematics as subsidiaries.

I got the lowest mark of those who passed Maths but on the strength of this I was able to get a job as a teacher of the subject at Ankara College. The idea was to return to Britain – the term 'gap year' had not yet been coined – and do research in English history. I had a number of possible subjects for research – the 1868 General Election, the political influence of Primitive Methodism or the meaning of Whiggism.

I defied the advice of the well-intentioned Careers Adviser, and also the anxieties of my parents, read Bernard Lewis's *Emergence of Modern Turkey* and bought *Teach Yourself Turkish*. At the end of August I travelled overland with another teacher bound for Ankara. He had already been at the College for several years.

We drove across Europe and entered Turkey at Edirne just after midnight, Bulgarian time, which turned out to be 2am, Turkish time. We did not stay at a hotel and I wandered around the town until morning. I found an all-night café, scruffy, informal and friendly. Dirty, diseased and emaciated dogs also wandered around the town, shunning human company. One dog would bark and this triggered off a fugue of howls and barkings. From time to time a shrill whistle would pierce the night, producing a response a few streets away. The whistles were less random than the noises of the dogs. I later learned that these were *bekcis*, policemen on patrol.

Architecturally the city was dominated by a superb and lofty mosque with four minarets. As the day dawned, the tops of the minarets were gently bathed in sunlight and I watched, fascinated, as the light moved down, revealing first one balcony and then the next, until the whole of the mosque was drenched in bright sunlight.

We drove the following day all the way to Ankara. I had three weeks before the school term started to get used to the food, drink, heat, local transport, language and company. There were about thirty British teachers at Ankara College and they provided welcome advice and assistance – finding a flat, buying furniture, introductions, the best restaurants.

Ankara College was a grey grim two-storey building built in the early 1950s. It looked more like a penal establishment than a school, but the administrative staff were cordial.

The school was fee-paying and coeducational. The teaching of mathematics and the sciences was through the medium of English. There was a preparatory year – Hazirlik – followed by three intermediate years – Orta – and then to the senior three years – Lise, pronounced lycée. Children had to pass each grade before continuing to the next and repeats meant that some of the older (and presumably less academic) students were in their early twenties. I was allocated five classes, three Orta first year, and two Orta second year. Children between eleven and fourteen.

The school was transformed on the first day of term. The deserted prison-like buildings became filled with excited, uniformed, well-scrubbed children. The children were from the privileged classes of the city. I learned that one was the son of the former Prime Minister, Adnan Menderes, who had been hanged the year before. Another was a grandson of the President of the Republic, General Gűrsel, who had led the coup against the Menderes government. All the pupils assembled in the asphalted school yard in front of a plinthed bust of Mustafa Kemal Atatűrk and bawled out the national anthem and the school song. They dispersed and I faced my first class.

Facing me were forty pubescent girls in blue dresses who, dark-eyed, gazed at me, seeking out my vulnerabilities. I looked back, trying to simulate cheerfulness, nonchalance and self-control. I had now been in Turkey for nearly a month. I had come across one or two Turks socially but mostly my contacts with the people of the country were officials, waiters, shop-keepers or shared-taxi drivers. I had come to Turkey to teach maths – a larky idea, but until this moment, nothing more than an idea. Turkey too had, till this moment, been an idea. From now on, there was the reality of teaching maths and reaching some kind of personal relationship for twenty-five hours a week with Turkish people, starting with forty young girls. If I was a male chauvinist it was from idle habit rather than conviction. These girls could be charmed, I thought. But the mutual contemplation had to be broken. I had to do something. And fortunately there was something to be done. The register. Before each lesson it was the teacher's task to read out the names of the children and to sign a register in triplicate. Hoots of girlish laughter greeted my attempts to read out names like Hadice Memençioğlu. I forced a smile, thinking, 'It's better that they laugh with me, than against me.' I hoped my smile would convey the message, 'We're going to get along famously.' When the hoots turned to gales, I feared they were thinking, 'We're going to have some fun, girls.' My 'we' included the girls but their 'we' did not include me.

The lesson proceeded. I had prepared it carefully but was relieved when I heard the bell announcing the end of the lesson.

'See you tomorrow,' I blithely said as I left the room. The girls cheered derisively. I went back, distressed and angry and told them off. I left again. They cheered again but with less conviction. I stormed back, not only distressed but very angry.

'If you do that again,' I shouted, 'I'll pick on four girls and make them responsible for the whole class.' I was not sure, even as these words came out of my mouth, how I could make them responsible. And I had misgivings about the justice of the threat. These anxieties, fortunately, were not detected by the girls. My bluff succeeded and I escaped with as much dignity as the situation allowed and took refuge in the staffroom, to sip a glass of milkless tea and to be consoled by advice and sympathy from colleagues.

Outside the school hours there were parties most evenings. More experienced teachers returned from holidays on the Black Sea or Lebanon. Beirut was a city to visit to buy all sorts of things — like Nescafe and games of scrabble — unavailable in Turkey. I accepted every invitation in the first few weeks. All the teachers in their twenties or early thirties were invited to all the parties which varied only in venue and host. The guests all seemed to be on edge and sought solace in heavy drinking. Older teachers had a different social world. I was struck by a lack of curiosity about our surroundings. 'Some things,' one teacher told me, 'are taboo — the Turks. You never invite them unless you are on your best behaviour.' Conversation was limited to complaints and grievances. Obstructive red tape. Water that could not be relied on — either to be fresh and free of germs, or to be available at all. Tummy upsets. One new teacher listened to these tales of gloom, stayed a fortnight and then fled home to Britain.

But I found life not too troublesome. I spent the afternoons — free of teaching commitments — on the balcony of my flat reading Gibbon's *Decline and Fall of the Roman Empire*. The clear dry air gave a sharp edge to the remarkable skyline – the Byzantine castle and walls of the old city, the Atatürk mausoleum and the impressive backcloth of the grey mountains. I also enjoyed the whole experience of living abroad and contemplating the months ahead. Everything was an adventure. Nothing could be taken for granted. It was a novelty to buy provisions in Turkish and to be understood. Milk bottle tops and eggs had the day of the week on them. This helped me to learn the days of the week. I derived an intense satisfaction in accepting these experiences as part of the landscape of my daily routine.

The humiliations of my first day of teaching were not repeated, and I got to enjoy the children who were mostly friendly and helpful. One day I was trying to explain something to a rather dim boy and was using simpler and simpler terms. I expected the rest of the class, who were mostly much brighter, to be impatient and scornful, but no – they were rapt with attention and I could sense waves of sympathy for the boy.

The days soon were slipping by. A break was expected at the end of October and I went with some other new teachers for a few days in Istanbul. I was also beginning to make Turkish friends and to rely less on the exclusive social circle of my fellow-teachers. I joined the British Council library and also the American library. And I went to the first concert of the Presidential Symphony Orchestra. Just before the concert started the audience all stood up and applauded the entry of the Prime Minister, Ismet Inönü. He had been Atatürk's right hand man from the 1920s. Now seventy-eight years of age, he was small and stooping, hesitant and weaing a hearing aid. I was thrilled at the sight of him: here was the man who had outwitted Lord Curzon at Lausanne forty years ago.

Nor was I bereft of historical stimulus of the old academic kind during those first months. Sir Steven Runciman lectured at the British Council on the Seljuks, the pre-Ottoman Turkish Muslims of Asia Minor. He observed the peaceful transition of Anatolia from being predominantly Christian to being predominantly Islamic within a few centuries. Arnold J Toynbee also lectured at a Turkish cultural centre. Toynbee, then aged seventy-three, talked about his first visit to Ankara in the early 1920s. I savoured his wide approach to history. He compared Atatürk to an innovating ancient Egyptian king I had never heard of. He also recalled an extended visit to China and Russia and returning to Western Europe, flying in to Cologne. After months of oriental pagodas and Orthodox churches he saw Cologne cathedral with fresh eyes. Having been brought up on Gothic architecture and taken it for granted, he had not before appreciated its majesty.

One of my Turkish friends, Mustafa, obtained some tickets to see the Whirling Dervishes at Konya. I found out more before we went. The thirteenth century poet, Jalāl ad-Dīn al-Rūmi – I learned – had founded a religious brotherhood which became known as the Mevlevi order or tarike. He died at Konya and his tomb became a focus of pilgrimage and devotion. Jalāl ad-Dīn wrote in Persian and was a citizen of one of the Seljuk states of Anatolia. He was given the name al-Rūmi by people further south and east. The land now known as Turkey was for centuries part of the Byzantine Empire, the successor or continuation of the Roman Empire. The land was known as Rome or al-Rūm, even after it was taken over by the Seljuks. Hence al-Rūmi, the Roman. The religious brotherhoods wielded great influence in the eighteenth and nineteenth centuries and formed a network of resistance to modern secular reforms. Men of the brotherhoods would periodically meet and remind each other of God by repeating His name in unison combined with physical acts of corporate worship. In Konya this took the form of men gyrating together to simple music. They became known as whirling dervishes, not a term they chose for themselves. In the 1920s, Mustafa Kemal, with his secularising zeal and ruthlessness suppressed the brotherhoods and their rites.

Although Atatürk was, by practice and instinct, a dictator, he was in theory a democrat and in his later years tried to stimulate political pluralism. In the decade after his death in 1938 opposition parties gained in strength and in 1950 the Democratic Party, led by Adnan Menderes, won an election and became the governing party, replacing the governing party of Atatürk and Ismet Inönü, the Republican Peoples' Party. During the 1950s Menderes made a number of gestures that offset Atatürk's militant secularism. Mosques were built. Restrictions on going on the pilgrimage to Mecca were lifted and the dervishes of Konya were allowed to whirl in public once again. But in 1960 the Turkish army, which saw itself as the custodian of Atatürk's revolution, thought Menderes had gone too far and took over the country. Menderes and some close associates were arrested, tried and four leading Democratic politicians were found guilty and hanged. But the annual ceremonies commemorating Jalāl ad-Dīn al-Rūmi were allowed to continue. It was for this that Mustafa had obtained tickets for some friends.

With some other teachers we drove down to Konya. We went to a restaurant for lunch, after which I wanted to wander around the town.

'There's nothing to see in Konya,' said one teacher in his fourth year at Ankara.

Stimulated by Steven Runciman's talk, I had bought and read *The Seljuks* by Tamara Talbot Rice, and, accompanied by a Turkish friend, Attila, I went to look around the town. In 1962 Konya had a population of 133,000 and there were more horse-drawn vehicles than cars. It had the reputation of being religiously very conservative. A museum was attached to the mosque and tomb of Jalāl ad-Dīn al-Rūmi. We took off our shoes and visited the tomb in a darkened room. It had, I observed, similarities to an English church tomb of the same period. But there were two great differences. The roof of the tomb was pitched and at its head was an enormous disintegrating turban. Attila and I gazed and moved on. It was cold, for Konya is set high up in central Anatolia – over 3000 feet above sea-level, higher than Snowdon. And it was December.

We went on to see the portal of the mosque known as Ince Minare. This is about forty feet high and fifteen feet broad, a solid vertical rectangle of white stone, completely carved in relief. There is an inner archway but what was most staggering were two central vertical flat ribbons of stone that embraced the door and intertwined to rise up to the lintel. Quranic verses had been chiselled into the bands, the writing at right angles to the horizontal. Over the lintel the two bands intertwined again. Arabic writing completely filled the bands. The rest of the rectangle was filled intensively with geometric and floral decoration. Two spandrels were filled with a spiky representation of the word 'Muhammad'. I learned later that the designer was a man called Kalūk bin Abdullah and the work dated from the 1260s, while Jalāl ad-Dīn al-Rūmi was writing his poetry and Salisbury cathedral was being built.

I had seen pictures of this doorway but its physical presence moved me as I had never been aesthetically moved before. (And, I may add, fifty three years later, rarely since.) I have only once been back to Konya, in the 1990s. Cars had driven out the horse drawn vehicles and there was a severe air pollution in the city. The white stone of the buildings including the portal of Ince Minare was discoloured. It was still impressive but the pollution had lessened the impact of the sharpness of the reliefs.

Why was I so moved? I was unable to read the script and, even if I had, would not have understood the message. The magnificence of this doorway was out of proportion to the ordinariness of the rest of the building. It was as if the creative genius of the designer was concentrated on the doorway. Such a style lacked any possibility of further development. It embodied a kind of perfection. I was unfamiliar with any such architectural form but was deeply moved by it. What was the mind, the imagination behind such a creation? How did Kalūk embark on such a design? Which bit came first? How long did he take? What about the craftsmen who executed the design? And what was the relationship between those who commissioned the work, designed it and executed it? How could I think myself into the personality of somebody for whom that doorway was a norm, something to be taken for granted, in the way that I took a Gothic parish church in England for granted?

Attila and I rejoined the others and we strolled off to where the ceremony was to take place. It was not in any of the religious buildings but in a modern school gymnasium. On the wall of which was a huge floor-to-ceiling Turkish flag. The gymnasium was flanked by galleries holding seats for about 800 spectators.

For two hours there were speeches and recitations of the poetry of Jalāl ad-Dīn, the former in Turkish, the latter in Persian: I could understand neither. Then the whirlers came in, preceded by a two-man band, one playing a slender high pitched recorder, the other beating a drum. They were half a dozen men, in their forties and fifties, wearing long smocks and maroon fezzes – both articles of dress had been outlawed under Atatürk. Attila told me that they were the sons of the members of the brotherhood that had been suppressed in the 1920s. The men turned gravely round and round to the music, not very fast but steadily, without hesitation or variation in pace. The skirts of their smocks blew out so that the lower halves of their bodies took on a white conical form. Attila explained that this 'dance', this whirl, was called a zikr and that the men had to forget themselves and their bodies. They had to daze the spectators so that all would forget their fleshly reality and reach a kind of mystical union with God. The men continued for half an hour without a pause and without collapsing.

I looked round at the other spectators. About half were European tourists, some of whom seemed to be either bored or indulgent. All very interesting, but two hours of talk and poetry! And were the men we were looking at not supposed to levitate? Had the trip been worth the effort?

I then turned and looked at some of the others sitting in the galleries. Some smart young Turkish men in suits were gazing at the performance in a detached and watchful way. There were also some poorly dressed Turks, men and women, who must have come from the city of Konya or neighbouring villages. Some swayed rhythmically and murmured 'Allah, Allah' under their breaths. I suddenly became aware that I was witnessing the impact of an intensely religious experience. The 'whirling dervishes' were not, for them, as they were for the tourists from the capital, the local equivalent of the Morris dancers of Thaxted. They were performing an act of devotion. And this, I realised, is what gave the smart-suited young officials a feeling of unease. I became conscious of the unfamiliar power of a popular religious culture that could not be wished away by schools or by legislation. The same activity was being viewed in three contrasting, almost irreconcilable, ways: devotedly by the local people, suspiciously by officialdom, and curiously by the trippers.

It was the spiritual aspect that intrigued me most. Here was a psychological involvement that my own education and cultural background could not come to terms with. To be true to that background I could only scoff, dismiss, marginalise or ignore. But I perceived the power of the religious feelings in the local people and saw it as comparable to the physical intensity of the Seljuk doorway. Both manifestations – the architectural and the spiritual – eluded the kind of rational categorisation to which my education had conditioned me. I recalled, that afternoon, something Toynbee had said the previous month, comparing Jalāl ad-Dīn al-Rūmi to St Augustine of Hippo. Jalāl ad-Dīn, Toynbee argued, was deeply affected by the fall of Baghdad, the Abbasid capital of the Arab Empire, to the Mongols in 1258. St Augustine had been similarly affected by the fall of the Roman Empire in the west. Both Jalāl ad-Dīn and Augustine had turned to mysticism. I thought this was an intellectual rationalisation. Would the local women in a swoon over the ritual be bothered with such a point? What did it matter?

I turned these questions over in my mind in the weeks and months ahead. I started to read books that focussed on the world of Islam. Unfortunately for me, the only works available in the American and British Council libraries were books by Western scholars – Brockelman, Grunebaum and Wilfred Cantwell Smith. But I read these and tried to imagine how things appeared from the perspective of the people of the Turkish, Arab and Islamic worlds.

At that time there was very little literature by Turks available in English. There were the classic writings of Arnold J Toynbee's friend, Halide Edib (still alive in 1962), some novels by Yashar Kemal and one book on the Turkish village by Mahmut Makal.

In the following eight months that I remained based in Turkey I had many other exciting experiences that left a deep impression on me. Over Christmas and the New Year I travelled overland to make my first visit to Syria. Aleppo was overwhelming with its great citadel and miles and miles of medieval souks. I reached Palmyra on Christmas Day and made friends with a Syrian teacher of English with whose family I am still in touch. I travelled to Damascus and Beirut. During another break in the spring I went south to Jordan, saw Petra and travelled to the old cities of Jerusalem and Bethlehem before they came under Israeli occupation. I travelled around western and southern Turkey – the east was a closed military area – and saw Pergamon, Ephesus, Izmir (Smyrna) and Bursa. I went to Antakya (Antioch) and the classical sites on the Mediterranean coast. I spent time in small towns and villages, exploiting my limited Turkish to the limits. When the school year ended I continued to explore the eastern Mediterranean – a few days in Cyprus (eleven years before the partition into Greek and Turkish sectors) and ten days in Egypt, returning to Ankara by boat from Alexandria to Beirut, train from Beirut to Adana and by bus through the Taurus mountains to Ankara and my flat.

In all these later journeys I travelled alone. The day in Konya made me want to see the world from the standpoint of the people I met. The company of other people was inhibiting. The antiquities and the historical places were stirring but I became more interested in the people who inhabited those places. How did they see the world? What were their hopes and expectations? 'Orientalism' had to wait another fifteen years to acquire its loaded ideological baggage, but I suppose I was becoming an orientalist. I was a secure outsider from Britain wandering around, taking hospitality in people's homes, listening to stories and trying to empathise. I certainly had no hidden agenda, evangelical or colonial. My own views became irrelevant and superfluous. I listened and observed.

At the end of the year I returned to Britain and resumed my interrupted academic career, researching on . . . historical whiggism. Although I completed my research, obtained a PhD and produced a book on this very anglocentric subject I was constantly restless. I was like Walter de la Mare's character:

> Still eyes look coldly upon me,
>
> Cold voices whisper and say —
>
> 'He is seized with the spell of far Arabia,
>
> They've stolen his wits away.'

I was reading books of travel, history and the politics of the Middle East. I travelled a little in Europe but ached for the long distance buses of the Levant, the fraternity of traveller and host, the conversations in languages I struggled to communicate in.

Four years after returning to Britain I joined the British Council overseas career service and asked to be posted in the Middle East. I was sent to Jordan. I asked for Arabic language training and spent a year in Lebanon studying how to learn the language. From there I was posted to Sudan for six years. I used my Arabic and started another career as a translator, putting a book on the Battle of Omdurman by a Sudanese soldier into English. I travelled around the country and walked over the battlefields of the 1880s and 1890s. I was interested in the various Sudanese narratives that offset the received versions, mainly derived from Winston Churchill's *The River War*, of the reconquest of the Sudan by Anglo-Egyptian forces in 1898.

I continued my British Council career in Yemen, Tunisia, the United Arab Emirates and Syria. All the time I tried to identify with the people of the country. How was my country seen from the perspective of the people of the countries I lived in? I never doubted or disowned my own background and never saw myself as a cultural imperialist. Insofar as I had a mission statement it was to find areas of common ground with people of the host country and to make friends for Britain. I started to read contemporary literature of these countries, thereby again shifting my own point of vision; and translated some novels, stories and plays.

But the starting point for this career, this insatiable curiosity and quest for empathising with this other world was that day in Konya – the impact of its architecture and the experience of the commemoration of Jalāl ad-Dīn al-Rūmi. That day has made me intellectually restless ever since. I was never tempted to become a Muslim. I have been suspicious of intellectual certainties that exclude others. I have tried to see myself as a product of my generation, education, class and nationality. But I felt passionately about the significance and power of the cultures of the Islamic worlds, and the decency of the thousands of ordinary Muslims I have met, a decency that owes it roots to Islam. Those worlds were connected to my own heritage – European and Christian – through wars, conflicts, trade and mutuality. I had no interest in claiming precedence or justification. In the last twenty-five years a passing acquaintance with India and China made me realise that the world of the Mediterranean and western Asia have been closely linked. Reading *Glimpses of World History* by Jawaharlal Nehru taught me that notions of 'Islam and the West' were both parochial and ephemeral.

I sometimes wonder how I would have developed if I had not been to Konya on that day in 1962. I might have become an authority on Whiggism.

ARTS AND LETTERS

TANPINAR AND THE
HERITAGE WARS

Nagihan Haliloğlu

'A classic' Alan Bennett says, 'is a book that everyone is assumed to have read and often thinks they have'. Ahmet Hamdi Tanpınar's *A Mind at Peace*, a long, stream-of-consciousness narrative about the upper middle classes languishing by the shores of the Bosphorus, getting entangled in futile love affairs, contributing a sense of unease rather than progressive zeal to the early republican Zeitgeist, has long been seen as such a classic. The book was long hailed as a psychodrama, with less discussion of its criticism of the republic's failure to instate a new set of workable social relations to replace the old one. With the declassification, as it were, of the Turkey's Ottoman and early republican intellectual and literary history in the last twenty years, *Time Regulation Institute*, with its much more open criticism of the early republican era, started to replace *A Mind at Peace* as the Tanpınar classic that no one dare admit they haven't read.

The interest in Tanpınar (1901–1962) seems, at least partly, to have been generated in the international world of letters by Orhan Pamuk repeatedly naming him as an influence, an international popularity that then trickles back to Turkey. One is tempted, maybe unfairly, to ask, if this renewed interest in Tanpınar is not similar to the renewed interest in Ottoman paraphernalia at home and abroad. Today, more than fifty years after his death, Tanpınar is still regarded as the author who, having lived both through the Ottoman and Republican eras, has expressed, almost comprehensively, the effects of Europeanisation on the Turkish psyche. I first became aware of him as a writer to be reckoned with in the noughties, when I read a reference to him in a book by a Turkish sociologist, from what one may call the enlightened, secular, ruling classes. The reference was an eye opener because until then I had only heard of Tanpınar from the mouths of moustachioed men who tended to lament the irrevocably

Westernised state of Turkish culture. The period that he wrote in, the 1940s through to the 1960s, was a time of consolidation of the values of the new republic, which were, on the face of it, brought in from Europe. It was a period that was not amenable to Ottoman nostalgia or to looking towards the past, as Tanpınar tended to do now and then. The only legitimate direction was forward, the future, where great things were waiting for the Turkish nation set free from its Ottoman shackles.

Tanpınar's writing helps us follow the trajectory of a certain type of Turkish intellectualism since the 1830s, a type that has been trying to reconcile European learning with a strong local heritage. In both his fiction and non-fiction writing Tanpınar gives us a panorama of a modernising Turkey, as the country experiences all the possible pitfalls in the process. Tanpınar was one of few the figures who recognised that something had gone wrong in this transformation, and that the country had to find a way to reincorporate Ottoman ways back into daily lives. The terms that Tanpınar uses when naming the difference between the religious life of the Ottomans and the secular worldview of the republic are 'our old life' and 'our new life'. His old-new dichotomy treats Ottoman and Republican cultures not so much as antithetical but as continuation of one another, with the possessive pronoun making sure that the reader knows that Tanpınar and his narrators have a sense of belonging to both. Raised and educated in the Ottoman period and well versed in the ways of 'the old life', Tanpınar was loath to let go of this Ottoman heritage, and particularly language at one stroke as the Republican Party ordered everyone, especially those with a public voice, to do. His Ottoman nostalgia was a few decades too early to find full support in public opinion.

For a very long time, both before and after his death, those yearning for the Ottoman way of life claimed Tanpınar as their spokesperson. Even the publishing house that his books appeared from, Dergah, had a fuddy-duddy name, calling to mind broken bookshelves, moth eaten books, and the scent of naphthalene, associated with conservative and religious scholarship and book-reading. The association of the name was only appropriate, Dergah, (along with *tekke*) being the name given to sufi dervish lodges in Turkey. These religious establishments were locked down by the secular republic in the 1930s and are now making a comeback in different guises as schools and arts centres under the supervision of the current government's municipalities.

When Tanpınar's diaries were published in 2008, the conservatives (in the sense of conserving Ottoman ways) found out that the Dergah author wasn't quite the Ottoman-Turkish patriot they understood him to be. Tanpınar called the observant Muslim masses – the term he uses is 'the right'yearning for the 'old life' – ignorant and thick-headed (and much more besides). The diaries also revealed an adoration for all things European in the most republican way imaginable. With the taint of being the go-to man of the pro-Ottomanists thus lifted, the new liberal brand of the secular establishment started to take to Tanpınar in the 1990s and the noughties, which culminated in Pamuk declaring him to be one of his influences. The battle lines were never quite as clearly demarcated as I make them out to be, but Tanpınar acted very much like the rope in this tug of war. In Turkey, sociologists left and right (more left than right) are now making references to Tanpınar as an excellent observer of the changes that happened during the transition from an Ottoman to a republican way of life. And just as in Turkey, he is treated as a keen observer of Turkey's uneasy Westernisation in the international world of letters.

The first Tanpınar novel to be translated into English, in 2011, was *A Mind at Peace*, a novel, as the renowned Turkish critic Jale Parla explains, that is about a disquieted mind rather than one at peace. It is a novel about the complex relationships between four people narrated in symbolic language, to the extent that they become allegorical figures representing the various deadlocks of Turkey's Europeanisation project. The theme of Europeanisation and its toll on the country is taken up again in the recently translated *Time Regulation Institute*, but with a much lighter tone. The title of *Time Regulation Institute* suggests a comical zeal on the part of Turkish elites to keep up with Europe. However, 'regulating time', as the novel reveals, was a pastime in Turkey well before the republic.

In this Bildungsroman of sorts, we learn that the protagonist and narrator of the novel, Hayri İrdal, has spent his formative years apprenticed to Muvakkit Nuri Efendi, a master clock maker and time keeper who is very much a throwback to the times when Turks were obsessed with keeping time, not with Europe, but with the daily prayer times. Hayri's life then takes an unexpected turn, and from the conservative neighbourhood that he has grown up in, he is hurled into the epicentre of republican revolutions. He meets a bona-fide republican Halit Ayarcı, who uses Hayri's 'credentials' for time-keeping to found an institute to keep time. The byzantine process of the founding of *Time Regulation Institute*, its aims and sinewy bureaucracy are so in keeping with the real historical cultural revolutions and establishments in Turkey that one wonders why Turkish republicans did not think of such a time regulating institute at the time, though they did have a go at it by changing the day of rest from Friday to Saturday and Sunday.

Tanpınar treats the real, historical 'regulation' issues in early republican Turkey seriously and at length in his essays and newspaper pieces. His wide-ranging concerns both in his non-fiction and novels put him squarely at the centre of the discussions of progress. Tanpınar may owe his eminence today to the thorny subjects he covered, but what tells him apart from other Turkish authors exploring Westernisation is the literary structure and the psychological insights of his novels. The ignorance feigning, ironic voice of the narrator in *Time Regulation Institute* is not unlike those of Nabokov, to whom he was a contemporary. His articles and columns, in which he did not shy away from using Ottoman words, cover mini-treatises on the new time regime, language, architecture, music, and even medical care. His writing reminds us that such a cornucopia of issues can be held together meaningfully only through a great deal of literary artistry.

In *Time Regulation Institute* he uses an idiosyncratic narrative style that is able to connect things through unusual clauses, metaphors, patterns, codas and even rhyme. In their 'Note on the Translation' Maureen Freely and Alexander Dawe draw attention to the matrushka like clause within clause sentence structure enabled by the Turkish syntax, which keeps the reader in suspense till the verb is reached. Such complex sentences throw even seasoned translators like Freely (whose translations of Pamuk's much more modern Turkish are excellent), by her own admission, off track. The two translators describe this intricate clause structure as 'going out on a limb', which is very much a characteristic of the whole novel. Hayri seems always to be going on tangents, and not getting back to the main plot, and it takes him more than half of the novel to get to the founding of the institute which he keeps saying changed his life.

In the novel itself it is clear that Tanpınar is aware that his narrative will be read for its social observation and contemplations on the rift between the 'old' and the 'new' life of Turkey. People brought up both in the 'old' and 'new' ways are seen as oracles who can declaim the impasses the country faces. Leaving his 'old' milieu behind through a series of misadventures Hayri enters the modernising republican fold. For a while he feels a little uneasy about having to some degree 'denounce' his Ottoman, or 'eastern' upbringing, but then, with time he assumes his role as reformer fully in the *Time Regulation Institute*, a subsummation that Tanpınar allows his character but does not engage in himself. After a while Hayri feels so confident that he starts 'to make immoderate comparisons between the East and the West' and 'comes to conclusions the gravity of which alarmed even myself'. Tanpınar wants the reader to know that he is aware of the 'gravity' of the situation, that as an author he might be making tallish claims about the heritage wars going on in his country. Having already written *A Mind at Peace*, a rather 'grave' book on these issues, with *Time Regulation Institute* Tanpınar seems to have come to the conclusion that the story of Turkey's Westernisation should be told as a parody. Indeed, first as tragedy, then as farce. His narrative suggests that the banality of speaking about being pulled in by two different directions – the Ottoman heritage and the European future – can only be redeemed by a very strong, ironic narrator.

Tanpınar was a master in revealing the absurdities and the predicament of Westernisation, making his ironic fiction the stage set for Turkey's heritage war. He was reporting from the field, but where exactly did he stand on this rift between the 'old' and the 'new'? Tanpınar's writing on literature reveals that although he made his name as a champion of 'old' literature he was just as well lettered in the Greek and French classics, and felt his writing to belong, as his Lectures in Literature reveal, firmly in the European Literature tradition. This question of belonging is an impossible one to resolve for the author and his critic. Tanpınar was hoping for an audience that would appreciate his multi-layered references; however, the fact that he was just as well read and had an appreciation for the Ottoman classics seemed to be a bar to his being unreservedly toasted in the Turkish literary circles of his time. As a result of his failure of total dismissal of the Ottoman heritage, he was, in his own words, subjected to 'assassination by silence' by the literary establishment:

> What have I done? I represent a whole side of un-read Turkish literature, with
> *Five Cities*, the *Five Cities* that no one ever talks about, and with short stories and
> novels...The first short story in particular, 'Abdullah Efendi's Dreams', did it
> deserve to be so unnoticed and uncritiqued? *A Mind at Peace*, which all who
> have read it have liked, was to have only three reviews, and 'Summer Rain' was
> to have no reaction at all? Do they bring no value to Turkey? To Turkey and to
> the Turkish language? How about my poems?...Why this unfairness? What am
> I doing wrong?

This lamentation could well be the self-making of a writer who wants to
position himself as not well understood by his contemporaries, as the avant-
garde. While Tanpınar complains about not receiving any recognition, he was
still able to write several articles in the republican paper *The Republic*. Many
of these articles argued for the preservation of Ottoman literary and architectural heritage, as every other week there seemed to be a plan to demolish an
Ottoman building to make way for a road or for a new republican institution.
The fact that he was given such space in the mouthpiece of the regime and that
he was not 'shunned' enough to be denied a teaching post at the Istanbul
University (as some Islamic-leaning intellectuals were), make his cries of
'unfairness' ring a bit hollow. Still he felt ignored by both groups:

> The right do not consider me to be of them, they do not feel I am as mono-
> vocal, as ignorant as themselves. The left hate me. Those of my cultural status
> find my better peers among the Franks.

Clearly, the politically engaged right and the left were not the audience he was
writing for. His ideal audience were his contemporaries who were lettered in
Ottoman and European languages and literatures and cared equally, if not
more, about style. Most of the educated classes had crossed over to the republican side and had no time for Tanpınar's love for 'the old life' and Ottoman
literature. For republican form's sake, they preferred European writers to
Turkish ones and were keen to seek a lineage in Greek and French classics
rather than Ottoman ones.

Tanpınar's *Lectures on Literature*, collected and edited posthumously by his
students, show how he tried to build bridges between European and
Turkish writers. The way he approached the Turkish literature subjects he
was teaching at Istanbul University can be read as the beginnings of a
particular comparative literature approach in Turkey, a method that sadly

seems to have produced very few acolytes. Scarcely can Tanpınar mention an Ottoman author's name without naming his French predecessor or peer. Influence is not yet seen as an anxiety in these lectures, but as a force of nature that Tanpınar recognises fully. He is such a confident comparatist that he suggests that had Namık Kemal, an important name in the late Ottoman cannon, been influenced by Victor Hugo's *Notre Dame*, as he seemed to be influenced by many other French writers, he would have conceived of a novel centred around Süleymaniye Mosque, the epitome of Ottoman refinement in architecture. In his lectures Tanpınar also makes several references to his professor, Yahya Kemal, particularly the latter's understanding of the heritage that Turks can and should claim. One of Yahya Kemal's formulations for the heritage wars in Turkey, as he saw them, was 'being Mediterranean, having a Greek taste, and defining one's self in opposition to Christian nations'. Istanbul's *hüzün* was first described by Yahya Kemal, too, as a post-empire sadness that Turks inherited from the Greeks, a trope that then passed on to Tanpınar, and from him to Pamuk who worked on it diligently to make it an internationally recognised category of nostalgia.

In his introduction to the Penguin translation of *Time Regulation Institute*, Pankaj Mishra connects *hüzün* to belatedness, and places Tanpınar firmly in 'the waiting room of history', and rightly so, as in *A Mind at Peace*, Tanpınar says that 'the East is the place to sit and wait'. This 'waiting room', however, turns out to be a creative one in which, along with certain other non-European writers, Tanpınar articulates discontent concerning the patchy Westernisation project of the elites. Mishra observes that Tanpınar's whole aesthetic was informed by this belatedness, and what better story could Tanpınar have told than one about the setting up an institution to regulate time to reflect this temporal angst? Mishra speaks about a resistance against European time in this waiting room, however, his exploration lacks the acknowledgement that time and its regulation were already important for Turks before 'Westernisation' set in. A quick reading of the history of science will reveal that measuring time was a crucial field of study for Muslims at large, with their fascination for astronomy and several blueprints for ingenious clocks. Tanpınar clearly wanted this fact acknowledged, as he makes his hero Hayri an apprentice to a clock maker of Ottoman persuasion. Early on in the novel the protagonist Hayri says that 'our old life' revolved around the clock, that the Turks were the best clients of European clock makers as they were obsessed with keeping time for prayer, iftar and sahoor.

The first section of the book is entitled 'Great Expectations' and in many ways *Time Regulation Institute*, like *Great Expectations*, thematises how one may have to carry one's own heritage through life, often as a burden. Hayri, from an early age, becomes aware of the vicissitudes of time and fortune. As a child, he is made to recognise the different life-styles lived in the country, even within the same extended family. He speaks of his maternal uncle who would give him gifts that were different in style from the gifts he gave to his own children:

> The double balconied minaret made of cardboard that my uncle had given to me: my uncle, who would choose different, if we must use the terms of today, 'modern' and 'secular' gifts for his own children used to give me such gifts, maybe on account of the fact that my father was a qayyum, a mosque caretaker and that our house was right next to Mihrimah Mosque.

The minaret represents the 'old life' in Turkey, being part of the old time keeping apparatus. Certain mosques have/had 'muvakkithane', out buildings with big clocks and astronomical devices for keeping time. Prayer times would be calculated in them for cities, and then would be passed on to the *muezzin*, who would call the *azan* from minarets. So in a way, the uncle is giving Hayri a memento of the old time keeping system. Hayri says that though he loved the minaret, his attention was diverted when he was later given a watch as a present. He was so fascinated by the watch, in fact, that he became apprenticed to Muvakkit Nuri Efendi, who, keeping time for mosques, became his first mentor. His second mentor, we learn later, is Halit Ayarcı (his surname translates to English as 'regulator'), the founder of the *Time Regulation Institute*, engaged in time keeping of a different nature. Ayarcı makes Hayri a high official in his republican Institute, devoted to homogenising time on everyone's watches and clocks. Having learnt his trade in an environment where clocks are for keeping prayer time, Hayri will now help the nation keep secular, European time. Hayri calls Nuri Efendi and Halit Ayarcı 'the two poles' between which his life has been weaved. It is hard to imagine that Tanpınar did not use the word 'pole' advisedly, as in the Sufi context 'pole' means a saint, a great teacher. So indeed, like the pendulum of a clock, Hayri's life oscillates between these two worldviews.

One Ottoman clock that Hayri makes much of in his narrative is the grandfather clock called 'Mubarak' standing in his childhood home. Hayri assures the reader that his grandfather had bought it for a mosque he would build when he became rich. However, neighbours spread rumours that as a mosque caretaker Hayri's father must have stolen it from an abandoned or an arsoned mosque. This anecdote reveals to us not so much the possible criminal tendencies in the family, but the kinds of stories that were doing the rounds in Istanbul at the time. Many mosques lay abandoned and looted after 'accidental' fires; this was a common phenomenon that Tanpınar refers to in his newspaper articles as well. Fires, also referred to in Pamuk's *Istanbul: Memories of a City*, seem to be an inevitable phase of life for buildings from the Ottoman period, particularly for houses of worship. Given its chequered history and religious provenance, Mubarak is temperamental and keeps its own time, the clock that sits on the table in Hayri's childhood home is referred to as the 'secular clock', keeping official time. The time regime of the 'old life' and the 'new life' thus live side by side in Hayri's childhood home. It is not a coincidence that *New Life*, Pamuk's Anatolian noir, has quite a few clocks and watches cropping up throughout the story. Fascination with time runs as a thread through both the old and new life in Turkey and it complicates the work of those who want to depict a clear break from the Ottoman period.

Another Ottoman artefact that haunts Hayri and the text is the trellis embedded in the wall of the madrasa and mosque complex where Sheikh Lutfullah, another figure from Hayri's younger days, used to live. Lutfullah is described as a man who dabbled in the black arts in Ottoman style, and was also an interpreter of dreams. As a young man, long before he is recruited to the republican cause, Hayri spends much time in this mosque complex with a motley, multicultural crew that includes the Greek (al) chemist Aristidi Efendi, and they hatch plans to find hidden treasures in Istanbul. Hayri describes the crumbling garden wall and how one day the trellis just falls to the ground, disengaged from the structure:

> This building, which was said to have been built at the time of Mahmut I along with the small mosque, had started to crumble slowly, according to a meticulous plan, the very day that the architect had left the premises.

Tanpınar thus defines an aesthetics of ruins in which the mechanism of disintegration is understood to be already built into the structure of newly manufactured things. As all things, the mosque, too, has been decaying since the very day of its completion. Tanpınar seems to be pointing to the natural death of things, that Ottomans themselves, perhaps, did not expect their heritage to last forever. Such romanticism of ruins has been the staple of almost all authors who have made their name by writing about Istanbul, often belying the city's lived experience of bustling reality.

Crumbling and abandoned dervish lodges and mosques have prime place in this aesthetics of ruins. Pamuk's brief elegies to these buildings in his *Istanbul* written a decade ago, influenced as they are by Tanpınar's laments in the 1960's, already seem a piece of urban history. Contemporary Turkish authors are advised to act quickly, if they want to capitalise on these architectural fragments as the current municipality seems to be on a mission not to leave a single crumbling Ottoman ruin unplastered and/or un-redeveloped, more or maybe less according to the original model. Tanpınar's Hayri tells us that as a child his father used to take him to (clandestine) dervish lodges every Thursday and Friday night. These houses of worship loom large in Tanpınar's oeuvre in their decaying grandeur. However poetic this disintegration may sound, Tanpınar is also aware that the reason for this slow and sometimes assisted death is that the new regime does not care about these buildings any more.

While as a young man Hayri imagines earning enough money, or literally striking gold, to rebuild Lutfullah's madrasa and the mosque; as an older man with money worries and a family to feed he steals the trellis and sells it to an antiquarian, a moment that embodies the cannibalisation of a neglected heritage. Later, when he is a rich man, he chances upon the same trellis in an antiques shop and buys it at a considerable price. The story of the trellis provides a rather visionary allegory for the way Turkey has treated and continues to treat its Ottoman heritage. Ottomania is everywhere and with this trend even secular households feel compelled to display prayer rugs and beads, along with Ottoman calligraphy - items one would think may have been among any Turkish family's heirlooms. One imagines these items as having waited in some attic until the right moment of fashion to be incorporated back into the family life, if one can speak of mere display as incorporation. That would be the story of the lucky and prescient families that, trying to convince the authorities of their secular zeal, put them away somewhere in the attic rather than throw them away altogether, saving themselves from having to buy similar items from fashionable expensive Nişantaşı boutiques a generation later.

There were moments in the 1960s as well when republicans were compelled to show appreciation for the Ottomans, albeit not to the same extent as today's fashionable set. Those 1960s moments are very well reflected in Tanpınar's novel: even characters who are working hard for the secularisation and Europeanisation of the country recognise certain virtues in 'the old ways'. When Hayri informs his psychoanalyst, (the first psychoanalyst to appears in Turkish fiction according to the sociologist Besim Dellaloğlu, who also claims they appeared in fiction well before in real life), that the Ottomans also had a method of interpreting dreams, the psychoanalyst calls the 'olds' 'an inexhaustible treasure'. Unsatisfied by the dreams Hayri recounts at sessions, he gives Hayri a prescription of the dreams he should be having. And Hayri obliges him by having Freudian dreams about his childhood and Sheikh Lutfullah. The analyst, amazed at the rhetoric employed by the said mullah as recounted by Hayri, tells him that Lutfullah must have read Marx and Engels, and that indeed Lutfullah is the founder of the socialist school of thought in Turkey. This attempt on the part of the analyst to create a heritage, a genealogy of scholars is typical of the early republican era that tried on the one hand to deny Ottoman heritage and on the other to find Turkish predecessors for every possible field of scholarship.

The fact remains though, that when it comes to history and literature, 'the olds' are a bit difficult to access due to the Alphabet Revolution that happened in 1928. However, in *Time Regulation Institute* the inaccessibility of the past does not stop the creators of a new tradition. Like all newly minted traditions and establishments *Time Regulation Institute* needs a heritage to call its own. As founder of the institute, Ayarcı, due to what seems to be lack of 'time' rather than lack of alphabetical skills, asks Hayri to write what he calls a 'Europeanish' biography of an imagined master clock-maker of the Ottoman era. Hayri obliges by imagining a certain Ottoman scientist very much ahead of his time, Ahmet Zamani Efendi, who then, with the help of the press, enters the Valhalla of reclaimed Ottomans who were progressive republicans before their time.

After going on several limbs, Tanpınar provides something akin to a climax in the story towards the very end. *Time Regulation Institute*, standing in for republican reforms, is now at its most successful and powerful and Hayri is given the job to build the new institute headquarters – read a functioning government. Having no architectural training he designs a labyrinthine building with redundant staircases and bridges. The shape of the building is so preposterous that it gets a mention in Dawe and Freely's translators' note as proving too difficult to comprehend and translate even for the combined force of two. They tell us, as a prime example of intertextuality, that the shape of this strange structure was revealed to Dawe in a dream after trying to understand it for quite a while. It appears the translators themselves were not immune to the enchanted atmosphere of Hayri's earlier years in and around *tekkes* and holy sheiks, and the Freudian interrogation of Hayri's analyst.

Hayri's monster is at first applauded by the state's media apparatus for its 'unfathomable [sic] innovation'. A newspaper comment on the building summarises the concerns that Tanpınar expresses in his essays, as architecture and language become interchangeable metaphors: 'Here, we see that in an era when the new syntax has started in Turkish, the new architecture has given its first fruit. What will the enemies of the inverted sentence say in face of the resounding success of Hayri İrdal?' Satire is at full gallop here, but then an earnest moment occurs. From the start of the book, people have been portrayed as gullible and ready to take on any kind of innovation coated with praise from government officials. When they tell the workers of the institute that their houses will also be planned according to Hayri's impossible designs they are alarmed, and object to their homes being built in a similar style. Here, at last, this relationship of gullibility and exploitation hits a wall. Private space, then, is still sacred, and the public will let the state walk only so far to their doorstep. This is the point when Ayarcı realises that the 'revolution' has been in vain, that people were 'humouring' his innovations and not putting their faith in them. In a newspaper article Tanpınar says that the wholesale Europeanisation will never be possible in

Turkey because it has never been the sole option: when the going gets rough, there is always 'the old life' to default to. He seems to be saying that this attempt to change the people has been a failure that the republican elites will have to own up and come to terms with at some point.

This final point made by Tanpınar suggests that while there seems to be a heritage war going on in the public space, the Turks will continue to be who they are in the private space of their home, in the little time they have after their day's work at the *Time Regulation Institute*, the Circumlocution Office, or similar, is done. The existentialist questions raised by Hayri, Ayarcı and Tanpınar concerning cultural belonging are theirs alone. They struggle with anxieties of influence and set up whole systems of thought and institutions to compensate for them. For Tanpınar, preservation of Ottoman heritage was possible by actively engaging with it, teaching it, producing it and connecting it to both literature of his day and to the European influences that went into the creation of a new Turkish literature. As a member of intelligentsia himself, he was acutely aware of the double heritage of the late Ottoman and early republican Turkish intellectuals. As an author and critic, he was a keen observer of the oscillation between innovation from Western genres and reconciliation with old Ottoman forms, just as Hayri oscillated between his two poles. Tanpınar's now famous complaint of 'assassination by silence' was that his efforts in welding all these elements together was not appreciated enough.

While many of the intellectuals who have dealt with the pull between 'the two poles' have found it relatively easy to let go of Ottoman heritage, Tanpınar insists on preserving it in some form, if only because he believes it will in fact facilitate the transformation that the republicans are hoping for. In this, and many other ways *Time Regulation Institute*, as prescribed in the name, is in competition with official Turkish history, with its imaginative and hard-to-believe project of Europeanisation. Changes to time regime, European forms of the arts being advertised through the papers and the radio as detailed in the novel have basis in early republican history, and Tanpınar plays with the dimensions of the project, exaggerating them to full ironic effect, providing a distance that makes historical facts more accessible to the contemporary reader who has imbibed early republican history through set school texts. Although the current government and its culture and education policies may seem readier than

previous ones to champion Tanpınar as one of the Turkish greats, one
wonders how ready they are to adopt his finely tuned and resourceful sort
of criticism, as they go about with suggested and/or implemented heavy
handed cuts and additions to the national curriculum in an effort to restore
the legacy of the Ottoman Empire.

In *A Mind at Peace*, Tanpınar says that the Turks hardly have five books that
have been read continuously through generations. If the *Qur'an* and Rumi's
Mathnawi are the two default ones (never mind the fact that they were
quite inaccessible for a few decades when the Arabic alphabet was banned),
then we still have to find three to fill this quota for a cannon for Turkish
sensibility. Dealing as it does with this need for the invention of tradition
and the constant battle between our 'old' and 'new' life, *Time Regulation
Institute* seems like a good contender, and Tanpınar acts like a real life
version of **Ahmet Zamani Efendi**, embodying our eternal struggle and
fascination with transformation, continuity and time.

ORHAN PAMUK'S LEGACY

Abdullah Yavuz Altun

In what category should we place the writing of Turkey's only Nobel laureate novelist, Orhan Pamuk? Is it 'fiction'? Or perhaps, 'non-Western fiction'? But how can we define his work as 'non-Western', when it is not considered to be completely 'Western' by some? Even Pamuk has been quoted as saying, 'as someone who has sat at the table of a secular Republican family I live as someone affected by Western, Cartesian rationalism'. On the other hand, his fictional novels have been translated into sixty-one different languages around the world. It is surely a huge success for an author who belongs to a 'non-Western' literary world, or 'third-world literature'. Can we consider his work as a part of world literature canon or not.

Though Pamuk talks about his 'Cartesian rationality', he also says:

> I open myself to other texts, other books. I don't see those texts as a necessity, I take pleasure in reading them, I feel a joy. Where pleasure is felt, the self is affected. Where the self is affected, I also have the control of my reason. Perhaps my books find themselves without bickering or scuffling between these two centres.

This is one answer he always repeats in narratives of his work and to others in various interviews. In expressing views and artistic notions to suggest that the novel is a Western invention, Pamuk is certainly shaping his narratives using a Western form of thinking. On the other hand, he also brings Turkish and Islamic texts, themes and subjects into his novels. In such terms, Pamuk's novels would easily be categorised as continuity with modern Turkish authors such as Ahmet Hamdi Tanpınar, Oğuz Atay and Yusuf Atılgan. Similarly to Pamuk, these authors are also writing using Western novel technique that also includes references to Turkish Islamic texts. However, Turkish critics mostly enjoy remarking that Orhan Pamuk was writing his novels for a Western audience. These remarks come more often after his Nobel Prize achievement. In my opinion, these critics miss a very crucial point. Pamuk's fiction requires his readers to know and read most of Western classical novels in order to comprehend the innovations in his novel technique that include direct references to Western myths, themes and sometimes well-known passages and characters. But he also expects them to have substantial knowledge of Islamic classics by writers such as Rumi, Attar and Ibn Arabi.

This 'bipolarity' of Pamuk's novels presents him as a pro-Western intellectual to Turkish readers and critics. However, it also leads Western audiences to consider his works as coming from the periphery or East. In reality, Pamuk enjoys the paradoxical situation of being a modern novelist who outcasts himself from both intellectual fronts. In his article, 'My Turkish Library', published in *Die Zeit*, he explains this uniqueness as follows, 'it was after I turned forty that I learned that the most powerful reason for loving my library was that neither Turks nor Westerners knew about it'. The article, while telling the reader how he built his library as an intellectual, is also quite notable as it implies how Pamuk deals with Turkish history, culture and identity. For instance, he interprets his motivation, like a voyager, as collecting books from second hand book shops of Istanbul streets: 'I wasn't buying like a book collector but like a frantic person who was desperate to understand why Turkey was so poor and so trouble'. And, in a further passage, he clarifies what he was gaining from this research and what was his relation to those books and their stories as a public intellectual:

> When I am confronted by such affectations, I am in sympathy with Dostoevsky, who was so infuriated by Russian intellectuals who knew Europe better than they did Russia. At the same time, I don't see this anger, which impelled Dostoevsky to turn against Turgenev, as particularly justified. Extrapolating from my own experience, I know that behind Dostoevsky's dutiful defences of Russian culture and Orthodox mysticism — shall we call it the Russian library? — was a rage not just against the West, but against the Russian intellectuals who did not know their own culture.

Like many other (post)modern or avant-garde novelists, Pamuk esteems 'history' very highly in his works. For him, history is a spring of interesting and retrospectively unreasonable details. And he often filters absurd details from historical accounts such as history books, traveller narratives, and local texts. While he is transforming the cruel reality of his city, Istanbul, into Kafkaesque or Dadaist fiction, he most probably believes that the absurdity of today's culture is somehow inherited from the absurdity of past. In this sense, almost every Pamuk novel includes melancholic, hysteric, or self-reflecting historical interpretation of the world in which his characters and objects are living. Sometimes Turkish Islamic history is symbolised by a fuzzy character, and on other occasions, it lies under the narrative, as a basement for what Pamuk has constructed. According to his interviews and articles, Pamuk's curiosity for history comes from reading almost every book in their family apartment. It more specifically originates from Reşad Ekrem Koçu, a city historian, who intended to write the Istanbul Encyclopedia but was not able to finish. (Koçu is mentioned in *The White Castle* and the character Salahattin Darvınoğlu in *The Silent House* is a parody of Koçu's intellectual persona). Similarly to Pamuk, Koçu was also good at choosing intriguing topics from Ottoman history. Pamuk is also interested in Istanbul's and Turkey's 'alternative', unofficial, unwritten history. In this context, his books could be read as a pretext to understanding Turkishness, in terms of history, culture and identity.

Pamuk's first novel *Cevdet Bey and His Sons* (1982) was a modern family novel, emulating Thomas Mann's *Buddenbrooks* (1901). It narrates modern Turkey's epoch from its formation to late 1970s with the story of three generations. This novel is also an articulation of the tradition of Turkish Republic's first novelists, who commonly liken the fall of the Ottoman Empire to the disintegration of a large family. Pamuk, in his award-winning debut, proved his talent in writing a 'modern text' in terms of novel technique, storytelling and forming a worldly character in Turkish literature. After that, in his second novel, *The Silent House* (1983), he surprisingly innovated his novel techniques by narrating the plot from multiple points of view. In this novel, in order to deepen the relations with history, one of the narrators, Grandmother Fatma Darvınoğlu, hysterically remembers her dead husband Selahattin Darvınoğlu, who is a mockery of positivist and secular Jacobins of late Ottoman and early Republican eras. Also, another narrator and grandson of Fatma, Faruk

Darvınoğlu locks himself to the archives in Gebze, a town near to Istanbul, without purpose and juxtaposes ordinary stories with historical accounts. Each chapter was formed by first person narratives from characters in the novel and each of them was resonated around perception of Turkishness through personal and public history.

The first peak of Pamuk's career, as many critics would agree, was *The White Castle* (1985), which was translated into English soon afterwards, and appreciated widely by Western pundits. In the beginning of the novel, the audience realises that the author of this text is a Venetian ex-slave, who was enslaved by an Ottoman elite. More surprisingly, this historical account was found in Gebze archives by Faruk Darvınoğlu, the historian character of the previous novel. It is a valuable coincidence also as Faruk finally discovers a good, concrete historical document from his arbitrary searches in the archives, Pamuk also finds his literary voice by formulating *The White Castle*. Here, while Pamuk was reinventing and progressing on the genre of East-West novel, which according to Pamuk is 'an invention of the Ottoman-Turk', he, at the same time, discusses the identity crisis of Turkish Republic rooted in Westernisation process of the late Ottoman Empire. The relationship between slave-owner Hodja and his counterpart is a reproduction of Hegelian master-slave dialectic and these two characters' roles are juggled throughout the text. In this context, the novel ably expresses the Ottoman-Turk identity through the changing perceptions of self in the eyes of Ottoman elites. It almost perfectly clarifies the complications of Westernisation by reiterating the famous philosophical question, 'Why am I who I am?' Pamuk cleverly transforms historical context to an existential question.

Such subject-matter and stylistic discoveries of Pamuk in *The White Castle* led him to his masterpiece *The Black Book* (1990). And probably the best description of what *The Black Book* was about come from the author himself:

> I thought that the formula, the structure of *The Black Book*, the idea was that put together whatever you found interesting in Istanbul … (R)emember your childhood, and try to see the city as a sort of a place where layers of layers, things and images, history and myths and combine this with experimental, postmodern European avantgardism, all together with a classical Sufi text and see what happens.

This recipe-like explanation, which lead the readers to think that the narrative of the novel was arbitrarily constructed, only offers some insights about the referential ingredients of Pamuk's literary work, the aspirations of his experiments in novel techniques, and his discerning of what-kind-of-reader would appreciate such an outcome. The novel's rich intertextual hinterland tempted many critics to decipher the Pamuk's narrative. In an essay entitled 'The Turks are Coming', Güneli Gün, successfully predicted and announced Pamuk's introduction to the Western literature: 'here was Orhan Pamuk, a kid who was doing the right thing at the right time'. Another critic, Sevinç Türkkan, gathered critical approaches to describing what the *The Black Book* was as:

> a theory of the postmodern novel, a *bildungsroman*, a picaresque novel, a detective novel, an encyclopedic novel, an experiment in innovation of the Turkish language and syntax, a cultural history of Istanbul, a quest in the tradition of mystical Islam, and an elaborate mediation on identity.

One of the main themes of these remarks is how *The Black Book* and Pamuk's novels considered as equivalent to modern Western literature. For instance, Hülya Adak, in her essay, compares *The Black Book* to James Joyce's *Ulysses* (1922) in terms of the idea of 'national allegory' and interrelations with their national myths and historical texts which two authors deliberately reproduced in their narratives. Adak criticises Pamuk for not being able to recontextualise Sufism stories as Joyce skilfully did with Irish ones, and she claims that the reinvention of the novel remains at a 'mimetic' level. Beside Adak's comparison to *Ulysses*, the famous literary critic, Enis Batur, applauds Pamuk's success in *The Black Book*, and places his depiction of Istanbul alongside Joyce's Dublin and Robert Musil's Vienna. In 2006, the Nobel committee decided to broaden this list by adding Dostoyevsky's St Petersburg and Marcel Proust's Paris among cities distinguished by their literary heritage.

The Black Book's influence on Pamuk's novel style resumed in his next book, *The New Life* (1994). This time, the hero was a postmodern Sufi pilgrim, searching for the love and meaning of his life by travelling across the country on intercity buses. The heroine's name was Canan (beloved), a direct reference to Sufi texts in which Canan means 'the ultimate love, God'. The common theme of those two novels is the inexhaustible longing for meaning from images in daily life, things and stuff, streets and cities, other people and other stories. It is zeal similar to Pamuk's research to understand the world and Turkey's poor situation by collecting and hungrily reading books. However, in both cases, at the end of the search, a deep, melancholic 'meaninglessness' fills the stage, like a black hole that absorbs the things around it. This fancy 'meaninglessness' is a characteristic of Pamuk's literary works. Scholar of world literature and writer, Ian Almond, explains the very logic of this meaninglessness. According to Almond, Pamuk's protagonists frequently end their quest for meaning with a certain level of despair and sadness. Each character finally realises 'that he does not have a self, that his narratives possess no super-cosmic significance, that his life no longer has an object of adoration'. Almond suggests another term for this situation: 'a very postmodern *fana*' – 'I was nowhere and everywhere; and that is why it seemed to me I was in the nonexistent centre of the world'. *Fana* means, as Almond suggests, 'self-annihilation; becoming a nonexistent'. In this realm, Pamuk is, on the one hand, introducing symbols of Islamic literary tradition to the Western world and, on the other hand he is annihilating its magic. The final analysis of Ian Almond, who categorises Pamuk as a kind of Orientalist, is telling:

> A sensitive, open-minded, but ultimately empirical worldview underlies the texts of *The Black Book* and *The New Life*, a subtle empiricism which dallies and plays with the semantic wealth of Islam for a variety of purposes, but seldom allows it to escape from certain prearranged boxes – prohibitive dogma, nationalistic glue, source of exotic mysticisms, soroptimistic messianisms, uncompromising fundamentalism. A book in which Islam, in other words, is kept safely 'other'.

Pamuk's next move was to publish *My Name is Red* (1998), which combines a historical detective story – as Umberto Eco had conveyed in his first novel, *The Name of the Rose* (1980) – and his childhood passion to be a painter. Thus, it is full of autobiographical references. Besides that, Pamuk's successfully detailed description of sixteenth century Istanbul daily life and events, which are gathered from court registers of that era, implies that his affection to history had become deeper and more refined. Here, he shows how colours, forms and meanings in Western and Eastern visual arts are interplayed in a late sixteenth century Ottoman Palace. According to plot, the palace's calligraphers and painters are commissioned by Sultan Murat III to prepare Western-influenced, mostly imitation, paintings for a book. Obviously, it is a critical look at the Westernisation process of the Ottoman era in terms of 'imitation'. However, Pamuk was not harsh as V. S. Naipaul, another Nobel laureate non-Western author, was. Pamuk describes Naipaul's attitude against colonised South Asian people, who were trying to Westernise their society, in his famous novel, *The Mimic Men* (1967), as 'sad and insulting'. Rather, Pamuk argues that his novel originated from the 'happiness of painting' and his feelings while painting and seeing the work of a painter. Compared to *The White Castle*, *My Name is Red* has a flawless voice for his ideas about East and West in relation to the Turkish identity. Against the famous quote from Rudyard Kipling that 'East is East, West is West', Orhan Pamuk offers that the 'East should not be East and West should not be West.'. This idea is frequently encountered in his writings and interviews in relation to Turkishness: 'everyone is sometimes a Westerner and sometimes an Easterner – in fact a constant combination of the two.'

Pamuk's 'unintentionally political' next novel, *Snow* (2002), differentiates itself from others. During the years that Pamuk was writing this novel, there were several political crises around the world including a 'postmodern military coup' in Turkey and radical Islamists terror attacks on USA. Thus, the novel became a global bestseller. However, Snow's stylistic equivalent was Dostoyevsky's *The Possessed* (1872), in which the author criticised nihilistic and socialistic ideas in Russian political culture. In *Snow*, Pamuk imagines the city of Kars, where the story unfolds, as a microcosm of Turkey under military rule. Thus, reader can easily feel the tension between the secular elite's political will with military governance and the tendency for radical Islamist to capture political power. As Dostoyevsky did in his novel, Pamuk also scrutinises nihilistic ideas of the radical Islamist leader Mr Blue, the harshly modernist secular thoughts of military officials and some politicians, and mild religious atmosphere of Islamic cults through his Kafkaesque anti-hero Poet Ka's participatory observations in Kars and Turkey. At the end of the book, the author skilfully leads his narrative to an absurd parody of his narrative, which is, in fact, an absurd parody of what was happening in Turkey's political sphere or, more explicitly, as a 'national allegory'. In addition to the unfolding events in the political layers of the book, Pamuk pinned his novel's literary vision to Stendhal's famous quote: 'politics in a literary work is like a pistol-shot in a concert – crude but impossible to ignore'. The political stirring in the country is something that Pamuk cannot avoid reacting to as a novelist. He also criticised the forms of modern knowledge, secular daily life and Western influence over his characters. As Marshall Berman puts it, Pamuk's analysis of anti-Modern political Islamism is not about 'tradition'. According to Berman, it should be called 'Modernist Anti-Modernism'. Political Islamists and especially Mr Blue in the novel are also Modern characters in terms of their interrelation with Western modernism. Berman finally says that since Thomas Mann, Pamuk is the only person who understands the historical importance of 'Modernist Anti-Modernism'. What is 'democratic' in *Snow* is that its narrator, Pamuk, gives enough space to his characters in order to introduce and explain themselves. The Eastern-Western dichotomy, once again, appears in Pamuk's novels, this time, in a secular-Islamist version, which is also transitional.

A year after the publication of *Snow*, Pamuk produced *Istanbul: City and Memories* (2003), an autobiographical prose which covered his life until the age of twenty-two. This book includes Pamuk family's experiences in his neighbourhood, timely changes in the very core of Istanbul, and Pamuk's youthful thoughts. Here, Pamuk exposes bits and pieces about his personal life, which is deeply reflected in his novels. His observations about the changing character of Istanbul also reveal the transformation of Turkish identity and nationality through decades. Looking at the progress of his novels, Pamuk's texts are shaped by mingling reality and fiction, things and words. For instance, he created the historian character in *The Silent House*, Faruk Darvınoğlu by imitating his older brother Şevket Pamuk, who is a renounced economic historian. He gave his apartment address in one of *The Black Book*'s chapters by placing it into initials of the first words of each paragraph. He also narrated his own family life with his brother and mother, as if it was happening in the sixteenth century in *My Name is Red*. And finally he went to Kars, the city where Snow was staged, as a journalist and walked the streets and talked to people before he sent *Snow*'s anti-hero Şair Ka to the city. His best descriptions about Istanbul come from his long, late night walks in its streets. And, most probably, his excessive references to sadness and solitude are rooted in his personal life.

This very nature of Pamuk's literary style peaked in *The Museum of Innocence* (2008). The novel tells the story of a love affair between an upper class man, Kemal, and his long-distance relative, a lower class young woman, Füsun. Kemal tries to collect every object, however simple, that reminds him of his love and then opens a museum in which he can present his never-ending love to visitors by explaining each object. Embodying his love through those things also indicates the dissolvability of something called 'never-ending love'. In other words, Pamuk resumes his pattern of extracting 'meaninglessness' from a very dense narrative. As he broke the Islamic literature's spell in *The Black Book* and *The New Life*, he now deconstructs paraphernalia of worldly love through imprisoning them into daily life objects. Moreover, Pamuk opened a museum in real life in the exact spot and with the exact same objects he had written about in his prose; and imposed an entrance fee to the museum in the novel. This concrete connection between reality and fiction is the zenith of his legacy. He also resumes investigating the elements of Turkish nationality and identity through the idea of constructing a museum. To do this, Pamuk visits museums around the world and in last chapters of his novel he carefully discusses the cultural necessities of creating an adequate museum in terms of exposing private life. He subsequently moves the idea to public and argues that Turks are not an 'exposed' society, thus they cannot collect and evaluate their daily life objects. However, the novel's reluctant and naive character Kemal attempts to collect things because he could not show his love to Füsun in public because of several moral reasons. Pamuk problematises the idea of 'innocence' since society does not regard their love as such. That is why the museum is called 'innocence'. Just as Dostoyevsky did with the concept of 'crime' in *Crime and Punishment* (1866), Pamuk frees the concepts of 'innocence and happiness' from common patterns, stereotypes and even philosophical categories. This process is applied through things and words, which would be considered pretty much the basic material of both fiction and life.

The latest of Pamuk's novels is *A Strangeness in My Mind* (2014). Surprisingly his fictional tricks play very small roles in this novel. He gently crafts his main character Mevlut into a long narrative. He borrows the name of the novel from William Wordsworth's poem, *The Prelude*, which is a fine example of Modern Romantic Era in literature. The story of the hero, Mevlut, who is a part-time tallyman on Istanbul's well-known and rich streets, is narrated simultaneously with the story of Istanbul's illegally constructed slums, which exists adjacent to tall apartments and skyscrapers. Pamuk explores the relationship between illegally possessing property and crafting a self from this opportunism; and the lack of individualism in Turkey's lower classes through the crooked ownership of capital by migrating families from Anatolia to Istanbul. Here his narrative is shaped through the 'innocent' hypocrisies of those people who presume to be making a living and makes a strong statement about ordinary people's indecisive practices in between public and private spheres. This hesitant nature, according to Pamuk, is caused by the Turkish state's oppressing impositions on citizens. Mevlut, on the other hand, appears as a character, who does not interfere with the opportunistic behaviours of his kin and becomes a modern, lonely, but also happy character. Mevlut, as Jale Parla suggests, also sees the things and events around him with a little 'strangeness', a sign of transcendence that commonly appears as one edge of a pendulum in Pamuk's novels. The other edge of the pendulum is temporality and this pendulum's oscillations indicate the act of search in his narratives. Thus, Mevlut finishes his training and trial with the city at the end of the novel and becomes a *porteur*, a bearer who bears the city and his 'accidental' love inside himself. Such an inclusive modern character is rather different from Pamuk's other more nihilistic heroes.

So we return to the original question. Are Pamuk's novels a part of world literature? Or, as the postmodern literary critic and theorist, Fredrik Jameson, says, are they to be placed into the 'third-world literature' box? Jameson is boldly making the distinction between classical and modern novels by describing the former's context as the public sphere and the latter's context as the private sphere. He then argues that third-world texts are always dealing with the public sphere by transforming characters' private lives into national allegories: the 'story of the private individual destiny is always an allegory of the embattled situation of the public third-world culture and society'. Jameson's position has been severely criticised by several scholars. Most of them are right in asserting that Jameson's distinction between 'worlds' was a continuum of colonialist discourse. However, Jameson's 'third world' could be considered as a suppositional category; after our bitterness fades, we would see that his arguments are true for the most part. By reading Naguip Mahfouz's stories about the great and miserable Egyptian nation, looking at Salman Rushdie's reckoning against Indian history and myths, even thinking of Orhan Pamuk's *The Black Book* or *Snow*, we can see that Jameson has a point. While Rushdie was explicitly chaining the hero of *Midnight's Children* (1981) to Indian history and Pamuk was deliberately choosing to tell his nation's awkward history through Kafkaesque allegories, they are also, most probably, mocking the idea of being a non-Westerner. These authors are struggling to make Westerners understand that there is a world beyond the West, and in that world there are beautiful stories to tell. This is even an advantage to Pamuk, who indicates that feeding his novels with Turkish culture made them original for Western audience. For instance, in *Snow*, as Sibel Irzık notes, the narrative purposefully embraces the tension of 'national allegory' but it is also 'hopelessly striving to achieve instead ...the map of a perfect correspondence between poetry and a unique life'.

In an interview with *The Paris Review* for The Art of Fiction series, Pamuk seems to be aware of his 'localness'. Sadly, he tells the interviewer, 'when Proust writes about love, he is seen as someone talking about universal love. Especially at the beginning, when I wrote about love, people would say that I was writing about Turkish love'.

READING TURKISH COFFEE

Suzanne Mordue

In Turkey a *falcı*, or fortune teller, is often versed in the ancient art of coffee reading. Before I came to Istanbul I had never heard of anyone reading coffee grindings; although when I was a child my grandmother used to read the tea leaves that remained clinging to the inside a cup of tea after drinking it. This was in the days before teabags became more commonplace, and this small piece of social culture slipped away into insignificance.

Unquestionably, coffee has great import in Turkey. Turkish coffee has a long and distinguished history, going back to the early seventeenth century. The making of coffee in its present-day form is said to have originated here – on its passage from Yemen to Europe, where the beans were chewed, and in other parts of the Middle East where whole beans were boiled. The coffeehouse is essentially an innovation of the Ottoman Empire, first introduced in Istanbul to create a stable commercial market for coffee amongst Arab merchants.

Traditionally, a Turkish woman is considered marriageable when she can make a good cup of foamy coffee for her husband to be. As a practical joke the woman puts salt in the coffee she makes for her potential husband when both families first meet, which is when he officially asks for her hand in marriage. After lunch a strong black tea or Turkish coffee is considered an essential digestive. After so many years in Turkey I too feel that the meal is incomplete without this dénouement. Naturally, I have had plenty of opportunities in the last seven years to witness the reading of the cup.

There seems to be a range of different practices when it comes to the actual reading. I can only document the ones I know although if you have your fortune read through the medium of coffee you may encounter something substantially different. But all seem to agree that once you have finished drinking your coffee you must turn the cup upside down onto the saucer. Some give great significance to the direction of the handle or insist that you must turn the cup once or twice to seal the fortune. Many put metal onto the base of the cup, a coin or ring is common, to draw out the heat to help the cup cool down.

The first rule is that you cannot read your own fortune, so it is customary for friends to read each other's cups. The shapes in the grounds are studied and a meaning assigned. There is a range of common interpretations for certain symbols; such as the tree which is related to family. The symbols around a main image are also assimilated into the reading. Some state that with the handle facing away from you the left-hand side represents the past, the middle of the cup the present and the right-hand side the future. Others simply read the cup as a whole for future predictions. There is general agreement that as something at the bottom of your cup is further away you will have to wait for it or maybe it is even something inaccessible. Symbols around the rim show an event that will happen soon. If the left-over coffee spills onto the outside of the cup this is considered lucky. After the main reading the saucer must also be studied. When placed at an angle, if the grounds are fluid enough to move it indicates that everything in your cup will come true. The reader may also see symbols in the saucer.

Being from a design background I became fascinated by the images in my cups; many of which look like abstract pieces of art. I started to take photographs of them and the idea first sparked that this could be an interesting art project. I made a few individual *fal* paintings as presents for friends, and the positive reaction I received made the concept of a whole series inevitable. I created ten fortunes; delicate Turkish cups carefully marked out in water colours on hand-made paper. I kept each fortune related to good luck to create a positive ambiance. For the last five years or so I have been heavily involved in learning technologies which made producing something tactile all the more momentous. The full series once complete was displayed for a month in Molly's Café which briefly stood in the historical Galata area of Istanbul. Like many artists who have gone before and in all certainty those who will come after it is hard not to be inspired by Turkish culture and in particular the dynamic and vibrant city of Istanbul.

there are bells which indicates the person with this coffee will receive good news...

fortune #9 sw

EXODUS OF SMOKE

Tam Hussein

Inspector Hyder lit a cigarette, he knew it was illegal to smoke in private property other than one's own, but he smoked anyway. It was one of those idiosyncratic rules that the President had applied to the Nation.

He put his gun back and opened the shutters letting the miserable light in to the small one bedroom flat.

Inspector Hyder was upset, not because the smog still lingered over the city when the forecasters had promised to disperse it. Not even because of the lack of light – these last days had been gloomy. He was upset because someone had died on his watch: that just didn't happen here. The President, the Embodiment of the Nation, prided himself on that.

He informed Control that he had found her. He puffed at his cheap Kazakhi Duty Frees peering at the young woman lying on the red divan partially undressed. She was beautiful but then everyone was beautiful, even middle aged men like him. But it was something about the young woman's beauty that niggled away at him. It questioned his very outlook in life and demanded a riposte.

It was this impulse that made him bring out his thin rubber gloves and put them on. The same impulse made him bend down and inspect her the way a jeweller does a diamond. There was nothing perverse about this, why else had he joined Homeland Security Services, a sister company of SecuriCorp? The inspection wasn't enough, his mind demanded more.

True, the President's guidelines explicitly stated: 'it is prohibited to touch the subject prior to the arrival of the Forensics Team'. But they would tell him exactly the same thing he would record in his File: 'A classic case of asphyxiation. The attacker had probably attempted copulation, the victim had resisted and perhaps screamed. He had panicked pleading with her to stop. She had tried to scratch him and in the process broken some of her long nails that were decorated with pretty pink butterflies. He tried to calm her down using the pillow that had fallen on the floor. But she just wouldn't stop screaming. So he slapped her in the face. Her rage turned into fear. With all the strength she had in her legs she pushed and pushed and all the while his hands closed in on her throat. She couldn't breathe. She lost strength. She expired.

At first he was probably terrified realising the consequences of his actions. As he was about to bolt out of the door, he paused. He went to the Masterworks and selected some classical music so the neighbours wouldn't be alerted. He returned to her, he felt her cheek, she was still warm. Her hair was soft and luxuriant, and she was still so perfect in that black dress. Before she succumbed to rigor mortis he clawed at her ripping her scant clothing away, he kissed her lips, breasts; he bit her neck lamenting her lack of sexual responsiveness, that's what they all do. He had seen countless CSI files in the archives. Inspector Hyder took a peek, there it was; traces of dried semen on the inside of her thighs. Classic text book motive: Beautiful girl gets raped by a disturbed man she considered a friend but he thought otherwise. Wires were crossed. Now she's dead. Case closed.

But that was not the question Inspector Hyder wanted to answer. Her intelligence was not in doubt. How many foreigners had several dictionaries of languages; Chinese, Spanish, Persian and Arabic? How many can understand archaic titles like One Who Flew Over the Cuckoos Nest, or comprehend Bach and know Arabic?

He decided to tamper with the victim come what may. Let them argue with me. After they see her they will understand. He carefully turned her over. His mind began to calculate and catalogue. Her back was a galaxy of brown freckles of all sizes. Her face was exquisite with a touch of the orient with no sign of scalpel. Her brown hair even in death remained full of glossy curls – no sign of pro-vitamin implants at the hair base. Cheekbones were chiselled. Dentistry: perfect, not even a filling. Neck: like a swan. Shoulders: sculpted. Breasts: large (but not too large). Buttocks: plump (no cellulite). Legs: not too long, not too short. Skin:

unblemished apart from the bite marks. He dared not say it, his eyes widened, his throat became dry. Had he had found the Holy Grail?

He shook his head in denial. He brought out his optifier and placed it on his eyes. He went over her one more time, dismantling her into parts like he had been taught. He came to her Piedic zone. Paused, focused the optifier. He punched the air. He had found it. 'Not bad Mr. Hyder,' he congratulated himself, 'not bad.'

Inspector Hyder heard the low rumbling engine of the Morgue truck. He flicked the cigarette out of the window. He heard his partner, Richards, leap up the stairs giving the location of the crime scene: 34 Old City, Moorgate.

'You Okay?' said Richards pumping his hands.

'Yeah, Yeah. I'm fine' replied Inspector Hyder, trying to act as if his colleague's middle age trimness didn't bother him. The worst thing about it was; Richards knew it bothered him. Inspector Hyder was just waiting to straighten out his crow feet so his wife would stop nagging, his neighbours would stop sniggering and Richards would stop taking the mick out of him at the bar. Soon Inspector Hyder would be whole again.

'So what's the story?' Richards chirped.

'A classic case' replied Hyder.

'Yeah I know- looks like it doesn't it? Wow!' gasped Richards, 'she is perfect! Look at her cheek bones, her breasts doesn't even have a trace of scalpel- Amazing! I think she is a perfect 89.2 on the Continental scale and 235 on Klein ratio. Do you concur?'

Hyder got smug: 'Why don't you look again?'

Richards' dead blue eyes came alive. He brought out his rubber gloves, got down on his knees until his face was an inch away from her pale skin. He went over like an artist that had masterd Vogue and the school of aesthetics it had founded. He measured her proportions, melanin levels, hairs, softness, her glassy eyes, dental imprints- she was a perfect specimen of Neo-Homo Sapiens.

'She is perfect!' declared Richards, 'Perfect.'

Hyder looked at him almost with contempt the way he might look at a criminal.

'I'm telling you she is! She is! 89.5 And 236 Klein that's the highest!'

Hyder just pointed at her toes and threw him his optifier.

'Look at that pinkie over there, see that?'

'What about it?' said Richards inspecting it with the optifier.

'Don't be in denial Richards, nothing is perfect. Nothing in this world is perfect.'

'Six toes' said Richard hanging his head in disappointment, 'six bloody toes'.

Hyder nodded 'the gods are against you Richards, it's as simple as that. Nothing is perfect.'

'Yeah, yeah' said Richards he had just seen fame, glory and fortune vanish in front of his eyes, 'do we know who she is?'

'Control got a call in Ms. Olivia Santos, Mo is on the lead.'

'And what about the aggressor?' inquired Richards.

'Unknown-we have to send the dried semen samples to Bio-Tech.'

'Yeah if we haven't found him after that then it's an Alien.'

'Don't worry we'll find him, we'll give the cleaners a shake up and have a word with the warden.'

Hyder bent down to peer underneath the Divan to see if there were any other clues that he could spot before Forensics combed it over. There was just a business card and a poem by the famous Arab Neo-Romantic Abu'l Hassan entitled 'Exodus'. He picked it up and read to Richards in Arabic.

'How erotic and beautiful' said Richards.

'Yes' said Hyder turning the business card in between his thumb and forefinger 'how beautiful indeed.'

'What does the business card say?' said Richards looking at his colleague knowing that he was turning something over in his mind.

'Mansur' replied Inspector Hyder, 'Mansur Ayluni.'

Muzzammil sat in the designated HSS smoking room. He was looking at the stern but benevolent picture of the President, a ruddy man with a hint of eastern mystery, his friendly grapelike eyes urging him to stop smoking. But Muzzammil had just started smoking two days ago. He had received the call up for the interview by Special Delivery- he had to sign for it with his finger code. So there was no excuse to proffer. In any case you can't really refuse a Presidential Summons could you?

The place was depressing to be in. The bright stale EcoEnergy lights cut in to his eyes. He had tried to rub his eyes to soften the hard light but it was no use. He was tired from the night shift, only the Taurine Enhancers gave him that slow release energy to keep him going. He sipped synthocoffee from his polysterene cup and made a grimace that you make when battery acid hits your ulcer. He looked at his coffee cup; it would be nice to have some real beans as opposed to the synth with its daily allowance of C-vits. If he wanted C-vits he would buy an orange. Sometimes he just wanted a cup of good old coffee made from pure Arabica beans; the way it had been served to him in Masr City with a genuine smile by a real human being with all the wonderful idiosyncrasies of the human form. You could if you wanted to, spark a cigarette and no one would say anything. You could sit down in the evening with the anthology of Abu'l Hassan and you'd be just fine.

In fact, some would even think you are cultured! You could live there, chicken tasted like chicken. And kebabs! What kebabs! No bullshit, there was real brotherhood there too. In Masr city there wasn't a Citizens Decree 3109 that compelled you to help an old lady with a heavy bag. People just helped. It's true; the buildings weren't as clean, transport not as fast but still Masr city worked well enough. In all the anarchy there seemed to be a harmony created by shared goals and ambitions. The people seemed poorer but they smiled more.

He kept on drinking if only just to stop that hawk in his belly from flapping. He could hear the rumble of the BA Interjunction above. Crisp and clear announcements of Hyper trains leaving for Manchester Sector or Mercy City, Swan City, or October City transporting busy workers, administrators, officers, peace keepers all around the Nation chasing their daily subsidised bread courtesy of the Embodiment of the Nation. All had a purpose. All knew their role. Ants.

He continued to stare at the monitor that urged him to stop smoking. He was shown the future that was available to him. If he gave up he'd get free tickets to remote places, the Presidential office would provide free medical advice and pay for the expenses. This was the picture of the Nation: everything was provided for; there was simply no excuse for any socially detrimental activities. If you felt a criminal tendency just visit the Social Integrationist Officer and he would provide you with the means to channel your criminality in a fruitful way for the greater wellbeing of the Nation. Thus many would-be thieves, killers and rapists fell fighting in far of lands; buried in sodden red earth and remembered forever as blue helmeted heroes and peace-keepers in the annals of the Nation.

Muzzammil looked at the digicast admiring the pure grass so close up. He stubbed out his cigarette in the extinguisher and looked around him: Is this where John was kept during the dark years of the 30s? Is this where they presented him with the files; where they took away his leaving papers, where he heard the screams? It couldn't be. It was just so sanitised.

A perfectly crisp announcement called out Muzzammil's full name. He got up and headed for the interview room 756. As he walked along the corridors he thought he could hear muffled voices, raised voices, laughter, even, faint whimperings coming out of the countless rooms.

When Muzzammil entered the bright white room he found himself in front of a podgy but extraordinarily handsome man smiling at him. He had expected his interrogator to be in the grey HSS uniform but instead he was in wearing a white shirt and fashionable jeans.

The room had a two grey chairs, a white desk with a Photopix and an ash tray. In the corner of the room was a small sink and coffee dispenser. The man invited Muzzammil to sit down and offered him the ash tray and some synthocoffee. He introduced himself as Inspector Hyder, even asked his permission to smoke. Muzzammil slightly disarmed by his affability gave him permission. And when he himself had the urge to smoke the man nodded his assent; as if they were an ancient breed of hard core smokers that wouldn't give up their freedom to dominate their own bodies, even if it meant their own perdition.

'Don't worry Mr. Sheraz, those bad days are over, we have learned from our mistakes- go ahead smoke-Though I am legally obliged to inform you that it is bad for your health and that this friendly conversation will be recorded for training purposes. Should you wish to see a copy of the transcript you may do so according to the Revised Data Protection and Home Land Security Act of 2057, section 254, article 48. You merely need to apply for a licence to the department of Citizen Protection who will give you a letter to take to the House of Justice whereby you can apply for the transcript. Providing that your credit check and identity are correctly verified you will have access. All this, I should add, is courtesy of the Embodiment of the Nation. Do you agree?'

'I guess, yes' replied Muzzammil hesitantly.

'Very well, I am Inspector Zakariya Kemal Hyder, your interviewing officer and responsible for this case that you may or may not have followed on the broadcasts going out to the Nation. Should you have any complaints my supervising officer is Commissioner Chris Stein. Of course, this is an informal interview and you are free to leave any time you wish.'

'You mean this interview has no legal weight?' asked Muzzammil.

'Yes and no. It depends on the various circumstances of the case, and how this turns out. I mean if you wish we could get someone from Citizen Protection to apply for a Legal Senator to ensure that my questioning is in line with presidential decree No. 259 section 45 of the Emergency Act of 2036. You are perfectly within your rights, but you would have to remain in custody until a Legal Senator can be found. Mind you I should add two things, one, that our custody rooms are actually quite comfortable with all the creature comforts available to you. Two, that it could be a waste of time since we are not actually accusing you of anything. We are on a fact finding mission.'

'What's this all about?'

'Well it's actually quite complicated Mr. Sheraz, you know how important it is to protect the peace and security of this Nation don't you?'

'Yeah' replied Muzzammil almost apathetic as if he knew what Inspector Hyder was getting at.

'Tell me, how are your studies doing?'

'It's tough working and studying.'

'Yes last time some of the officers spoke to you, you were doing some work on Burnusi weren't you?'

'Yes I was.'

'What about now? Are we tired of researching an ancient old Sufi?'

'Not tired, it's just hard to multitask, night shifts aren't exactly conducive to study.'

'Yes understandably, I actually read your introduction to the man, it's a good piece. Even your supervisor likes the three chapters you wrote. I mean he was very radical wasn't he?'

'I wouldn't call Burnusi radical. I just think you need to contextualise his period.'

'Well your professor says that it's actually one of the weaknesses of your argument.'

'Well, I don't actually want to get dragged into an intellectual debate regarding the merits and demerits of my paper, at least not with you.' Muzzammil stopped himself abruptly looking at his questioner for signs of anger, when no signs of anger emerged, in a softer tone he continued: 'maybe we could just crack on with the matter at hand.'

'My goodness, look at me! I am sorry, just tell me when you need to go and we will finish. I always forget my lowly place amongst you intellectuals.'

'Its quite okay, now what's this all about?' asked Muzzammil with a polite smile that hinted at insincerity.

'Now' said the Inspector leaning back on his chair, 'do you know who Olivia Santos is?'

'Who?'

'Ms. Olivia Santos.'

'No. I don't think so.'

'Let me see if I could jog your memory, take a look at her picture.' Inspector Hyder pressed the Photopix and Muzzammil saw her in her full glory.

Inspector Hyder gave a commentary of the victim's background and the light form mimicked everything that the inspector said. Muzzammil's pupils dilated as he saw her talk in several languages, he saw her walk in centre park, he saw her sitting with friends giving him stolen glances, he saw her exercising and he saw her snuggling up in the evening.

'Beautiful isn't she? You should see her when she undresses,' said Inspector Hyder watching Muzzammil's reaction as the form began to undress, 'my colleague even thought she's an 89.5! I told him only in Paradise. Only in Paradise eh? Why would someone want to kill her?'

'I don't know,' said Muzzammil lowering his eyes as the Pixform was in her undergarments, 'but I don't know her.'

'Some of your friends think that you might have known her.'

'What do you mean 'might', replied Muzzammil startled, that's an ambiguous word: 'might'. Who said that I might know her?'

'Mr. Sheraz, you know that under the Civil Witness Protection Act of 2087, section 567 article 29, that any one supplying information regarding homicide.'

'Homicide!' said Muzzammil interrupting the monotonous voice of Inspector Hyder.

'Of course, Mr. Sheraz, it's homicide, rape and many other by laws and sub-penalties that has been broken in this gruesome crime. You understand why we need your help?'

'But it has nothing to do with me!' said Muzzammil raising his hands in frustration.

'Well it does because one of your friend's business card was found in the victim's room.'

'Well what a coincidence!'

'Come Mr. Sheraz you out of all people don't believe in coincidence. Contribute to making the Nation a success by eliminating sickos from our communities, a diverse, tolerant and beautiful community that adheres to all those ideals that you and I believe in, come let's find this Mansur.'

'Look Mansur and me didn't get along, I don't really know him.'

'Really? The neighbours said you guys talked all through the night.'

'The neighbours have swastikas tattooed on their arms and cheeks- why don't you go and harass them?'

'Well they are entitled to their beliefs as long as they hurt no one. Our Nation accepts them even though we disapprove, so you weren't close I take it?'

'Look, we were flatmates. If he did all his chores he would get no grief from me.'

'The neighbours say that you had many friends coming around with books and stuff- and they'd leave late'.

'That's not a crime, many of us are students.'

'But as I understand it some of these students as you call them, have control orders on them.'

'Correction monthly control orders, they have broken no law.'

'Yes, I am not implying they were. I am just thinking out aloud.'

'If it's just thinking aloud can I go?' asked Muzzammil.

'Yes yes, certainly just a few more questions, so what were they studying?'

'Usually languages.'

'You know about seven languages don't you?'

'Five.'

'It is quite interesting that these guys are learning English, it's probably to teach abroad, right?'

'I don't know.'

'I mean some of them have made the Exodus out of the safety of the Nation.'

'I don't know about Exodus.'

'Some' said Inspector Hyder leaning forward, 'were even caught crossing without a Presidential visa going to the Levant.'

Inspector Hyder was clearly enjoying his line of questioning. According to him he modelled his style on the legendary sleuth Colombo who behaved like an absent minded fool but was far from it.

'I don't know anything about that.'

Inspector Hyder noted an imperceptible jaw muscle move on his subject's face. He looked for nervous twitches and flickering of the eyes. Nothing. He would have study the recordings later. This guy knew the game, maybe even trained by experts in the business of Exodus.

'Did you know, said Hyder spitting some tobacco on the floor, 'that Mansur used to attend illegal gatherings on Fridays? He used to sermonise without a license. Why didn't he just apply for a presidential license, the Nation has the biggest mosque in the world. You prayed there haven't you? I certainly do every Friday.'

'I've walked past it Inspector, are we going to continue with this trivia or can I go?'

Muzzammil lit another cigarette; he offered one to the inspector. Inspector Hyder refused.

'Soon Mr. Sheraz, I understand it's an inconvenience but your cooperation will actually help us find the killer. You went to Masr city as well didn't you?'

'Yes. But if you're asking if I am planning to enter the Levant, the answer is no.'

'I was just checking. You withdrew a large amount of credits- we thought you were leaving that's all.'

'Business venture and holiday.'

'Great! Muslims have always been great merchants. Course you know the penalty for National Citizens if they cross over to the Levant without a Presidential decree?'

'Yes.'

Inspector Hyder got up from the chair. He walked up to the little sink in the corner of the room and washed his hands. He dried his hands and then took out a packet of Kazakhis and lit one. He knew his victim would get impatient so he took his time. With his back to the sink he inhaled the smoke and watched the broad shouldered young man with pock marks and joined up eyebrows look straight ahead as if he didn't exist. He couldn't understand why the young man was trying to undermine the Nation that united all peoples with complete disregard for creed, race and gender under its Blue banner perpetuating the glorious ideals of 24 October 1946. Was it because he was ugly? Is that why he hated the Nation?

'You know what I can't figure out?' said Inspector Hyder scratching his head, 'why would someone want to kill this beautiful young woman?'

'Maybe she knew something. Maybe she had something more than just great looks.'

'Then why would she know someone like Mansur? A nightshifter?'

'I don't know maybe he was teaching her?'

'Where is he?' he said laughing in disbelief.

'I haven't seen him for months.'

'Strange, people say you two were inseparable?'

'Who are these people?' exclaimed Muzzammil annoyed at the repetition of the question, 'It's not true. He used to come in and out of the flat, sometimes he'd disappear for days, can I go now?'

'Yes, just a few more questions' said Inspector Hyder. He sat down on the chair as if the questioning would last as long as he wanted. 'Now you're a Natural aren't you?'

'Yes' replied Muzzammil rubbing the stubble on his face self-consciously, his striking black eyes stared at Inspector Hyder's smooth hairless face.

'Do you think', said Inspector Hyder, 'that she was a freak?'

'What do you mean?' asked Muzzammil.

'You know she preferred unrefined sugar to refined sugar?'

'Does everything have to be about sex?'

'Don't be naïve Mr. Sheraz, how comes you haven't had any work done?'

'Not allowed too.'

'What do you mean?'

'It's forbidden, we don't play around with the Creation of God.'

'I know but I'm a Muslim and I get it done.'

'You can do what you like, I'm Old School Inspector.'

'But don't you think it's an outdated idea? Imagine if you have a one inch prick are you not allowed to adjust it a bit? Wouldn't it be great to possess a twelve-inch? Wouldn't you want to walk into the showers with a twelve inch dong and join the rest of us?'

'Well if you possessed a one inch piece that is a genuine medical issue. You would probably be allowed to go under the scalpel.'

'I see' Inspector Hyder making a mental note, the subject has good knowledge of religious law.

'Remember' said Muzzammil, 'It's what you do with it that counts Inspector, not how big it is.'

The inspector grinned at Muzzammil's ironic remark. In other circumstances maybe they could have been friends. Maybe they could have drunk a few beers and discussed how every historical figure had made that small step towards establishing the Brotherhood of Man. He couldn't understand why the young man rejected what every citizen, every school, every institution and brotherhood council saw as being self-evident truths? What is wrong with saving succeeding generations from the scourge of war? What is wrong in affirming faith in fundamental human rights? Establishing justice and respect for the obligations arising from treaties and other sources of international law? What is wrong with promoting social progress and better standards of life in larger freedom? Inspector Hyder could not understand why that was so problematic.

'So' said the inspector sighing, 'you are a true Muslim then?'

'No more true as you.'

'Sure- did you hear what the Embodiment was saying yesterday?'

'Yes, he was urging us to prevent the Mehdi Army from penetrating the Holy Sanctuaries.'

'Yes, don't really think he'll succeed. The President has sent ten Fighting Potemkins their way to protect the Prophet's mosque.'

'If that was all can I go? You understand I have work.'

'Sure, absolutely, let me just ask you one more question about Ms. Santos, if you didn't know her how comes we have Pix of you walking with her?'

'What are you talking about? I don't know anything about that?'

'If you want them, I have them.'

'Just exactly what are you accusing me of?'

'You sure you two weren't preparing for Exodus?'

'You are kidding me?' said Muzzammil staring at Inspector Hyder.

'I think Mr. Sheraz you are getting overly agitated. Why don't you sit yourself down' said Inspector Hyder.

'You are kidding me aren't you?' repeated Muzzammil.

'This is clouding your judgement. I think we will have to resume this interview at a later date.'

'Why?' We don't need to continue this at all.'

'For the moment I think we will put you on a weekly control order until the next interview.'

'I haven't done anything wrong! You can't do that!'

'I didn't say you did- it's standard procedure.'

'But what about my holiday?'

Inspector Hyder smiled. Game, Set and Match. The subject was going to join the Barbarian who calls himself the Saviour.'

'Well I guess you have to reschedule, please put your print here to acknowledge notification.'

'I want a Legal Senator!'

'You have waived that right Mr. Sheraz. If you want I can put you in custody until we conduct the next interview. The process will take a month but with the control order you can get along with your life.'

'I won't even be able to take a shit without you knowing about it.'

'Mr. Sheraz' said Inspector Hyder smiling, 'we knew that anyway.'

The inspector got up to leave and offered him a pack of cigarettes. Muzzammil refused.

'That's right' said Inspector Hyder, 'quit while you can Mr. Sheraz you're a poor actor. Now here's my card if you want help us, HSS has prayer rooms for Muslims who work hard to keep our Nation safe. We have discounted Hajj tours to the Holy Sanctuaries; Ramadan is catered for. Our Nation is better than anything that Barbarian in the Levant is offering. Take your time I know many Naturals like you who think you can't reconcile your ideals with this Nation but it's not true. '

'Ms. Santos? What about Ms. Santos' asked Muzzammil.

'What about her?' said Inspector Hyder smiling, 'we caught Mansur three weeks ago. He killed her because she was beautiful and he couldn't take it. He committed the most heinous crime a man could commit. You know if you work with us I can make you beautiful.'

'Is that what you think? Give me a cigarette.'

Inspector Hyder took out a Kazakhi and threw it on the table. Muzzammil lit it and dragged on it till the cherry was a red hot and then put the cigarette on his forearm so it started to sear his skin. He kept it there without a sound.

Inspector Hyder put his hands to his eyes. He couldn't watch this, his stomach turned. He could smell the cigarette smoke mingle with burning skin. Muzzammil moved the cigarette and made burn marks all over his forearm.

'Stop it' shouted Inspector Hyder, 'it's illegal. Stop it.'

Muzzammil continued.

Inspector Hyder rushed out of the room. He leaned on the wall breathing hard, he wanted to vomit. Once he caught his breath, he went in to the room next door. Richards was watching the whole scene visibly disturbed.

'What a psycho,' repeated Richards, 'what a psycho!'

Muzzammil had stopped burning himself and was staring at the business card smiling as if he knew Richards was watching.

'You are telling me he is a proper psycho' exclaimed Inspector Hyder, 'no wonder that barbarian wants his sort. Come on I need a beer.'

Richards agreed. He informed Control that they had checked out for the day. They left the subject next door for Control to deal with. They went down the hallway towards the bar. Inspector Hyder walked in silence.

Richards nudged him.

'Oi!' he said, 'what's eating you?'

'Nothing' replied Inspector Hyder.

'Come on man. I know you better than that. Spit it out.'

Inspector Hyder stopped.

'You think that psycho is right man?' asked Inspector Hyder, 'you think that maybe this isn't real?'

'What!? You too?' said Richards slapping his back. 'Are you going to listen to a barbarian who squats on his knees to take a shit and says he's going to free the oppressed?! What a joke, where are the oppressed? Where? The boy is lost and ugly I might add. We are real. We are free. We believe. They believe in nothing.'

Inspector Hyder felt reassured at Richard's contemptuous gesture.

'Come on', said Richards, 'let's go and see Martin and Rosa sing. Martin's not a bad looker but you know what the miracle is about Rosa?'

'No' replied Inspector Hyder.

'She's had four kids sucking at her nipples and you know what? She still manages to stay a 76.5 consistently day in, day out. I don't know how she keeps those boobs up there man!'

'Yes' said Inspector Hyder laughing, 'but there's nothing there. Nothing'.

For a moment they burst out in laughter; both pretended to be Rosa, singing, dancing, holding their imaginary boobs and running their hands down their bodies the way she did when she sang.

'You are right' said Richards, 'there is nothing there, you know she is 75?'

Inspector Hyder was struck by the nothingness of Rosa boobs. He became pensive and watched Richards' perfectly smooth face. It had no wrinkles, no sign of stubble, not a single eyebrow out of place. His teeth were white like the moon and his suit always seemed new.

'You know what?' said inspector Hyder, 'tomorrow we got Mansur to play with in the morgue best get an early start. He's gonna be an ugly feller after what those eels did to his face in the Thames. I'm going to have an early night.'

Richards didn't like it and tried to convince him to stay but it was no use.

'Make sure you debrief with Trauma. It's not every day you see a man burn his forearm.'

Inspector Hyder dismissed the idea with a wave. Richards continued on towards the bar to meet the rest of the gang. He was looking forward to watching Rosa and that spunky singer Martin performing their jazz duets.

REVIEWS

FOUND IN TRANSLATION

Samia Rahman

Come in, come in. Please, esteemed guest, kindly take off your shoes. If you wish you may recline on the *charpoy*. Are you comfortable? Can I bring you a glass of hot sweet *chai*? This heat is insufferable, no? Perhaps cool water instead? Or a hand fan? Perhaps you would like to meet the local Maulvi for some spiritual comfort? Or see a show from the village juggler?

The voices from Ali Akbar Natiq's collection of Urdu short stories permeate my subconscious. I am not here; I am there, immersed in an unfamiliar world I should recognise. Every story has left an imprint in my mind, his narrative leaping from the page and transporting me to rural Pakistan. The intermingling of fantasy and reality unravel in simple tales that bequeath a dark underbelly of contradiction and injustice. The themes are heavy: superstition, oppressive customs and tradition, religious bigotry, social hierarchy – a bitter and sarcastic pill in the guise of unadorned stories. These can be superficially devoured in quick succession and enjoyed for their macabre humour. But reflect on them and you will realise that Natiq is articulating the deeply troubling nature of the times we live in. His is a world of desolate universal emotion. It is no coincidence that these feelings encapsulate the media imagery informing our perception of rural Punjab for it is in this region that we enter the abode of his mind and locate his tales.

Natiq's stories, traversing the mundane to the remarkable, emerge from his own extraordinary life. There is nothing in his background that helped pave the way for a career as an Urdu writer and poet, who is now considered to be one of brightest stars of Urdu literature. He was born in a village that does not even have a name but is labelled with a number: '32-2L, District Okara'. Following his father, he became a mason, specialising in domes and minarets. But a mason's life in a land utterly unable to extricate itself from the binds of nepotism and rigid social hierarchy is harsh and brutal. Unable to feed his family, Natiq migrated to Saudi Arabia to work as a labourer; and like most labourers in the Kingdom faced hunger, homelessness, indignity and humiliation. He started writing after returning to Pakistan publishing a collection of short stories, *Qaeem Deen*, two volumes of poetry, and gracing the pages of *Granta*.

While Natiq's background is remarkable it is not unusual in Urdu literature. The late great Urdu poet, Ehsan Danish (1914-1982), also spent much of his early life working on building sites. His poetry reflected his love of fellow labourers; and he came to be known as *Shair-e-Mazdur* – poet of the labourers. Natiq's stories too have a distinguished pedigree. The landscape, the shimmering hate and shame, the sudden turn of violence are all familiar from the unforgettable tales of Saadat Hasan Manto (1912-1955) and Munshi Premchand (1880-1936).

Ali Akbar Natiq, *What Will You Give For This Beauty?* Penguin India, Haryana, 2015.

What Will You Give For This Beauty? is translated by the writer Ali Madeeh Hashmi, who also happens to be the grandson of celebrated Urdu poet Faiz Ahmed Faiz (1911-1984). It is to Hashmi's credit that he asserts Natiq's autonomy in the finished project. As he explains in his translator's note, 'a legitimate caution one must observe while translating the written word is to curtail the tendency to enhance the translation into a "transcreation", to embellish and exaggerate the translation in order to "improve" the original'. In a nod to the cultural rootedness of Natiq's tales, Hashmi describes the author's use of language as 'raw'. It is faithful to the communities it depicts. His words convey realities, which convey truths. For Hashmi, it is vital that nothing is lost in translation.

Natiq mines his life for his stories, drawing on the harsh poverty of his first three decades. His gift lies in sketching characters that stubbornly refuse to serve up a neat hypothesis on the state of Pakistan's political and religious quagmire. He is a keen observer of the humdrum detail of the everyday, carrying us effortlessly along as he stitches a patchwork of simplicity that forms a misshapen whole. This fulminates in the creation of characters that defy any stealth of design, invoking disgust and sympathy in equal measure as in the case of the protagonist of 'A Male Child', the unwashed, embittered barber, Sharfu 'Timepiece', who despises the children whose heads he shaves. Here the tale's conclusion leaves the reader contemplating his or her own connivance in the enjoyment of a man's torment. Natiq beckons us forth until we are forced to confront our own ugly (in)humanity. This is characteristic of most of the stories in this collection – the mood can easily turn on the reader and leave him or her at a questioning loss. The anti-hero of 'Jodhpur's End' astounds the reader's expectations and subverts the narrative to reveal man's cruelty to man. The scheming and calculating individuals leave the hapless dimwit Ghafoora at the mercy of the powerful Haji Sharif, with the entire village complicit in the cruelty. It is poignant that the *haji*, named for his religious piety due to having completed the pilgrimage to Mecca, is ruthlessly self-interested. The corrupting nature of power is a prevalent theme, as is the manner in which people are defined by the circumstances of their birth and their place in the social order. The strength of social convention cannot be underestimated, and has the power to condemn individuals and families to a life of humiliation and drudgery with no possibility for redemption. Natiq, however, does offer redemption to the misfits and the marginalised albeit, in Ghafoora's case, a violent and brutal redemption. The Robin Hood-esque thief in 'Qaim Deen' is awarded no such triumph. Instead, a devastating sequence of events leads to insanity and isolation and an unconfirmed yet highly probable grisly fate.

The tragedy of Pakistan has been endlessly analysed in numerous books, non-fiction and fiction, academic and popular. But Natiq's exploration and analysis of rural Punjab, with its emphasis on pain, satire and subtlety, is in a different class. Dreadful consequences await those who slavishly bend to the status quo whether it is tribal allegiances, irreproachable religious authority and dogma or superstition. His tales can be loosely regarded as a lament of the masses who blindly follow the directives of power-crazed *sahibs* or *pirs*. In 'The Maulvi's Miracle', for example, the esteemed cleric is a thoroughly despicable figure with a volatile temper and a penchant for maledictions. His curses always come true, whether as a result of Godly assistance or orders carried out by his followers. Conversely his prayers imploring divine blessings are never realised:

in fact they often showed results to the contrary. After *fajr* prayers one morning, Rana Farooq requested Maulvi sahib to say a prayer for his father's health. Rana Farooq was a wealthy man and the Maulvi led a prayer so humble and obsequious, it lasted a half-hour. No sooner had the prayer ended than Rana sahib's younger brother brought the news of their father's death. Similarly, the villagers had once requested Maulvi sahib to pray for rain. This resulted in such a drought that people cried in agony.

Yet, the villagers continue to regard the Maulvi in high esteem, without raising even an iota of doubt. 'This was due to the fact that, at least superficially, the majority of people thought about things in the same way as the Maulvi'. The Maulvi's downfall comes in the shape of a dog; he finds himself locked in a room with the unclean creature, tries to wrestle with it, and ends up biting and bitten. The reverence he is accorded disintegrates and the people of the village finally see him for the fraud he is.

Other stories also relate brutal falls from grace, as in the case of Achoo the acrobat who is remembered by his school friend as having great potential but who finally succumbs to the limitations of life that someone of his background is taught to expect. Then there is also the violent empowerment of Noora, the wretched son of a prostitute who submits to unrelenting and intense provocation throughout his life until one day he simply snaps.

The anthology closes with a powerful fable. 'A Mason's Hand' is a universal tale of cruel betrayal, suffering and shattered dreams. The story mirrors Natiq's own experiences as a skilled labourer in Saudi Arabia. Asghar goes to Saudi Arabia to look for work against the advice of his father: 'There is nothing but humiliation in those Arab places'. At every turn, he is degraded, despised and cheated by the locals and fellow ex-patriots who he thought would come to his aid. He ends up stealing a pair of shoes from a mosque and is given the standard punishment: he has his hands chopped off. Natiq conveys the horrific abuses almost in a matter of fact way, without descending into hyperbole. The story is stiflingly bleak yet loses none of the simplicity of style that is found throughout the collection. It is a fitting, almost-biographical, end to a terrifying, amusing and unsettling sojourn.

OLD JUICE IN NEW CARTONS

Ramazan Kılınç

The phrase 'New Turkey' has gained wide currency in Turkish politics and media. The Justice and Development Party (AKP) leadership and supporters use the phrase to describe the transition from 'secularist' Turkey to the one in which Islam plays a larger role in national identity, politics, and foreign policy. The opponents of AKP use the term to describe its recent authoritarian moves based on social polarisation and discrimination, decreasing transparency, weakening rule of law, increasing corruption, and fading press freedoms. The critics accuse the AKP of using religion opportunistically to justify its competitive authoritarianism that gained momentum during the last few years. The recent political contestation point to deeper debates on what a Turkish nation is and should be, and has implications for political institutions and their transformation. A careful examination of the political discourses and institutions of 'Kemalist Turkey' and 'New Turkey' reveals a common theme: both projects imagine a state that would impose a vision of homogenous nation in which pluralism is considered as a threat to the state and nation. The political discourses and institutions that constituted the basis of this shared vision are critically analysed in Behlül Özkan's *From the Adobe of Islam to the Turkish Vatan* and Ahmet T. Kuru and Alfred Stepan's edited volume, *Democracy, Islam, and Secularism in Turkey*. While Özkan traces the evolution of the idea of homeland and territorial national identity in Turkey, Kuru and Stepan analyse the historical roots, functioning, and transformation of the political institutions through which the state homogenises the nation.

Behlül Özkan, *From the Adobe of Islam to the Turkish Vatan: The Making of a National Homeland in Turkey*, Yale University Press, New Haven, CT., 2012

Ahmet T. Kuru and Alfred Stepan, editors, *Democracy, Islam, and Secularism in Turkey*, Columbia University Press, New York, 2012

Özkan provides a richly documented analysis of how the idea of 'homeland' evolved, changed over the last two centuries, and transformed from a conception of religious-based society in Ottoman Empire to an understanding of nation-state in modern Turkey. He analyses the construction of a modern national-territorial consciousness through various geographical imaginations that led to the creation of a meaningful link between territorial space and national identity at various epochs of Turkish political history. He shows how the idea of Islamic community in the classical age of the Ottoman empire first transformed to an imperial discourse of homeland based on territoriality in the late Ottoman era, and then to a nationalist discourse under the Young Turks rule, and finally to a secular nationalist idea of homeland under the Turkish Republic. However, Özkan's study is not simply a discursive analysis of the idea of homeland; he develops a very dynamic discussion by looking at how the idea of homeland has been utilised in the debates on politics, nationalism and foreign policy. In doing so, he relies on a variety of primary sources such as archives, textbooks, newspapers, and maps.

Özkan argues that, after the French revolution, the Ottoman elite conceptualised the imperial homeland as territorial space for multiple religious and ethnic identities. However, political events transformed the thinking of the Ottoman ruling and oppositional elite during the last fifteen years of the empire. He documents oscillation between Islamism, Ottomanism and Turkism among the elites and demonstrates how the Ottoman defeats in the Balkan War and World War I led to the abandonment of its original ideas and its replacement with the notion of a homogenous Turkish nation. The nationalist vision was pursued through education in early Republican Turkey; the national shift is documented through comparison of education, particularly geography textbooks, before and after 1923. Foreign policy was also used to provide legitimacy to this notion – from defending the homeland from European imperialism in the early Republican period, facing the Soviet and Communist threat in late 1930s and 1940s, involvement in the Korean War in the early 1950s, defending the rights of Turkish Cypriots in the 1960s and 1970s, to using Cyprus as a negotiation item in Turkey's membership of the European Union in the 2000s. Foreign policy also served as an instrument for silencing domestic critics.

Özkan's book is a significant contribution; it sheds light on key debates in contemporary Turkey such as the Kurdish Question, issues related to Alevis and non-Muslim minorities, neo-Ottomanism, and the rise of Islamism in domestic and foreign affairs. By discussing the ways in which the state constructed territorial nationality at different political epochs in Turkish history, the book offers great insights into the struggles for the soul of Turkey today. The book's strength is its empirical richness based on primary and secondary sources, its balance of political theory and comparative politics, and Özkan's exploration of social and political context of each period. The background history is explained without sacrificing the theoretical and philosophical depth of his analysis.

One minor shortcoming: Özkan does not examine the recent developments in the Kurdish Question or the rise of Islamism and its influence on the discourses on territorial nationality in depth. He discusses how the early Republican elite gradually embraced a discriminatory rhetoric against the Kurds, but he could have examined the transformation after the 1980 coup when the Kurdish question entered a new stage after the Kurdistan Workers Party, formed in the mid-1980s, employed terrorism as an instrument to defend Kurdish interests. Similarly, after AKP came to power, Islamism might have offered a strong challenge to territorial nationalism. Incorporating the new debates into the general framework of the book could have enriched the analysis.

In their edited volume, *Democracy, Islam, and Secularism in Turkey*, Ahmet Kuru and Alfred Stepan bring leading political scientists, sociologists, and historians together to examine the consequences of the construction and development of the idea of homeland and territorial nationalism in Turkey. The nationalist identity is unpacked in its relationship with Islam, secularism and democracy through historical and comparative analyses. The book examines the roots of Kemalism, its social and political consequences, its impact on institutions of state and society, particularly secularism, the military and semi-authoritarian institutions of representation and governance. A two-dimensional methodology is employed. On the one hand, the historical context is explored through continuity and change from the Ottoman Empire to modern Turkey. This makes the unique aspects of the Turkish case more visible. On the other hand, a forum is provided for the readers to put Turkey into a global context through comparisons with France, Senegal and the Christian democratic experience in Europe.

Karen Barkey and Şükrü Hanioğlu provide historical accounts of the relationship between state and society relations in modern Turkey. Barkey examines the nature and development of the Ottoman state's management of diversity, particularly its relationship with non-Muslim religious minorities and concludes that the Ottoman tolerance can be utilised in challenging the nationalist conception of modern citizenship in Turkey. Barkey is critical of AKP's handling of pluralism, particularly its relationship with Alevis and non-Muslims. Hanioğlu studies the historical roots of Kemalism by focusing on the three main principles of the ideology: secularism, Westernisation and nationalism. He concludes that Kemalists offered a singular concept of modernity that is based on a vision of a homogenous society and state-centred social and political development.

The institutional consequences of Kemalist singular modernity are well analysed by Ergun Özbudun and Ümit Cizre. Özbudun, who has two chapters in the book, first highlights the contradictions between the Kemalist state's vision of a homogenous society and the empirical reality of the pluralist Turkish society; then he shows how the incompatibility between the state vision and social reality is reflected in the decisions of the Turkish Constitutional Court that were used to legally impose these ideals on society. Cizre examines the changing strategies of the Turkish military to keep its influence over politics especially after its weakened position in recent years. She argues that the military adapted to the new conditions that prioritise society over the state, and moved towards establishing coalitions with social actors instead of pursuing an exclusively state-centred approach.

Ahmet T. Kuru, Alfred Stepan, and Stathis N. Kalyvas compare Turkey with other experiences of secularism and religious mobilisation. Kuru and Stepan, in their co-authored chapter, compare Turkish secularism with its French and Senegalese counterparts by using the categories of passive and assertive secularisms, developed by Kuru in his previous work, as well as similar categories Stepan developed in his previous analysis of Senegal, Indonesia, and India. They find that Turkish secularism is assertive, excluding religion from the public sphere; Senegalese secularism is passive, developing cooperation with religion and incorporating it in the public sphere; and French secularism is in between. Stathis Kalyvas compares 'the Turkish model', which is 'based on the combination of moderate Islamism, liberal reforms, and democratic consolidation', with Christian democratic experience. He finds common ground between the Turkish model and the experience of Christian democracy that emerged as an outcome of Catholic mobilisation within liberalising and democratising Europe. Though it is not a comparative analysis, Joost Lagendijk's essay also makes similar points in its examination of Turkish politics in the context of the European Union. Lagendijk, a journalist and a former Dutch politician, evaluates how Turkey's relationship with the European Union under the AKP, during the 2000s, led to initial reforms of institutions but the party's limitations meant that they could not be expanded further.

Kuru and Stepan's volume offers strong analytical and critical insights for understanding contemporary Turkish politics as well as broader debates on secularism and democratisation. It is well-crafted, provides excellent historical and comparative perspectives on the relationship between Islam and Secularism, and speaks to a wider audience.

But Kuru and Stepan are also somewhat muted on the Kurdish issue. They may argue that they have given less emphasis to this issue because the book's major focus is secularism and democracy. However, many issues of identity that are relevant for secularism are also relevant for the Kurdish Question as a singular modernisation project, analysed so well by Hanioğlu, is at the root of both. Similarly, Barkey addresses the issues around the discrimination of Alevis in her chapter briefly, but a full chapter on the Alvis could have added to the value of the volume.

The scholarly engagement on identity issues requires going beyond static and binary distinctions, and needs a nuanced analysis that does justice to varying political discourses, dynamic relationships that political actors establish in domestic and international settings, and multiple religious and nationalist (re)interpretations that the actors conduct to meet the social and political challenges. Both books do an excellent job in providing nuanced and contextualised analysis of Turkish politics with historical and comparative depth. While Özkan shows how territorial nationalism gradually excluded religious and ethnic differences and prioritised a homogenous vision for national identity, Kuru and Stepan's volume charts the historical evolution of singular modernity and its consequences for social and political institutions in Turkey.

Since the publication of the books in 2012, Turkey has turned toward more authoritarian governance and experienced significant transformations. Although the state evolved toward pluralism in the first decade of the 2000s, the state-centric singular understanding of modernity won over pluralist alternatives, and has emerged in different clothing during the last few years. Although the books do not cover the recent developments, they still offer significant insights into current debates in Turkey. The only caveat is the optimism of Kuru and Stepan, which is understandable given the time the book was published. Given the fact that the Turkish government continues to use Kemalist institutions to justify its own policies and demonise the opposition the outlook is less than positive.

The AKP government harks back to the Ottoman Empire, but this nostalgia has not produced tolerance toward ethnic and religious minorities as discussed by Barkey. Rather, by creating social polarisation, the public debates on the Ottoman legacy are being used to impose a monolithic vision of a homogenous nation. The AKP government shares the Kemalist ideal of homogeneity and singular modernity in a new form. The state-centric institutions of the 1980 coup, a manifestation of the Kemalist state vision, are still in operation. Although the government initiated a new reform process for the resolution of the Kurdish Question, its authoritarian and non-pluralist approach prevented the emergence of a more inclusive national identity discourse that could have facilitated the process.

The historical and institutional background explored in these books tells us why both Kemalism and Islamism are incapable of creating pluralist, inclusive citizenship and society.

ET CETERA

ON TURKISH DELIGHT

Merryl Wyn Davies

Sweet! Never was there a confection more sugar saturated nor so gluey gummy. Chocolate perfume it has been called, and not by way of any compliment. This small square of chocolate coated scented jelly is remembered in the mind's eye in ways that far transcend anything to do with its taste. It is not its distinctive place on shop counter displays among the veritable cornucopia of different brands available to tempt a nation's sweet tooth that whets the sense of nostalgia. It is not the incomparable taste, definitely not – did anyone ever eat a second bar? No, Fry's Turkish Delight lives in the memory of generations for the advertising slogan it generated that still trips faultlessly off the tongue: 'full of eastern promise'!

To those of a certain age the mere mention of Fry's Turkish Delight comes with wafts of haunting music that conjure images of desert dunes, sheikhs and obligatory diaphanously clad maidens. However it was that Fry's arrived at the recipe for their inimitable chocolate bar, their advertising department most certainly imbibed the entire history of Orientalist phantasmagoria and indelibly imprinted all its jumbled ambiguities into the consciousness of new generations.

This was and is no innocent confection. The eastern promise that fills this Turkish Delight may appear located among sand dunes or palm fringed oasis but truthfully its delights can all be traced to the Grand Saray of Istanbul. The Topkapi Palace, *Topkapisaray*, founded in 1465 as the primary residence for the Ottoman sultans has garnered, re-inscribed and became a generic hub for the ongoing legacy of Europe's Orientalist imagination. The Topkapi stands on Seraglio Point, and one might say that is precisely the point. The term *seraglio* is a complex of ideas that sprawls more expansively and resonates more evocatively than the reality of any piece of earth. Fry's slogan and adverts exploit the sprawling complex of ideas associated within the bounds of Seraglio Point.

What is advertising if not the condensation of cultural literacy, the semiotic art form par excellence? Advertising relies upon signs, symbols and the ideas they generate, ideas so embedded in common acceptance, so well-known they are instantly recognisable, instantly available to communicate just the meaning the company wishes to convey, just the stimulation needed to make a product distinctive and desirable. Not just a chocolate bar, Fry's Turkish Delight is an exotic indulgence because it stimulates an allure that has titillated European curiosity down the centuries. The advertising explains why it is both Turkish and a delight. If the imagery seems to travel far from the reality of Istanbul, the city by the sea, the connections are taken as read and understood.

Fry's chocolate coated bar is far removed from *rahat lokum*, the classic Turkish confection that is a gel of sugar and starch flavoured with rose water, mastic, Bergamot orange, lemon, cinnamon or mint and encasing chopped dates or pistachio or other nuts. Its name derives from the Arabic *rahat al hulkum*, meaning throat comfort. The sweet itself is said to have been invented by one Bekir Effendi who set up shop in Istanbul in 1777 and became confectioner to the Sultan. He became the eponymous founder of Haci Bekir, the company which still operates in Istanbul producing the sweets.

In contrast, Fry's Turkish Delight could be described as the outcome of some loose mistaken association with the actual original product. Something similar but much older applies to the imagery used in the adverts that popularised the British confection. In *Harems of the Mind*, Ruth Bernard Yeazell argues that the Turco-Persian word for palace, *saray* was mistakenly associated with the Italian word *serrare*, meaning to lock up or enclose. It was used to signify the women's apartments within the Grand Saray, the locus of the harem a place closed to and guarded from prying eyes. The Italian word generated the English 'seraglio' and the French 'serail' and all came to mean not merely buildings that housed women but a nexus of social customs concerning

Muslim gender relations and ultimately the women themselves. Yeazell' makes it abundantly clear how seraglios have fascinated, indeed obsessed the European mind and has become central to conceptions of the generic condition of that most mysterious of all creatures – Muslim womanhood.

Fry's adverts toyed with all aspects of the inheritance of the Orientalist imagination. In the 1960s the ad was set in a desert oasis. A woman dressed in the regulation outfit associated with belly dancers and inmates of the seraglio, harem pants and top with a long diaphanous veil attached to her headdress, emerges from a tent and grasps a tray opulently overflowing with jewels upon which sits a bar of Turkish Delight in its distinctive wrapping. Furtively she runs through the camp nervously looking over her shoulder as she searches out her objective: the suitably luxurious tent of an appropriately turbaned and robed sheikh to deliver this exotic offering. Is this woman fearful of prying eyes seeing what should be hidden from all except her master? Does she carry off illicit riches to pleasure her master as the voiceover states – 'exotic, delicious; full of eastern promise'?

Just a moment. This is all a little confusing. Who exactly is the target market here? Are men such notorious consumers of scented chocolate that straightforward titillation is sufficient lure to sell this product? Or is the more embedded message that the frisson of being a sex slave, of serving the pleasure of a potent powerful man is every woman's heart's desire? Answers within the foil wrapper no doubt.

By the 1970's the advert had morphed. In this incarnation a woman sits within her tent. She is clad in black, lightweight Muslim cloth draped decorously over body and head. Enigmatically her ringed fingers lift a chocolate morsel to her lips. This woman actually eats a Fry's Turkish Delight as, we are told, 'a rich red secret, a rare eastern essence.' Outside the tent two men fight, an exaggerated balletic wrestling match. The winner, golden and glistening, emerges from the contest and makes his way to the woman's tent where she opens an opulent casket to reveal 'a long luxurious taste of the east' in the shape of a Turkish Delight which is of course 'full of eastern promise.'

The 70s may have been wordier but let us stop and reconsider. This may have been the era of women's lib and true the woman gets to eat the confection but, thereby, is she ingesting and thus becoming the essence of eastern promise? In which case has she been empowered to consume herself in seclusion while awaiting the fulfilment of the arrival of a hero worthy of her allure? I hardly think Germaine Greer would approve.

By the 1980s we have reached an even lusher embodiment of the desert setting. The sinuous sensuality of idealised sand dunes transform into a women with exotic hair and characteristic diaphanous attire who, to the haunting refrain of musical accompaniment, sheds a single silent tear. Bounding though the sand dunes comes the very embodiment of an ardent sheikh. He caresses a mound of sand which morphs into another woman again suitably attired. He bends to share his breath with what appears to be a third woman. Cut to something nestled in silk. Is this object nestled in the sensuous curves of a woman's silk clad thigh or resting on a silken handkerchief strewn on the desert? The man reaches to grasp the Fry's Turkish Delight from its purple silken resting place, whatever that be. A snake slithers across the sand towards the man. The sheikh raises a silver scimitar and strikes. We see a Fry's Turkish Delight cleaved to reveal its rich red interior. The only words, spoken in the drippling dulcet tones of voice-over actors Anthony Valentine or John Carson – voices of liquid opulence, or money, as they were known – tell us the scene is 'full of eastern promise.'

So let me try to get this clear in my mind. Women are the very essence of the desert? Sensual indeed but barren and neglected until awoken by the caress of a man? How post women's lib is that? And what's with the snake, or should that be serpent – the enduring symbol of temptation – and what is all that sword play suggesting? Well, modesty forefends that I suggest the associations of the sudden thrust that reveals 'the rich red secret' within so full of eastern promise.

The Orientalist lexicon begins with the seminal idea of sexual licence and libidinous behaviour as an essential characteristic of Muslim religion and society. The tortured denial of sensual temporal pleasures was inherent in Western Christian thought from its inception. Little wonder then that the Fathers of the Church who vaunted the moral superiority of celibacy allowing the rest of fallen sinful humanity only the monogamous procreative indulgence of marriage recoiled at reports of the multiply married Prophet Muhammad and the supposed Qur'anic permission for Muslims to take up to four wives. The inversion of Christian norms is prominent in the account of John of Damascus (c. 676–749 or 54 AD), the Christian saint brought up at the heart of Umayyad administration in the time of Yazid I. Last of the Church Fathers St John of Damascus' work, *Concerning Heresy*, canonical for both the Roman and Eastern Orthodox churches, saw Islam as Christological heresy, number 101 of that ilk by his tally.

Prurient obsession with sexual arrangements may be foundational to Western interest in Muslim society but its encapsulation in the harem and the idea of the seraglio gathers force from growing interest in the inner life of the Ottoman Empire. The growing power of the Ottomans and their threatening encroachment on Europe was a pressing 'terror of the world' in the words of the English statesman and philosopher scientist Francis Bacon (1561–1626). This father of empiricism expressed the common dread of the Ottomans which reached its high watermark in 1529 when the forces of Suleiman the Magnificent reached the gates of Vienna. Fear demonised but by the time another Ottoman surge was defeated at the Battle of Vienna in 1683 the balance of power had decisively shifted. The global expansion of European interests in this period was accompanied by the perception of the waning power of the east. The Ottomans along with other eastern potentates were seen as stultified in superstition hidebound by tradition, slaves to their past while the West embodied the march of progress. Curiosity, the urge to know and understand the quaint and exotic differences that characterised the rich lands of the Orient Europe desired and sought to dominate and control came to the fore as erstwhile fear was transmuted into recoils of horror at the barbarism, despotism and violence the east could visit upon itself.

In medieval times the east had been the subject of Books of Wonder, a far distant place of marvels. This was an especially potent idea derived from centrality of the Holy Land in Western consciousness. The land where miracles had happened was the gateway that influenced all ideas of what existed in the unknown fabled east. By the late seventeenth century the east was visited and reported in increasing numbers of traveller's tales that sought to demystify the little known inner life of the region and peoples with their eye witness accounts. In 1678 the French traveller

Jean Baptiste Tavernier published his *Nouvelle Relation* offering a detailed portrait of the seat of Ottoman power located in the Grand Saray of Istanbul. He observed: 'I am writing a chapter on the women's quarters only to persuade the reader of the impossibility of really knowing them.' As Ruth Bernard Yeazell notes, 'if distant places and peoples have always tempted human beings to fantastic projections of their own wishes and fears, then the blank space of the harem, sealed by definition from the eyes of Western men, only magnified the temptation.' Of the secrets of the harem Tavernier could only say: 'Unless one wishes to compose a fiction it is difficult to talk about them.' And of course he was right, that's exactly what everyone did.

The seraglio/harem entered the annals of Western culture as ethnography and essential topic that had to be included in poetry, plays, operas, visual arts and pornography. The *haremlik* within the Topkapi was reputedly home to some 400 women. When contact with reality was precluded the identity, life and status of these 'birds in gilded cages' had to be constructed on their behalf. What could not be known could be embroidered effortlessly with evocative details borrowed from the *Arabian Nights*. Antoine Galland, the first to translate the Arabic tales of *Thousand and One Nights* for European readers, became secretary to the French Ambassador in Istanbul in 1670. His 12 volume French version *Les mille et une nuits* published from 1704 through 1717 was swiftly retranslated into various European languages and quickly established itself as a most serviceable utility for the fictions of the Western imagination. So central was Ottoman power to the control of Muslim lands most proximate and known to Europe that the interest in and cluster of ideas gathered around the Grand Seraglio became the basis for all understanding of the customary practice and mores of Muslim life everywhere. Old ideas found new outlets in the profusion of diverse and divergent interpretations each of which, no matter how much a figment of the imagination vied to claim learned authority. Footnoted poems and plays citing scholarly sources as warrant for their elaborate detail were common. In the profusion of representations all the confusion of licentious abandon, allure, sexual indulgence jostled with sex slavery, intrigue, jealousy and despotic domination with overtones of barbaric brutality in the frustrated desire that festered in the European imagination.

There is no single consensual narrative of Orientalism. A welter of ideas twist, turn and morph into contradictory formulations. True the confusion of ideas are always compliant to the control and desire of Western observation but that does not mean a coherent monolith of detail. The fascination with Muslim womanhood is consistent as in many ways is what its portrayal represents yet the representations of different eras can be diametrically opposite. In medieval European *chanson de geste* literature set in the context of the Crusades, for example, Muslim women far from being submissive alluring coquettes were usually portrayed as sharp tongued termagants, shrews who gave their enfeebled men folk no end of grief for their lack of resolve and success. These women were inversions of ideal European moral tropes and the best thing for them was to be carried off by Christian knights, married, converted and thus acquire the silent invisibility appropriate to proper womanhood – which was their formulaic fate in the chanson genre.

When the Ottoman seraglio became the type site of Western interest the exotic, opulent abundance of male opportunity, wives and concubines galore, fed the imagination with a different kind of inversion of moral norms. Behind the veil of seclusion which so effectively excluded direct access therefore must be contained the protean sexual potency of Muslim women, a force that must be controlled, dominated, and made submissive to male power. What could modesty have to do with it?

When European women became travellers in eastern lands they could legitimately lay claim to access to the seraglio impossible for their male counterparts. However, superior opportunity did not bring a coherent alternative portrait. Indeed, many women writers merely sought to demystify the harem by explaining the comforts and little freedoms that came with confinement and a life of lassitude within the walls of constraint. The contrary mode emphasised by other women writers portrayed the demeaning condition akin to slavery that trapped even free inhabitants of the harem. It was an expression of indignation that did no more than rearrange the priority of element in the extant conventions of description.

What best defines Orientalism is not so much its monolithic consensus but the confusion of its tropes and the facility it affords for infinite variety deployed to the same end. The confusion can endlessly be rearranged to support the thesis of the incomprehensibility of the Other based on whichever inversion of Western norms and expectations best fit the argument being made. Difference is the key and necessitate that 'them' are separated from 'us'. Only by acquiring and becoming like 'us' can the Other ever truly be known – which is as much the philosophy of modern development programmes as the moral of medieval chanson literature. Plus ça change...

The Orient that is the Muslim World has been dreamed and imagined so often with such consistent themes that their inherent confusion is the accepted norm. What its variant representations are telling Western audiences are reflections not of a reality that is 'out there' but the character of their own cultural imagination. Nothing better exemplifies the longevity of the old and familiar of Western imagining than their recycling in Fry's ads for Turkish Delight. All the exoticism and allure is the fulfilment not of eastern promise but Western desiring. As with so many previous incarnations of Orientalist lore the model for Fry's ad was nothing real and distant but cinema's most famous exploitation of the east. The adverts visually reference and draw on the cultural memory of *The Shiekh*, the 1921 film that made Rudolf Valentino a global megastar of the silent screen.

The drama of the *The Shiekh* is set in train when an adventurous female traveller, Lady Diana, determines to learn for herself about the 'ancient custom' of a strange land that has 'a marriage market where wives are bought by wealthy men.' To gain access to what 'is closed to all except Arabs' she steals the costume of a dancing girl and enters a 'casino' where 'Brides are won on the turn of the wheel.' Inevitably Lady Diana lands in trouble, carried off in the teeth of a sandstorm to his opulent desert tent by Sheikh Ahmed Ben Hassan, played by Rudolph Valentino, who asserts: 'when an Arab sees a woman he wants he takes her'.

Lady Diana, resists the brooding passionate attentions even of Valentino and attempts suicide rather than submit. When the Sheikh is reproached for his lamentable want of etiquette Lady Diana is to be returned to home and family only for her to be kidnapped again, this time by a villainous sheikh, Omair [sic] and his 'barbarous' bandits. At which point Valentino's Sheikh rescues the damsel in distress which should be cue for a romantic climax. The trouble was in 1921 miscegenation, romantic let alone sexual relations across racial lines was strictly forbidden in Hollywood lest it outrage the sensibilities of segregationist American audiences. On the other hand, the film makers could not permit all the pulsating sexual tensions aroused by Valentino, once called 'catnip for women', to be wasted and thus disappoint the hordes of swooning ladies he was drawing to cinemas. The film became the first to use the ingenious device that exposes the true nature of the Orientalist project. At the eleventh hour Sheikh Ahmed Ben Hassan is revealed to be Viscount Caryll, Earl of Glencaryll, a true Englishman orphaned and raised in the desert by a friendly sheikh, educated in Paris before returning to the desert to succeed his foster father. All dreams of Orient begin and when necessitated by circumstance end at home ever serviceable to the needs and exigencies of Western desire and determination. What should an Englishman be but the most desirable of desert sheikhs? What more fitting outcome for a venturesome English Lady than to be wooed by an English earl? Western wish fulfilment is the metier of the Western imagination, a fictive environment more closed, confined and enduring than ever was harem or seraglio that might ever have existed in any real time or place.

Fry's Turkish Delight is anything but Turkish. It is an appropriation, over sweet, cloying designed to adhere, possibly immovably to the interior of eager consumers. Overladen with the narcotic power of that devil's juice, sugar, the product so basic to the expansive project of Western empire and its overwriting and reimagining of distant lands. The problem - for problem it surely is - is that like sugar on teeth enamel the legacy of Orientalist imagination is so long lasting in its effects that it corrodes the contemporary ability to hold informed dialogues, indeed polylogues of mutual respect and understanding. The noise of errant old familiar fictive ideas construct false baselines for debate. Muslim women, Muslims in general, find themselves faced with the need to answer for and against things that never were nor ever took the form, scale and meaning ascribed them. The detritus of old imaginings resists revisionary learning – myth and legend remain more companionable. The urgent needs of an all too real world smothered in a chocolate coating that is not sweet and has no promise eastern or otherwise.

I am forever glad that I don't eat chocolate or sweets.

TURKEY'S TOP TEN ENCHANTMENTS

Being in Turkey can make people imagine that they are at the midpoint of the world, and in many ways there is no other place on earth that provides such a sense of being centred. Turkey is the proverbial bridge of civilisations: a place affected by almost every major Empire, at one point or another, whether in retreat or expansion. It was not just the nucleus of the Ottoman Empire for over six hundred years, but also the centre of the Eastern Christian Empire for a thousand years. It is the junction, highway and intersecting point between numerous, diverse cultures that have shaped and moulded what Turkey is today.

The Ottoman Empire encompassed a huge landmass during its pinnacle, containing many different ethnicities. At its peak in the sixteenth century, it extended from Basra to Vienna and for a considerable time challenged Europe's hegemony. One of its main legacies was the great diversity of the people who lived under the empire including millions of Christians and Jews who were shown greater tolerance than their co-religionists experienced in Europe. Art, science and culture flourished as the Ottomans absorbed cultural traditions from conquered empires into new intercultural forms.

The modern Turkish Republic reduced its borders, but within them remains a tremendous diversity of people whose differences in language, heritage, religion, cultural traditions and historical memory linger. Some of these diversities are suspended within a profound sense of nationalism that has become the Turkish political statement to many outside of the country. In Istanbul, there is often the homogenisation of the Eastern and the Western, but in other parts of the country these ethnic linguistic and cultural differences are unreservedly noticeable, and wholly fascinating to the discerning observer. Every Turk is a proud Turk whether they are

Islamist or secular, Conservative or Liberal, leftist or rightist, pro-European or anti-European – leading to all sorts of deeply held ideological perspectives that do not always yield or transform in the light of social exchange and interaction. Rather, the tendencies are for polarities to remain acutely embedded in the political, religious and cultural sphere. At times of national crisis, for example in the case of the 2013 Gezi Park protests, different factions can unite under a collective sense of disenfranchisement and dislocation at the hands of a seemingly neo-liberal authoritarian administration.

Turkey is always fascinating, enchanting and never, ever dull. There is much to like and love about the country but our list is limited to a top ten of Turkish delights.

1. History

All countries have their particular history and historical properties but in Turkey history positively oozes from every nook and cranny. Ottoman mosques, mausoleums, and monuments are staring at you from all directions. But there is also a wealth of archaeological and cultural significance from the ancient Hittites, the Persians, Romans, Christians, Seljuks to the cultures of Neolithic times such as Catalhoyuk in Anatolia. There is Troy, city of Homer's Iliad, and along the Aegean Coast you will find Ephesus from Ancient Greece, one of the most impressive cities of the ancient world. Then there is Bodrum, famous for being the location of one of the seven ancient wonders of the world, the Mausoleum at Helicarnassus. One of the most stunning Roman structures is the Aqueduct of Valens which today is bisected by a six-lane highway in Istanbul. It is impossible to over-estimate the vast archaeological treasures within Turkey; the country is a living museum – but not all is innocence – of humanity.

2. Istanbul

Not just one of the greatest cities of Islam but of the world. Today, the city is home to nearly 18 million people who live compactly in densely concentrated zones of urban settlements that are loosely connected by major roads and thoroughfares. But for the people of the world who come to see Istanbul for the first time, there is the famed Blue Mosque, built by the young Sultan Ahmet 1, with its hierarchy of increasingly large domes dominating the city skyline, and vast complex that is truly an architectural wonder. Right opposite is the sixth century Hagia Sophia, built by the Byzantine Emperor Justinian, the best preserved building of the ancient world. Then there is the legendary Topkapı Palace, brimming with cultural treasures. And of course the Galata Tower, built in 1348, with a sub-city that stretches down to the Bosphorus. It was from the Galata Tower that Hezârfen Ahmed Çelebi flew across the Bosphorus from Europe to Asia in 1638, thus inaugurating the first ever intercontinental flight! The romantic Basilica Cistern, constructed in the sixth century, that shows how the water was brought to the city, fitted with light and music. The city is chock-a-block with museums including the Archaeological Museum, the Calligraphy Museum, Devan Literature Museum, Museum of Turkish and Islamic Arts, and Islamic Science and Technology History Museum. Oh, we nearly forgot to mention the Grand Bazaar.

The locals may not even notice what lies within, but for those who are new to the city the romanticism is overwhelming. Within the old quarters there are various stores, cafes, boutiques, bookshops, restaurants and second-hand furniture outfits that cater for every conceivable taste and preference. There are churches, synagogues and late Ottoman architecture that is invisible, hidden or transformed. Istanbul is genuinely the place where the East and the West meet now as they have done in the past.

3. Sinan

Sinan Abdur-Mennan (1489/99–1588), known simply as Mimar Sinan, is the greatest architect of all time, he has built more buildings than any other architect who has ever lived, and many of his works are considered unrivalled masterpieces. Before he was made the Royal Chief Architect of Sultan Suleyman the Magnificent, he was a slave, a soldier, a janissary and Sultan's bodyguard. His greatest achievements include the Sultanahmet Mosque in Istanbul, the Stari Most in Mostar, and his crowning glory: the Selimiye Mosque in Edirne. Involved in over three hundred constructions as chief royal architect, he designed colleges, palaces and even hospitals. Outside Turkey, his work can also be seen in Damascus and Belgrade. Such was Sinan's influence that he is considered to be an inspiration in the majestic design of the Taj Mahal. He has been often emulated but never bettered.

4. Rumi

'Come, come, whoever you are', said Jalal ad-Din Muhammad Rumi (1207-1273), poet, jurist, theologian, philosopher and, of course, one of the greatest mystics of all time. Known simply as the Mawlana ('our master), the author of the *Masnawi* and *Diwan-e-Shams-e Tabrizi*, has become one of Turkey's most famous exports, with his poetry and verse remaining enormously popular in the West. His shrine in Konya is a place of pilgrimage for mystics and non-mystics alike from all over the world; and his Sufi order, the Mevlevi (aka the Whirling Dervishes), has hundreds of thousands if not millions of devotees. Today, the whirling dervishes perform the Sema to dedicated followers and swathes of tourists are enchanted by the symbolism, sounds and serenity of the whirling dance.

5. Cappadocia

Imagine a dry, dusty land pierced by volcanic peaks and pinkish lunar landscapes dotted with enchanting villages sprouting fairy chimneys and still, inhabited caves. No it's not Tolkien but Cappadocia in Central Anatolia, a place which has been inhabited since the time of Herodotus. Cappadocia's unique historical and cultural heritage is characterised by the rock-cut churches of Goreme and their beautiful frescoes, while the nearby cities of Derinkuyu and Kaymakli provide subterranean refuge with their labyrinthine delights. A highlight is staying in the cave hotels, a must for any visitor. As with the rest of the country, history plays an important part in the region. Cappadocia has been at the crossroads of many empires since the Hittite Empire. Persians, Greeks, Romans fought over the land while Cappadocia became an important Christian region during the Byzantine Civilisation. Subsequently, the region became a Seljuk stronghold.

6. Kebab

Meat or vegetables roasted or grilled on a skewer has a long history. Even though kebabs are associated with the Middle East, they were not uncommon in Central Asia and ancient Greece; even Homer enjoyed a kebab or two. And the Ottoman army marched on the humble kebab (and, it had to be said, *raki*). Today, kebab has become synonymous with Turkish food: it is the fastest of fast food before fast food was invented. In Europe and America, kebab means shish kebab (cooked on a skewer) or doner kebab, which is (horrible) thin sliced meat wrapped in flat, pitta bread. It is generally accepted that the method of grilling meat vertically originated in nineteenth century Bursa courtesy of Iskender Efendi who is known as the father of the doner kebab. There are many variations of the doner such as durum, halep and iskender kebab, the staple in a Turkish restaurant. There are other incarnations in other countries such as shawarma in the Middle East and Central Asia. In South America, it takes the form of Churrasco Turco. But there is more to Turkish food then kebab.

Much of Turkish cuisine reflects what is common across the region in terms of meats, sweets and breads, but there are huge localised variations to consider. In the South and south-east regions of Turkey the food is noticeably spicier, while in the North and north-east parts the food is more vegetable and fish based. But it is the Turkish breakfast which is legendary. Home-made jams, cheeses, yoghurts, natural honey, breads, eggs, olives, vegetables, fruits, sauces, pickles, dips and spreads are the norm. For Turkish families and friends, meeting for breakfast is not just about consuming delightful food, but also an opportunity to catch up and engage in all sorts of conversation, taking breaks in between courses as required. A breakfast lasts up to two hours, but it can set someone up for the rest of the day. The other aspect of the cuisine is the sweets in general, for they are as diverse as they are delicious. Baklava, Dondurma, Aşure and Tavuk göğsü, which is made from chicken breast, are all decidedly Turkish even if their origins emerge from a wider domain.

7. Coffee

After a Turkish breakfast, a Turkish coffee is a must: roasted and finely ground beans are boiled in a special pot, called *cezve*, and served in a cup where the grounds are allowed to settle, with or without sugar (we prefer 'medium'). While coffee probably originated in Yemen, coffee houses were established by the Ottomans – the first opened in Istanbul, then Constantinople – around 1555. Coffee houses established by the Ottomans in the centres of Europe during the end of the seventeenth century became the fuel for discussions that led scholars, thinkers and originators to inspire each other to dream up the Renaissance. Today, connoisseurs of coffee throughout the world cannot but wonder at the sight, smell and sip of a perfectly brewed Turkish coffee. An intense shot of caffeine is unavoidably followed by a rush of energy in thought and action. For the more dedicated, a Turkish coffee follows every substantial meal, morning, noon or night. The reading of the coffee cup residue is deemed an amusing pastime. Happily, few take the utterances of self-proclaimed soothsayers seriously.

8. Yılmaz Güney

What should be taken seriously are Turkish films. Turkey has the most vibrant cultural scene of all Muslim countries. Literature, art and music have distinguished histories and are thriving industries. But, for us, it is the Turkish film industry that is truly original and brilliant. The country has produced a plethora of legendary film directors from the late Lutfi Akad (*Law of the Border*, 1966) to Zeki Demirkubuz (*Innocence*, 1997), Yesim Ustao (*Journey of the Sun*, 1999), and Nuri Belige Ceylon (*One Upon A Time in Anatolia*, 2011). But the greatest is Yılmaz Güney (1937– 1984). Güney, a Turkish Zaza, spent considerable time in prison, accused of being a communist and anarchist sympathiser, and often directed his films from prison – his assistant, Şerif Gören doing the technical leg work. His masterpiece is *Yoli* (1982), which like most of his films, deals with the dispossessed – the titles reflect the theme: *Elegy* (1972), *Pain* (1971), *The Hopeless* (1971), *The Miserable* (1975). *Yoli* portrays Turkey after the 1980 military coup and tells the stories of five prisoners on a week's leave. But these real-life prisoners are also prisoners of tradition. A grim, allegorical film, it takes us deep into the unsavoury underbelly of Turkey.

9. Hospitality

While the Turkish authorities and elite are not very hospitable to dissidents and critics, the Turkish people are another story. Even in Istanbul's crammed Metrobus, younger Turks always give up their seat to the elderly, mothers, those with special needs and tired visitors. But true Turkish hospitality is to be found outside of Istanbul, where the pace of life is markedly gentler, and where the environment is more soothing to the eye and to the body. It is here that the extreme generosity and hospitality of the vast people of Turkey can be witnessed in full. Much of it is nested in the Sufi traditions of humility and piety, but it is also seen among others from different backgrounds. Kindliness is found everywhere in Turkish society, from the store keeper keen to sell his wares, to the bus driver who directs passengers to their destinations, or to the family who are the hosts for dinner, feeding their guests the finest of home-made foods until no more can be eaten, and then offering them even more.

10. Coastline

And finally there is the devastating and diverse coastline. Sandy beaches, jagged shorelines and hidden coves, popular for yachting and boating and obscured by stunning mountains, Turkey's Southwestern coast is called Turquoise Coast for good reason. In ancient times it was known as Lycia: the distinctive rock tombs can be seen near the resorts of Dalyan and Fethiye. This is a place of contrasts with conifer forests hugging the mountainous coastline. Further north is the Aegean coast where the scenery is picture-perfect and idyllic beaches are scattered among popular resorts such as Marmaris and Bodrum, which also boast numerous Classical sites. More discerning is the Black Sea Coast, which extends from Istanbul to Georgia and is climatically similar to

Northwestern Europe with walls of mountains plunging to the sea contrasting with pristine empty beaches.

There is only one thing missing in Turkey: sensible politics and governance.

CITATIONS

The False Promise by Ahmet T. Kuru

For the historical background on Turkish democratization and its relations with Islam, see Nilüfer Göle, *The Forbidden Modern: Civilization and Veiling* (Ann Arbor: University of Michigan Press, 1996); and Reşat Kasaba, ed., *The Cambridge History of Turkey: Vol. 4, Turkey in the Modern World* (New York: Cambridge University Press, 2008). For recent debates on secularism, Islam, and democracy in Turkey, see Ahmet T. Kuru and Alfred Stepan, eds, *Democracy, Islam, and Secularism in Turkey* (New York: Columbia University Press, 2012); Ahmet T. Kuru, 'The Rise and Fall of Military Tutelage in Turkey: Fears of Islamism, Kurdism, and Communism,' *Insight Turkey* 14, 2 (2012), pp. 37-57; and Ahmet T. Kuru, 'Turkey's Failed Policy toward Arab Spring,' *Mediterranean Quarterly* 26 (3): 94-116.

The Ambiguity of Turkish Secularism by Edip Asaf Bekaroğlu

The sources for quotations from various politician and academics are: 'PM Erdoğan's surprising message in Cairo,' *Hürriyet Daily News*, September 9, 2011, accessed February 2, 2015, http://www.hurriyetdailynews.com/default.aspx?pageid=438&n=pm-erdogan8217s-surprising-message-in-cairo-2011-09-15; Veit Bader, 'Post-Secularism or Liberal-Democratic Constitutionalism?,' *Erasmus Law Review* 5/1 (2012): 13; Dankwart A. Rustow, 'Turkey's Liberal Revolution,' *Middle East Review* 12 (1985): 1-11; Yael Navaro-Yashin, *Faces of the State: Secularism and Public Life in Turkey* (Princeton: Princeton University Press, 2002): p133; 'İslamcı basın Hoca'ya gülüyor (Islamist press laughing at Hoca [Erbakan]),' *Sabah*, 29 May, 1997, http://arsiv.sabah.com.tr/1997/05/29/p09.html; *Mustafa Erdoğan, 28 Şubat Süreci* (Ankara: Yeni Türkiye Yayınları, 1999), 273; 'Kıvrıkoğlu'ndan Ecevit'e: 28 Şubat daha bitmedi (From Kıvrıkoğlu to Ecevit: February 28 is not yet over),' *Haber Türk,*

February 28, 2012: http://www.haberturk.com/gundem/haber/720006-kivrikogludan-ecevite-28-subat-daha-bitmedi-; Jürgen Habermas, 'Notes on Post-Secular Society,' *New Perspectives Quarterly* 25/4 (2008): 20; Seda Demiralp, 'White Turks, Black Turks? Faultlines beyond Islamism versus secularism,' *Third World Quarterly* 33/3 (2012): 517; the quotes from the Ministry of National Defence's White Papers of 1998 and 2000 and other military statements are from Ümit Cizre, 'Demythologyzing the National Security Concept: The Case of Turkey', *Middle East Journal* 57/2 (2003): 216; and Umit Cizre and Menderes Çınar. 'Turkey 2002: Kemalism, Islamism, and Politics in the Light of the February 28 Process.' *The South Atlantic Quarterly* 102/2-3 (2003.): 309-332 p313, 316, 318; and the excerpts for the Turkish army statement, see *Turkish Daily News*, April 30, 2007.

See also: Veit Bader, 'Secularism, Public Reason or Moderately Agonistic Democracy?' In *Secularism, Religion and Multicultural Citizenship*, G.B. Levey and T. Modood, eds, pp110–135. (Cambridge: Cambridge University Press, 2009) and 'Post-Secularism or Liberal-Democratic Constitutionalism?' *Erasmus Law Review* 5/1 (2012): 5–26; Niyazi Berkes, 'Historical Background of Turkish Secularism' in *Islam and the West*, Richard N. Fyre, ed., pp41-68, The Hague: Mounton & Co, 1957; Alper Bilgili, 'Post-Secular Society and the Multi-Vocal Religious Sphere in Turkey' in *European Perspectives* 3/5 (2011): 131-146; Faruk Birtek and Binnaz Toprak 'The Conflictual Agendas of Neo-Liberal Reconstruction and the Rise of Islamic Politics in Turkey' in *Praxis International* 13/2 (1993): 192–212; Umit Cizre, 'Demythologyzing the National Security Concept: The Case of Turkey.' *Middle East Journal* 57/2 (2003): 213-229; Umit Cizre and Joshua Walker. 'Conceiving the New Turkey after Ergenekon' in *The International Spectator: Italian Journal of International Affairs* 45/1 (2010): 89-98; Ismail Çağlar, *From Symbolic Exile to Physical Exile: Turkey's Imam Hatip Schools, the Emergence of a Conservative Counter-Elite, and its Knowledge Migration to Europe* (Amsterdam: Amsterdam University Press, 2013); Demiralp Seda, 'White Turks, Black Turks? Faultlines beyond Islamism versus secularism' in *Third World Quarterly* 33/3 (2012): 511-524; Ernest Gellner, 'The Turkish Option in Comparative Perspective' in *Rethinking Modernity and National Identity in Turkey*, Sibel Bozdoğan and Reşat Kasaba, 233-244 (Seattle: University of Washington Press, 1997); Nilufer Göle, 'Secularism and Islamism in Turkey: The Making of Elites and Counter-Elites' in *Middle East Journal* 51/1 (1997): 46-58.; William Hale, *Turkish Politics and*

Military (London: Routledge, 1994); Michael Hardt and Antonio Negri, *Empire* (Cambridge: Harvard University Press, 2000); Metin Heper, *The State Tradition in Turkey* (Beverley, UK: The Eothen Press, 1985); Metin Heper and Aylin Guney 'The Military and the Consolidation of Democracy: The Recent Turkish Experience' in *Armed Forces & Society* 26 (2000): 635-657; Serder Kaya, 'The Social Psychology of Ergenekon Case: The Collapse of the Official Narrative in Turkey' in *Middle East Critique* 21/2 (2012): 145-156; Ahmet Kuru, 'Passive and Assertive Secularism: Historical Conditions, Ideological Struggles, and State Policies toward Religion' in *World Politics* 59/4 (2007): 568-594; Serif Mardin, 'Center-Periphery Relations: A Key to Turkish Politics?' in *Daedalus* 102/1 (1973): 169-191; Ergun Özbudun, 'The Nature of the Kemalist Political Regime' in *Atatürk: The Founder of a Modern State*, A. Kazancıgil and E. Özbudun, eds, 79-102 (London: Hurst, 1981); Binnaz Toprak, 'Islam and Democracy in Turkey' in *Turkish Studies* 6/2 (2005): 167-186; Nur Yalman, 'Some Observations on Secularism in Islam: the Cultural Revolution in Turkey' in *Daedalus* 102/1 (1973): 139-168; and Hakan Yavuz, 'Cleansing Islam from the Public Sphere and the February 28 Process' in *Journal of International Affairs* 54 (2000): 21-42.

A longer version of this article was published in Turkish at *Insan & Toplum* (*Human and Society*) Vol. 5 N. 9 (2015): 103-122.

Gazi Warrior and Sufi Mystic: Turkey's Erdoğan-Gulën Breakup by Sophia Pandya

I extend profound gratitude to my graduate research assistants for their help: Marie Brown, Jessica Grace Howell, Keri Hughes, and Brenda Oliden.

The quotes from Gulën's work are from M. Fethullah Gűlen, *Towards a Global Civilization of Love and Tolerance* (New Jersey: Light, 2004), p172, 1, 27 and 29; the quotes from Clifford Geertz are from *Local Knowledge: Further Essays in Interpretation of History* (New York: Basic Book Publishers, 1983), pp123, 125, 198-199 and 146. Other quotes are from: Graham E. Fuller, *The New Turkish Republic* (Washington D.C.: United States Institute of Peace Press, 2008), p9; M. Hakan Yavuz, *Towards an Islamic Enlightenment: The Gülen Movement* (Oxford: Oxford University Press, 2013), p122; Mark Juergensmeyer, *Terror in the Mind of God: The Global Rise of Religious Violence* (Berkeley: University of California Press, 2000), p188 and 199; Amanullah De Sondy, *The Crisis of*

Islamic Masculinities (London: Bloomsbury, 2015), p156, 178 and 52; Salih Yucel, 'Fethullah Gülen: Spiritual Leader in a Global Islamic Context,' *Journal of Religion and Science* Vol. 12, (2010) pp4 and 11; Nil Mutluer, 'Disposable Masculinities in Istanbul,' *Global Masculinities and Manhood*, Ronald L. Jackson and Murali Balaji, eds, (Chicago: University of Illinois Press, 2011), 84; and from Selin Akyűz, *Political Manhood in 2000's Turkey: Representations of Different Masculinities in Politics*, Ph.D. Dissertation (Department of Political Science, Ihsan Doğramacı Bilkent University, Ankara, May 2012), piii. And the quote from Syed Abul A'la Mawdudi, is from *Sondy*, p52.

Articles mentioned include: Zeynep Kurtulus Korkman, and Salih Can Açıksőz, 'Erdoğan's Masculinity and the Language of the Gezi Resistance,' *Jadaliyya* (June 22, 2013), which can be accessed at: http://www.jadaliyya. com/pages/index/12367/Erdoğan's-masculinity-and-the-language-of-the-gezi; Zeynep Kurtulus Korkman and Salih Can Açıksőz, 'Erdoğan's Masculinity and the Language of the Gezi Resistance,' *Jadaliyya* June 22, 2013, which can be accessed at: http://www.jadaliyya.com/pages/index/12367/ Erdoğan's-masculinity-and-the-language-of-the-gezi; Margaret Malamud, 'Gender and Spiritual Self-Fashioning: The Master-Disciple Relationship in Medieval Islam,' *Journal of the American Academy of Religion* LXIV/1 (1996), 89-117; and Salih Can Açıksőz, 'Sacrificial Limbs of Sovereignty: Disabled Veterans, Masculinity, and Nationalist Politics in Turkey,' *Medical Anthropology Quarterly* 26:1, (2012), 12.

Media reports include: Daren Butler, 'Turkish Prime Minister Tayyip Erdoğan accuses supporters of US-based Islamic cleric Fethullah Gűlen of "vile betrayal,"' *The Independent* Thursday 7 August 2014, at: http://www. independent.co.uk/news/world/europe/turkish-prime-minister-tayyip-Erdoğan-accuses-supporters-of-usbased-islamic-cleric-fethullah-gulen-of-vile-betrayal-9655312.html; 'Turkey's Erdoğan Accuses New York Times of meddling in country's affairs,' *The Guardian*: Agence French-Press available at: http://www.theguardian.com/world/2015/may/26/turkeys-Erdoğan-accuses-new-york-times-of-meddling-in-countrys-affairs; *The Sunday Times*, 'Gulën awarded 2015 Gandhi King Ikeda Peace Prize,' *The Sunday Times*, April 26, 2015, available at: http://www.sundaytimes.lk/150426/sunday-times-2/ gulen-awarded-2015-gandhi-king-ikeda-peace-prize-146074.html. : Murat Onur, 'Brief Summary of Turkey's Intelligence-Judiciary-Government Crisis,' *Foreign Policy Association*, at: http://foreignpolicyblogs.com/2012/02/26/

summary-turkeys-intelligence-judiciary-government-democracy-crisis/; Mustafa Akyol, 'What you should know about Turkey's AKP-Gülen conflict,' Turkey Pulse. January 3, 2014 at: http://www.al-monitor.com/pulse/originals/2014/01/akp-Gülen-conflict-guide.html#; Fehim Taştekin, 'Kurds Abandon AKP,' Al-Monitor, 20 May 2015 which can be downloaded from: http://www.al-monitor.com/pulse/originals/2015/05/turkey-pious-kurds-abandon-akp-in-droves-hdp.html# and Laura Smith-Spark and Gul Toysuz. 'Rights groups slam Turkey's Erdoğan over remarks on women,' CNN, 25 November 2014, available at: http://www.cnn.com/2014/11/25/world/europe/turkey-Erdoğan-women/, accessed on May 28 2015.

Lyndal Roper, "Blood and codpieces: masculinity in the Early Modern German Town," Oedipus and the Devil: Witchcraft, sexuality and religion in early modern Europe (London: Routledge, 1994), 116-117, 120.

Ahmet T. Kuru, "Secularism and State Policies toward Religion: The United States, France, and Turkey," (Cambridge: Cambridge University Press, 2009), 161-163.

İhsan Yılmaz and Hüseyin Gündoğdu, "Secular Law in an Islamic Polity: The Ottoman Case," European Journal of Economic and Political Studies, 6:2 (2013), 58, 77.

Gülen, Fethullah, "471. Nağme: 'Affetmeye Hazır Olun!' Tenbîhi," Herkul, May 19, 2015. The title of this article in English is "Be Ready to Forgive." Found at: http://www.herkul.org/herkul-nagme/471-nagme-affetmeye-hazir-olun-tenbihi/. Accessed on May 31, 2015. Interview, Istanbul, October 2012.

The Headscarf Debate: Recognition and Citizenship by Yusuf Sarfati

The Mustafa Kemal quotation is from Bernard Lewis, The Emergence of Modern Turkey (New York: Oxford University Press, 2002), p. 271. Other citations include: Nilüfer Göle, The Forbidden Modern: Civilization and Veiling (Ann Arbor: Michigan University Press, 1997), pp. 4 and 73; Jenny B. White, 'State Feminism, Modernization, and the Turkish Republican Woman', NWSA Journal 15:3 (2003), pp. 157-158; Ayşe Kadıoğlu, 'The Headscarf and Citizenship in Turkey', Social Science Research Council blog, Immanent Frame, (23 April

2008), available at: http://blogs.ssrc.org/tif/2008/04/23/the-headscarf-and-citizenship-in-turkey/; Hilal Elver, *The Headscarf Controversy: Secularism and Freedom of Religion* (New York: Oxford University Press, 2012), pp. 75 and 77; Gülşen Demirkol Özer, *Psikolojik Bir İşkence Metodu Olarak İkna Odaları*, (Istanbul: Beyan Yayınları, 2005), p. 71; Yeşim Arat. 'Group-differentiated rights and liberal democratic state: Rethinking the headscarf controversy in Turkey', *New Perspectives on Turkey* (2001) 25, pp. 33-34; Murat Akan, 'Contextualizing Multiculturalism,' *Studies in Comparative International Development* 38: 2 (2003), pp.58 and 72; Charles Taylor, *Multiculturalism: Examining the politics of recognition,* Princeton: Princeton University Press, 1994, p.25; and Elizabeth Kiss. 'Democracy and the politics of recognition', in I. Shapiro and C. Hacker-Cordon (eds) *Democracy's Edges* (pp.193-210). Cambridge: Cambridge University Press, 1999, p.193; Ziya Öniş, 'The Political Economy of Export-Oriented Industrialization in Turkey', in Çiğdem Balım (ed.) *Turkey: Political, Economic, and Social Challenges in the 1990s*, (Leiden: Brill, 1995), pp.114-15; Sammy Smooha, 'Types of Democracy and Modes of Conflict Management in Ethnically Divided Societies', *Nations and Nationalism* 8 (2002), p. 424; Ahmet Kuru, 'Two forms of Secularism', in *The Justice and Development Party and the Emergence of a New Turkey*, Hakan Yavuz (ed.), (Salt Lake City: University of Utah Press), p. 147; Nilüfer Göle, 'Secularism is a Woman's Affair', *Global Viewpoint*, 18 February 2008, (accessed 6 May 2011), http://www.digitalnpq.org/articles/global/246/02-18-2008/nilufer_gole; Nancy Fraser, 'Rethinking Recognition', *New Left Review* (2000) 3, pp. 108-109; 113-114; Iris M. Young, 'Polity and group difference', *Ethics* (1989) 99 (2), p. 261; Iris M. Young, *Inclusion and Democracy*, New York: Oxford University Press, 2000, p.137; 144; 121-153; Nancy Fraser. 'Rethinking the public sphere: A contribution to the critique of actually existing democracy'. *Social Text* (1990) 25/26, p. 67.

The interview with Numan Kurtulmuş was conducted on 4 March 2007; and the interview with Mehmet Çiçek on 26 February 2007. The Erdoğan statement appeared in *Zaman*, 'Başbakan Erdoğan: Başörtüsünün dinimizin bir emri olduğunu bilmeyecek kadar cahil' (31 October, 2013). For Leyla Şahin case, see Talvikki Hoopes, 'The Leyla Şahin v. Turkey: Case before the European Court of Human Rights', *Chinese Journal of International Law* 5:3 (2006), p. 720.

Fatma Akdokur's statement is quoted in Gül Aldıkaçtı Marshall, 'A Question of Compatibility: Feminism and Islam in Turkey' *Critique: Critical Middle Eastern Studies* 17:3 (2008), p. 235; Ali Bulaç statement appeared in 'Başörtülü Aday', *Zaman*, (2 April 2011); and the Erdoğan's reprimand is taken from CNN Türk, 'Erdoğan'dan peşpeşe bombalar!' (13 April 2011).

See also: Benjamin Barber, *Strong Democracy: Participatory Politics for a New Age*, (Berkeley: University of California Press, 1984); Leila Ahmed, *Women and Gender in Islam*, (New Haven: Yale University Press, 1992); Anna Korteweg and Gökçe Yurdakul. *The Headscarf Debates Conflicts of National Belonging* (Stanford: Stanford University Press, 2014); Leslie McCall, 'The Complexity of Intersectionality', *Signs: Journal of Women in Culture and Society*, 30:3 (2005); Berna Turam, 'Turkish Women Divided by Politics: Secularist Activism versus Pious Non-Resistance', *International Feminist Journal of Politics* 10:4 (2008), p. 482; Ahmet Kuru. 'Passive and Assertive Secularism: Historical Conditions, Ideological Struggles, and State Policies toward Religion', *World Politics* (2007) 59 (4), pp. 568-594; Ahmet Kuru and Alfred Stepan. 'Laïcité as an "Ideal Type" and a Continuum: Comparing Turkey, France, and Senegal' in A. Kuru and A. Stepan (eds) *Democracy, Islam, and Secularism in Turkey* (New York: Columbia University Press, 2012); and Naciye Kaynak, 'İkna Odaları Kitabının yazarı Gülşen Demirkol ile röportaj' Yeni Asya, (4 May 2005); Dilek Cindoğlu, *Headscarf Ban and Discrimination: Professional Headscarved Women in the Labor Market*, (Istanbul: TESEV Publications, 2011), p. 36; pp. 71-95; Şeyla Benhabib, 'The Return of Political Theology: The scarf affair in comparative constitutional perspective in France, Germany and Turkey', *Philosophy & Social Criticism* 36 (2010), p. 466.

Memory and Forgetting in Istanbul
by Charles Allen Scarboro

This essay is based on two articles published in *Today's Zaman*: 'Memory and Forgetting,' March 29, 2011, http://www.todayszaman.com/expat-zone_an-american-in-avcilar-memory-and-forgetting_239451.html, and 'Memory and Forgetting II,' April 5, 2011, http://www.todayszaman.com/expat-zone_an-american-in-avcilar-memory-and-forgetting-ii_240139.html.

The report on 'French Senate passes the controversial Armenian genocide bill' appeared in *Foreign Policy News* and can be accessed at: http://

foreignpolicynews.org/2012/01/23/french-senate-passes-the-controversial-armenian-genocide-bill/. For the controversy on Mehmet Aksoy's 'Monument to Humanity' see 'Turkey-Armenia friendship symbol being demolished.' BBC News Europe, April 26, 2011, which can be accessed at: http://www.bbc.com/news/world-europe-13199787.

The quote by Niall Ferguson, *The War of the World: Twentieth-Century Conflict and the Descent of the West* (Allen Lane, 2006) is from pp176-177. David Fromkin's *A Peace to End All Peace: The Fall of the Ottoman Empire and the Creation of the Modern Middle East*, is published by Owl Books (New York, 1989); and Taner Akcam's *From Empire to Republic: Turkish Nationalism and the Armenian Genocide* is published by Zed Books (London, 2004).

On Raphael Lemkin see John Cooper, *Raphael Lemkin and the Struggle for the Genocide* (Palgrave, London, 2015). The full UN definition can be found on the website for the UN Convention on the Prevention and Punishment of the Crime of Genocide.

EU and Turkey's 'Self' and 'Other' by Melek Saral

The Iver B Neumann quotation is from European Identity, EU Expansion, and the Integration/Exclusion Nexus,' *Alternatives: Global, Local, Political* (1998), p.399.

The sources for quotations from various politicians are as follow: Bulent Ecevit from 'AB, ırkçılık ve Hıristiyan kulübü eğilimi etkisinde', *Hürriyet*, 4 May, 2000; Sükrü Sina Gürel from 'AB süreci zorlasacak', *Cumhuriyet* 26 November 2000; İsmail Cem from 'AB'den dayatma yok. Disisleri Bakani Helsinki Zirvesi'ni degerlendirdi', *Milliyet*, 14 December, 1999; Gül from 'Otoritiseni kaybeden elbette bagiracaktir', *Milliyet*, 7 July 2003; 'Gül, Birinci önceliğimiz AB'ye girmek', *Hürriyet*, 3 December 2003; from Baykal from various newspaper articles: Sevrcilere taviz yok, Cumhuriyet, August 15, 2005; AB ile iliskiere reset atalim, *Hürriyet*, 25 September, 2009.

The quotations from the Bahceli are from the following newspaper articles: 'Bahceli'den Basbakan Erdoğan'a Israil suclamasi', *Milliyet*, 6 January 2009; 'Basbakan tuzaga düsme', Cumhuriyet, 17 August 2009; and from Erdoğan from the following newspaper articles: 'Erdoğan, AB Kriterleri taviz değil',*Hürriyet*, 29 May, 2003; 'Erdoğan, Türkiye AB'ye girme derdinde degil', *Hürriyet*, 3 April 2006; 'Medeniyetler ittifakinin yolu Türkiye'den gecer', *Yeni*

Safak, 7 November 2005. Finally, the Davutoglu quotes are from: 'Davutoglu, Masaya ilisenlerden degil kuranlardan olacagiz', *Milliyet*, 21 May, 2010; and 'Türkiye'nin AB üyeligi stratejik hedefimizdir', *Yeni Safak*, 22 June, 2009. See also: Thomas Diez, "Europe's others and the return of geopolitics," *Cambridge Review of International Relations*, Vol. 17, No. 2, (2004) pp 319-335; Thomas Diez, "Constructing the Self and Changing Others: Reconsidering 'Normative Power,'" *Millennium-Journal of International Studies* Vol. 33, No. 3, (2005) pp. 613-636; Alaistar Ian Johnston, *Social States, China in International Institutions, 1980-2000*. (Princeton, Princeton University Press 2008; Wendt A. "Anarchy is What States Make of It: The Social Construction of Power Politics" *International Organization* 46 (1992), pp. 391-425; Risse, T., Daniela E. M., Knopf H. J. and Roscher K. "To Euro or Not to Euro? The EMU and Identity Politics in the European Union" *European Journal of International Relations* 5 (1999), pp 147-187; Chambers, Samuel A. and Carver Terrell (Eds) *William E. Connolly: Democracy, Pluralism and Political Theory* (London, Routledge 2008); Meltem Müftüler-Bac, *Europe in Change: Turkey's relations with a changing Europe* (Manchester, Manchester University Press 1997); Ayla Göl, "The Identity of Turkey: Muslim and secular" *Third World Quarterly*, Vol. 30, No. 4, (2009) pp. 795-811; Caglar Keyder, "Whither the Project of Modernity? Turkey in the 1990s," in *Rethinking Modernity and National Identity in Turkey*, ed. Sibel Bozdogan and Resat Kasaba, (Washington, University of Washington Press 1997) pp. 37-52; Mahmut Bali Aykan, "The Palestinian Question in Turkish Foreign Policy from the 1950s to the 1990s" *International Journal of Middle Eastern Studies* Vol. 25, No. 1, (1993), pp. 91-110; Beyza C. Tekin, "Human Rights as a Security Challenge: An Examination of Turkish Nationalist Discourse on Minority Rights Reforms," in *Nationalism and Human Rights. In Theory and Practice in the Middle East, Central Europe, and the Asia-Pacific*, ed. Grace Cheng (New York: Palgrave Macmillan, 2012) pp. 21-46; Fatma M. Göcek, *The Transformation of Turkey: Redefining State and Society from the Ottoman Empire to the Modern Era*, (New York, I. B. Tauris 2011); Hakan Yilmaz "Euroscepticism in Turkey: Parties, Elites and Public Opinion," *South European Society and Politics*, 16 (1) (2011), pp. 185-208; Kemal Kirisci "Turkey's Foreign Policy in Turbulent Times" *Chaillot Paper*, No. 92 (2006); L. Hovsepyan, "The Fears of Turkey: the Sèvres Syndrome", *Information and Public Relation Center* (2012); Baskin Oran Türkiye'de Azınlıklar: Kavramlar, Teori, Lozan, iç Mevzuat, içtihat, Uygulama, (Istanbul: Iletisim Yayınları 2010)

Saving Hasankeyf by John Crofoot

The sole manuscript of ibn al-Munshi's *History of the Ayyubid Dynasty* is to be found in the Austrian National Library (Die Ergötzung des Lesers und die Erholung des Geistes; Cod. Mxt. 355; http://data.onb.ac.at/rec/ AL00230477). A summary has been published by Claude Cahen in *Journal Asiatique* (1955); a Turkish translation by Eyyüp Tanrıverdi and Adnan Çevik has yet to be published. The ibn al-Munshi quotes are from the pages 73b and 25b of the manuscript. The Al-Jazari quotes are from *The Book of Knowledge of Ingenious Mechanical Devices*, translated by Donald R. Hill (Dordrecht, Holland: D. Reidel, 1974), pp 157-69 and 107-109.

On the history and cultural property of Hasankeyf see: M. Oluş Arık, *Hasankeyf: Üç Dünyanın Buluştuğu Kent* (Hasankeyf: The City Where Three Worlds Meet) (Ankara: Türkiye İş Bankası Kültür Yayınlar, 2003) and 'Turkish Architecture in Asia Minor in the Period of the Turkish Emirates' in *The Art and Architecture of Turkey*, edited by E. Akurgal (New York: Rizzoli 1980), pp. 111-13; Çevik, Adnan, *Hasankeyf: Medeniyetlerin Buluştuğu Başkent* [Hasankeyf: The Capital where Civilizations Meet]. Ankara: Doğa Derneği, 2012; Oktay Aslanapa, *Türk Sanatı I Başlangıcından Büyük Selçukluların Sonuna Kadar* (Turkish Art I From Its Beginnings to the end of the Great Seljuks) (İstanbul: Milli Eğitim Bakanlığı Kültür Yayınları, 1972); Baer, Eva, *The Human Figure in Islamic Art: Inheritances and Islamic Transformations* (Costa Mesa, California: Mazda Publishers, 2004); Aziz Basan, *The Great Seljuqs: A History* (London: Routledge, 2010); Murat Biricik and Recep Karakas, 'Birds of Hasankeyf (South-Eastern Anatolia, Turkey) Under the Threat of a Big Dam Project.' *Natural Areas Journal* 32.1 (2012): 96-105; Muharrem Çeken, 'Materials, Techniques and Kilns used in the Production of Seljuk and Beylik Period Glazed Tiles' in *Tiles Treasures of Anatolian Soil: Tiles of the Seljuk and Beylik Periods,* Rüçhan Arık and Oluş Arık, eds, (Istanbul: Kale Group Cultural Productions, 2008) pp. 13-23; Albert Gabriel, *Voyages Archéologiques dans la Turquie Orientale*. Vol. I. (Paris: Boccard, 1940); Mohammad Gharipour, *Persian Gardens and Pavilions: Reflections in history, Poetry and the Arts* (London: I.B. Tauris, 2013); Carole Hillenbrand, 'The History of the Jazira: 1100-1250' in *The Art of Syria and the Jazira, 1100-1250,* Julian Raby, ed.,(Oxford: OUP, 1985) pp. 9-20; Michael Meinecke, *Patterns of Stylistic Changes in Islamic Architecture: Local Traditions versus Migrating Artists* (New York: New York UP, 1996); Gönül Öney, *Anadolu Selçuklu Mimari*

Süslemesi ve El Sanatları (Architectural Decoration and Minor Arts in Seljuk Anatolia) (Türkiye İş Bankası Kültür Yayınları, 1992); A C S Peacock, *Early Seljuq History: A New Interpretation* (London: Routledge, 2010); Scott Redford, *Landscape and the State in Medieval Anatolia: Seljuk Gardens and Pavilions of Alanya, Turkey* (Oxford: Archaeopress, 2000); and Estelle J Whelan, *The Public Figure: Political Iconography in Medieval Mesopotamia* (London: Melisende, 2006).

For more information on the campaign to save Hasankeyf see: http://www.hasankeyfmatters.com/

Our Man in Havana by Ken Chitwood

On the issues surrounding the building of a mosque in Cuba, see Ishaan Tharoor, 'Turkey's Erdoğan wants to build a mosque in Cuba. It's based on a historical fallacy', *The Washington Post*, February 12, 2015; and Lora Moftah, 'Turkey, Saudi Arabia Compete Over Cuba Mosque Project: Erdoğan Determined to Build Havana Mosque Alone,' *International Business Times*, February 13, 2015. On the rivalry between Turkey and Saudi Arabia, see Reza Akhlagi, 'The Sunni Divide: The Ideological Rift Between Turkey and Saudi Arabia', *Diplomatic Courier*, January 8, 2015 and Abdulmajeed al-Buluwi, 'The Saudi-Turkey cold war for Sunni hegemony', *Al-Monitor*, available at: http://www.al-monitor.com/pulse/originals/2014/04/saudi-arabia-turkey-muslim-brotherhood-sunni-middle-east.html

The quote from David Harvey is from *The Condition of Postmodernity*, (Malden, MA: Blackwell Publishing, 1990), p234. Other works mentioned include Asef Bayat, *Post-Islamism: The Changing Face of Political Islam*, (London: Oxford University Press, 2013); Benedict Anderson, *Imagined Communities*, (New York: Verso Books, 2006); and Arjun Appadurai, *Modernity at Large: The Cultural Dimensions of Globalization*, (Minneapolis: University of Minnesota Press, 1996). On the so-called Muslim discovery of America, see Abdullah H Quick, *Deeper Roots, Muslims in the Americas and the Caribbean from before Columbus to the Present* (Cape Town, ZA: DPB Printers and Booksellers, 1996); and Youssef Mroueh, 'Precolumbian Muslims in the Americas': http://www.sunnah.org/history/precolmb.htm

See also: Nester Garcia Canclini, *Hybrid Cultures: Strategies for Entering and Leaving Modernity* (Minneapolis, MN: The University of Minnesota Press, 1995); Alev Çevh, *Modernity, Islam, and Secularism in Turkey: Bodies, Places, and*

Time (Minneapolis, MN: University of Minnesota Press, 2005)'; Marvine Howe, *Turkey Today: A Nation Divided over Islam's Revival* (Boulder, CO: Westview Press, 2000); Sena Karasipahi, *Muslims in Modern Turkey: Kemalism, Modernism, and the Revolt of the Islamic Intellectuals* (London: I.B. Tauris, 2009); Peter Mandaville, *Global Political Islam* (London: Routledge, 2007); Adil Ödil ur and Kenneth Frank, *Visible Islam in Modern Turkey*, (London: Macmillan, London, 2000); and Bnu Gökiriskel and Anna Secor, 'Post-secular geographies and the problem of pluralism: Religion and everyday life in Istanbul, Turkey', *Political Geography* 46 (2015): 21-30.

Tanpınar and the Heritage Wars by Nagihan Haliloğlu

Ahmet Hamdi Tanpınar's *A Mind at Peace*, translated by Erdağ Göknar, is published by Archipelago Books (New York, 2008 and 2011); it was first published in 1949. *Time Regulation Institute*, translated by Alexander Dawe and Maureen Freely is available in Penguin Classics (London, 2014). *Lectures in Literature* (Edebiyat Dersleri) is published in original Turkish by Yapi Kredi Yayinlari (Istanbul, 2002).

Orhan Pamuk's *Istanbul: Memories of A City*, translated by Maureen Freely, is published by Faber and Faber (London, 2006).

Orhan Pamuk's Legacy by Abdullah Yavuz Altun

Orhan Pamuk's novels are widely available. The English version of his *Die Zeit* article, 'My Turkish Library', was published in *New York Review of Books*, 18 December 2008; it is available at: http://www.nybooks.com/articles/archives/2008/dec/18/my-turkish-library/

His description of *The Black Book* is from the interview with Horace Engdahl, given when he won the Nobel Prize for Literature, which can be viewed at: http://www.nobelprize.org/nobel_prizes/literature/laureates/2006/pamuk-interview.html

His comments on V. S. Naipaul appear in the foreword to *My Name is Red*. His *Paris Review* interview appeared in issue 187, 'The Art of Fiction' (Fall/Winter 2005) and can be read at: http://www.theparisreview.org/interviews/5587/the-art-of-fiction-no-187-orhan-pamuk.

Pamuk's confession about the localness in the book is from *The Naïve and Sentimental Novelist* (Faber and Faber, London, 2011) which is a collection of his lectures at Harvard University.

The Ian Almond quotations are from, 'Islam, Melancholy and Sad, Concrete Minarets', *New Literary History* (Winter, 2003), pp. 75-90, Enis Batur is cited in this paper; Stendhal's quote is from his novel, *The Charterhouse of Parma* (Penguin Classics, 2006), p. 414; 'East should not be East' quote is from Aylin Bayrakçeken and Don Randall, 'Meetings of East and West: Orhan Pamuk's Istanbulite Perspective', *Critique: Studies in Contemporary Fiction* (2005), p. 203; and the Fredrik Jameson quote is from his article, 'Third-World Literature in the Era of Multinational Capitalism' *Social Text* (1986), p. 69.

See also: Güneli Gün, 'The Turks Are Coming: Deciphering Orhan Pamuk's Black Book', *World Literature Today* (Winter, 1992); Sibel Irzık, 'Allegorical Lives: The Public and the Private in the Modern Turkish Literature' *The South Atlantic Quarterly* (2003), p. 564; Marshall Berman, 'Orhan Pamuk and Modernist Liberalism' *Dissent* (2009); and Hülya Adak, 'Pamuk'un 'Ansiklopedik Romanı', in Kara Kitap Üzerine Yazılar (İletişim Yayınları, Istanbul, 1996).

There are comments on *A Strangeness on My Mind*. The comment about "pandulum" belongs to this article: "Jale Parla, Tuhaflıklar Diyarında Tuhaf Bir Karakter: Mevlut ve İstanbul, on the website K24 (published on February 4, 2015)."

And the comment about the character being a "porteur" belongs to Murat Belge's review on Pamuk's novel in Milliyet Kitap (December, 2014).

Last Word: On Turkish Delight by Merryl Wyn Davies

Fry's Turkish Delight ads can be watched on numerous places on the YouTube, for example: https://www.youtube.com/watch?v=qAY_o36paQ0

Ruth Bernard Yeazell's *Harems of the Mind* is published by Yale University Press (New Haven, 2000); various reprints of Jean Baptiste Tavernier's 1713 *Nouvelle Relation* are available; a kindle version appeared in 2013; and John of Damascus on heresy can be read in the 'New Translation' of *The Fathers of the Church: Writings: The Fount of Knowledge: The Philosophical Chapters, On Heresies, The*

Orthodox Faith by Saint John of Damascus (The Catholic University of America Press, Washington DC, 1958).

See also: Ziauddin Sardar, *Orientalism*, Open University Press, London, 1999; and Ziauddin Sardar and Merryl Wyn Davies, *Distorted Imagination: Lessons from the Rushdie Affair*, Grey Seal, London, 1990.

CONTRIBUTORS

Tahir Abbas is a Professor of Sociology at Fatih University in Istanbul and currently a Remarque Visiting Fellow at New York University ● **Abdullah Yavuz Altun** is editor of *Püff*, a political satire magazine ● **Edip Asaf Bekaroğlu** is an Assistant Professor of Political Science at Istanbul University ● **Ken Chitwood** is a PhD student at the University of Florida and writes frequently on religious issues ● **Peter Clark** is a renowned author of many books, including *Istanbul* and *Marmaduke Pickthall: British Muslim* ● **John Crofoot** is a community volunteer in Hasankeyf, Turkey, and co-founder of www.hasankeyfmatters.com ● **Merryl Wyn Davies** is co-director of the Muslim Institute ● **Nagihan Haliloğlu** is an Assistant Professor at Fatih Sultan Mehmet University, Istanbul and writes for *Lacivert* ● **Aamer Hussein** is a well-known short story writer and Professorial Writing Fellow at the University of Southampton ● **Tam Hussein** is a writer and journalist ● **Ramazan Kılınç** is an Assistant Professor of Political Science and Director of Islamic Studies Program, University of Nebraska at Omaha ● **Ahmet T. Kuru** is an Associate Professor of Political Science at San Diego State University ● **Suzanne Mordue** is an e-learning consultant working in international teacher development ● **Sophia Pandya** is an Associate Professor of Religious Studies at California State University ● **Samia Rahman** is deputy director of the Muslim Institute and is busy putting together the next issue of *Critical Muslim* ● **Melek Saral** is a postdoctoral researcher on the University Research Priority Program on Asia and Europa at the University of Zurich ● **Yusuf Sarfati** is Associate Professor of Politics and Government at Illinois State University ● **Charles Allen Scarboro** is a Professor of Sociology at Fatih University in Istanbul ● **Rebecca Soble** has worked as an English instructor in Istanbul since 2006 and has a keen interest in travel and photography.